The Editor

ERIK GRAY is Assistant Professor of English and Comparative Literature at Columbia University and a specialist in Romantic and Victorian poetry.

LIBRARY

This book is due for return on or before the last date stamped below

D1380271

A NORTON CRITICAL EDITION

Alfred, Lord Tennyson
IN MEMORIAM

AUTHORITATIVE TEXT
CRITICISM

Second Edition

Edited by

ERIK GRAY
COLUMBIA UNIVERSITY

W • W • NORTON & COMPANY • *New York* • *London*

Copyright © 2004, 1973 by
W. W. Norton & Company, Inc.

All rights reserved.
Printed in the United States of America.

The text of this book is composed in Fairfield Medium
with the display set in Bernhard Modern.
Composition by Binghamton Valley Composition, Inc.
Manufacturing by the Maple-Vail Book Group.
Book design by Antonina Krass.
Production manager: Ben Reynolds.

Library of Congress Cataloging-in-Publication Data

Tennyson, Alfred Tennyson, Baron, 1809–1892.
    In memoriam : authoritative text : criticism / Alfred, Lord Tennyson; edited by Erik Gray.—2nd ed.
        p. cm.—(Norton critical edition)
    Includes bibliographical references and index.

ISBN 0-393-97926-1

1. Hallam, Arthur Henry, 1811–1833—Poetry. 2. Tennyson, Alfred Tennyson, Baron, 1809–1892. In memoriam. 3. Hallam, Arthur Henry, 1811–1833—In literature. 4. Elegiac poetry, English—History and criticism. 5. Friendship in literature. I. Gray, Erik Irving, 1972– II. Title. III. Series.

PR5562.A2G73 2003
821'.8—dc21   2003051298

W. W. Norton & Company, Inc., 500 Fifth Avenue, New York, N.Y. 10110
www.wwnorton.com

W. W. Norton & Company Ltd., Castle House,
75/76 Wells Street, London W1T 3QT

4 5 6 7 8 9 0

FOR KATHERINE

Dear friend, far off

Contents

Preface

For thirty years Robert H. Ross's Norton Critical Edition of *In Memoriam* has furnished a reliable and helpful text of Tennyson's poem. In preparing this new edition I have frequently referred to Professor Ross's annotations, and on occasion I have reproduced his notes exactly or with only small alterations. The text of the poem has been reset to allow for a clearer and more readable layout, and I have taken this opportunity to correct a few misprints. Five of the critical essays included in the first edition reappear here; they have been supplemented by a selection of criticism from the past three decades, including examples of formal, contextual, reader-response, queer, and genre criticism. Given the availability of continually updated bibliographical databases, I have not tried to assemble a comprehensive bibliography but instead have supplied a more selective annotated bibliography; criticism of the poem is extensive, and I hope this will serve as a useful guide to those doing further research. Also new to this edition is the introduction, which aims to provide readers with necessary background information and a critical overview of the poem's most distinctive formal and thematic peculiarities.

In the notes I have frequently quoted the annotations Tennyson himself provided for the Eversley edition (see Bibliography); these are marked [T.]. I am greatly indebted to the two chief modern editions of the poem, that by Christopher Ricks and that by Susan Shatto and Marion Shaw, both of which are described in the bibliography. Like Ross, I follow the Eversley text, retaining Tennyson's distinctive abbreviations (*thro'*, *tho'*, endings in -*'d*), but also retaining, unlike Ross, the Roman numerals that Tennyson used in all printed editions to number his sections. I have followed Ricks in reverting to one earlier reading, a comma rather than a period at the end of LXXII, 16.

I am grateful to Harvard University for its financial support in the preparation of this volume and to the libraries that allowed me to consult the major manuscripts of the poem: Houghton Library, Harvard University; the Wren Library, Trinity College, Cambridge; and the Tennyson Research Centre, Lincoln. I would like to thank Gerhard Joseph and Herbert Tucker for their helpful suggestions, and I am especially grateful to Christopher Ricks for his guidance and advice: I remember with great pleasure the day we worked through some of Tennyson's "wordy snares" together.

Introduction

Tennyson, Hallam, and the Poem

In October of 1833, Alfred Tennyson (he would not become "Lord" Tennyson for another fifty years) was living at the rectory in Somersby, Lincolnshire, where he had grown up. His father had died two years before, while Tennyson was studying at Cambridge; Alfred, although he was not the eldest son, had left the university without completing his degree in order to take on the duties of the male head of the household for his mother and his numerous younger siblings. Life with Tennyson's father had been extremely difficult for the entire family, and it did not get much easier when he died. The Reverend George Tennyson had been the rector at Somersby; after his death his family, which was always in want of money, was faced with the probability that they would have to leave the rectory that had always been their home—as eventually they were compelled to do in 1837, an event commemorated in sections C–CV of *In Memoriam*.

One bright spot in Tennyson's life at this time, and in that of his whole family, was Arthur Henry Hallam. Tennyson had met Hallam in the spring of 1829 at Cambridge, where they were both students at Trinity College, and they immediately formed the deepest and most profound friendship of Tennyson's life. Tennyson's childhood had been dark and unquiet, and he had not liked Cambridge at first, but with his newfound friend he flourished. Hallam was a sensitive and brilliant young man, later remembered not just by Tennyson but by many of his friends (including the future prime minister William Ewart Gladstone) as the member of their circle most clearly destined for greatness. Together he and Tennyson became members of "The Apostles," an undergraduate society for intellectual discussion and debate. Hallam fervently admired Tennyson's poetry and encouraged him to publish it. The result was a volume of poems in 1830, which Hallam very ably (and very favorably) reviewed in an article the following year, and then another, larger volume of poems in 1832, which Hallam was instrumental in getting published.

Meanwhile, Tennyson brought Hallam to Somersby, where he became an immediate favorite, particularly with Tennyson's younger sister Emily, with whom he fell in love. The two were soon engaged to be married—a move that angered Hallam's father, who forbade Hallam and Emily to see each other until Hallam turned twenty-one. But their love survived the separation, and when Hallam did come of age in February 1832, the engagement was renewed; Hallam finished his degree at Cambridge and moved to London to study law, hoping to begin a career that would allow him to marry soon. In the meantime his friendship with Tennyson continued as close as ever. When Hallam left for a long tour of the Continent with his father in late summer of 1833, Tennyson went down to London to share his final days in England and to see him off.

Such was the situation when in early October 1833, Tennyson received the following letter:

> My dear Sir,
>   At the desire of a most afflicted family, I write to you because they are unequal from the abyss of grief into which they have fallen to do it themselves. Your friend, sir, and my much-loved nephew, Arthur Hallam, is no more. It has pleased God to remove him from this, his first scene of existence, to that better world for which he was created. He died at Vienna, on his return from Buda, by apoplexy, and I believe his remains come by sea from Trieste. * * * May that Being in whose hands are all the destinies of man, and who has promised to comfort all that mourn, pour the balm of consolation on all the families, who are bowed down by this unexpected dispensation!

Tennyson was faced with the duty of breaking the news to his sister Emily, and then of learning to cope with it himself.

Tennyson's reaction was to begin writing poetry that, directly or indirectly, confronted the grief that seemed to have cut his life in two. Within a week of receiving the news of Hallam's death, he composed one of his greatest short poems, "Ulysses," and over the following weeks he began work on other major poems, including "Tithonus" and "Morte d'Arthur." All of these dealt obliquely with his loss. But at the same time Tennyson drafted a more explicitly personal lyric, "Fair ship, that from the Italian shore," addressed to the boat that was bearing Hallam's body back to England for burial in Somerset, near the family estate. (The ship finally arrived and the funeral took place in early January; Tennyson could not bring himself to attend.) This lyric later became section IX of *In Memoriam*.

So began the drawn-out and piecemeal process of composition that was not to conclude until the elegy was published at last in May 1850, nearly seventeen years after it was begun. Indeed, for many years after Hallam's death Tennyson published very little at all, until

1842, when he came out with a two-volume edition of old and new poems—including "Ulysses" and "Morte d'Arthur"—that securely established his reputation as a major English poet. He continued to compose his elegies for Hallam, and by 1845 the poem we know as *In Memoriam* had reached nearly its present length, but he remained reluctant to publish it. Eventually, early in 1850, he printed a small number of copies for private distribution to his friends. This so-called trial edition had no title, though Tennyson had considered such possibilities as *Fragments of an Elegy* and *The Way of the Soul*. After some further revisions the poem was finally published a few months later; the author's name was not given, and the title (perhaps suggested by Tennyson's fiancée, Emily Sellwood) was simply *In Memoriam A.H.H.*

The effect of the poem's publication, both on the reading public and on Tennyson's life, was immediate and enormous. *In Memoriam* was hailed as a masterpiece, and Tennyson—who despite the anonymous publication was quickly identified by most reviewers—was widely celebrated in the press. The practical repercussions for him were twofold. The post of poet laureate had been left vacant by the death of William Wordsworth in April, and Queen Victoria was searching for a worthy successor. Tennyson's name had already been suggested, and his nomination was secured when the queen's husband, Prince Albert, read *In Memoriam* and expressed his admiration. Second, Tennyson was enabled to marry Emily Sellwood, to whom he had been engaged, on and off, for over ten years. The marriage had been delayed both by Tennyson's lack of steady income and by Emily's concerns about his religious faith. But *In Memoriam*, although it expresses much doubt as well as faith, apparently allayed her misgivings. And profits from the sale of the poem, which quickly ran through several printings, together with the modest stipend attached to the laureateship, provided Tennyson with a sufficient income to support a family.

The popularity of *In Memoriam* continued to grow after its initial success. It appealed to the Victorians for a number of reasons, in addition to its sheer poetic beauty. The rituals of mourning were a central feature of Victorian culture: there were elaborate codes concerning everything from dress to stationery for months or years after the death of a loved one. After the death of her husband in 1861, Queen Victoria spent the last forty years of her life in mourning, and she told Tennyson, "Next to the Bible *In Memoriam* is my comfort." It filled a similar role through all levels of society. Contemporary readers also appreciated Tennyson's poem because it frankly confronted the crisis of faith that troubled so many mid-century thinkers. For several decades scientific discoveries had challenged the Bible, particularly the biblical account of creation, and by 1850 the scientific and technological progress on which the Victorians so prided themselves seemed painfully at odds with the religious beliefs and practices of earlier times. Readers were therefore grateful to Tennyson for combining a poetic exploration of such concepts as evolution with an ultimate affirmation of faith. To understand how he managed to do this, it is important first to consider the form and structure of *In Memoriam*.

Unity and Division

The *Memoir* of Tennyson written by his son, Hallam Tennyson, records a number of the poet's comments about the way he composed *In Memoriam*. "The sections were written," says Tennyson, "at many different places, and as the phases of our intercourse came to my memory and suggested them. I did not write them with any view of weaving them into a whole, or for publication, until I found that I had written so many." This information confirms what the reader of *In Memoriam* feels while moving through the poem: that *In Memoriam* is simultaneously one poem and one hundred thirty-three poems, almost any of which could stand independently as a separate elegy. This fragmentation is one of the most surprising features of Tennyson's poem. Most elegies have a single movement or trajectory: the speaker reacts to the death of a loved one by moving steadily from grief to some form of consolation. That continuity, however, is shattered in *In Memoriam*. One section will reach some form of consolation, only to be contradicted by the next section, in which the sense of grief is renewed. Most elegies present a reaction to death; *In Memoriam* presents what T. S. Eliot called a "diary" of reactions to Hallam's death. The fictional time of the poem extends over nearly three years from the moment the speaker learns of his friend's death, and its fragmentary nature reflects the fluctuations that typify such a period: you continue to have good days and bad days, even after you feel you have overcome the immediate shock of grief.

And yet for all its fragmentation, *In Memoriam* also displays an admirable unity. Although it endures more doubts and setbacks along the way than most other elegies, it contains the same overall movement from near despair to a sense of consolation. Moreover, its different sections are often tightly woven together: they react to each other, and sections that share particular concerns (those addressing the ship or those that speculate on the possibility of seeing the spirit of the dead) are grouped together. Above all, the poem is written throughout in a single, unusual stanza form. Tennyson's claim that each section was written independently of the others is a little misleading: he must have been conscious early on that all of the poems he was writing about Hallam shared a meter and rhyme scheme that he had only rarely used before. The consistent use of a single stanza—what has come to be called the *In Memoriam* stanza—reinforces the sense that although the speaker may feel himself to be filled with conflicting, even contradictory feelings, nevertheless he retains some integrity, a hope of eventually resolving the disparate impulses he feels.

The conjunction of division and unity is not merely an aspect of the poem's structure but its most pressing concern. Tennyson feels himself to be divided into two—a former self, who was young and happy in Hallam's company, and a new self who, at twenty-four, feels already aged. His sense of identity is therefore shaken, leaving him asking "Who am I?" or even on one occasion "What am I?" (LIV, 17). This identity fragmentation is even more painfully acute in the case of Hallam. Tennyson knows that he longs for his friend, but who is his friend? Is he the Hallam so vividly remembered at Cambridge and at the Tennyson home in Somersby? Is he the corpse being brought back on the ship? Is he an angel looking down from above? Or is he the person that Hallam would be now had he survived, as section LXXXIV suggests? These are the pieces that the poem must put together again. How can the poet reassure himself that there is some sense in saying "I" or saying "Hallam"?

Even the stanza itself, the formal feature that provides the greatest unifying force, contains elements of brokenness or dividedness. Each line of the *In Memoriam* stanza is shorter than one would expect. The typical meter for serious English poetry is the pentameter, a line consisting of ten syllables (five "feet"); *In Memoriam* uses a tetrameter line, which is two syllables shorter. Furthermore, what is usually called the "elegiac stanza" in English poetry is a quatrain (a four-line stanza) with interlaced rhymes, *abab;* the stanza of *In Memoriam* rearranges the rhymes *abba*. These may seem like small variations, but they have an immense effect, and together they make the stanza form so unusual that Tennyson thought he was the first to use it: "I believed myself the originator of the metre, until after 'In Memoriam' came out, when someone told me that Ben Jonson and Sir Philip Sidney had used it."

There are several important effects Tennyson achieves by using a tetrameter line rather than the more standard pentameter. The tetrameter or four-beat line is the standard meter for ballads, nursery rhymes, songs—in other words, for what are considered to be the more spontaneous or immediately appealing forms of poetry. The shorter line allows *In Memoriam* to appear more unpremeditated. The poem often wishes to present itself as inarticulate or unthinking, poured forth as naturally as the lament of a bird that has lost its fledglings (section XXI) or as the cry of an infant in the night (sections LIV, CXXIV). These assertions are still paradoxical—a poem that claims to be speechless—but the self-deprecation derives credibility from the use of the simpler, abbreviated meter. Pentameter had for centuries been used for long or important poems, such as epics and elegies, because it conveys a sense of confidence; this derives in part from the fact that a ten-syllable line is long enough to contain a complete statement. Consider, for instance, the opening line from a major elegy written in pentameters a few decades before *In Memoriam*, Percy Shelley's "Adonais":

> I weep for Adonais—he is dead!

The theme and motivation of the poem are summed up neatly. Contrast the opening stanza of section I of *In Memoriam*:

> I held it truth, with him who sings
> > To one clear harp in divers tones,
> > That men may rise on stepping-stones
> Of their dead selves to higher things.

"I held it truth with him who sings": by itself it is an incomplete and almost meaningless line. We must wait until the second line to get a sense of who this singer is and until the final two lines to learn what "truth" is being repudiated. Tennyson emphasizes the brokenness of the tetrameter stanza, the way that each line falls short of expressing a complete thought—just as words fall short of expressing his emotion, as he insists throughout the poem. Words "half reveal/ And half conceal the Soul within" (V, 3–4); they are insufficient, and the shorter line insists upon this by being itself insufficient.

Like the meter, the rhyme scheme Tennyson employs expresses the poem's self-doubt, or rather its mixture of faith and doubt. In one sense, the *abba* stanza conveys a sense of fulfillment: it begins with one rhyme sound, which is then temporarily lost as we move on to the couplet in the middle; but in the end the initial rhyme returns, clinching the stanza and seeming to redeem or justify the open-endedness of the beginning. The second stanza of section I offers both an example and an image of this forward-looking trustfulness:

> But who shall so forecast the years
> > And find in loss a gain to match?
> > Or reach a hand thro' time to catch
> The far-off interest of tears?

Like the expectant hand in line 3 (a symbol that recurs throughout the poem), the opening rhyme, "years," is extended in good faith and

then left waiting, until it is finally rewarded with the satisfying closure of a matching rhyme at the end.

Yet this hopeful or redemptive reading is only one side of the *abba*
rhyme scheme, and even the stanza just quoted seems doubtful: it
is phrased, after all, as a question. The same rhyme scheme also
conveys the opposite sense, a feeling not of looking forward but of
falling back. It begins surely enough with a progression, *a* to *b*, but
then it seems almost to give up, to turn around and retreat into what
it knows. This sense is conveyed in the third stanza of section i:

> Let Love clasp Grief lest both be drown'd,
>   Let darkness keep her raven gloss:
>   Ah, sweeter to be drunk with loss,
> To dance with death, to beat the ground.

Instead of moving beyond grief toward some eventual reward, a "far-
off interest," the poet wishes to turn around and "clasp Grief," to
cling to the past and to what he already knows. It is therefore appropriate that the rhyme scheme itself is one of clasping—the *a* rhyme
embracing the *b* and the stanza as a whole ending where it began.
Both of the poet's impulses, then—the impulse to move hopefully
on and the desire to turn back—are equally represented by the
stanza.

But it is worth pausing to consider the notion of *clasping,* which,
like the hand, reappears as one of the central images of the poem.
The command given at the beginning of the third stanza seems to
be backwards: "Let Love clasp Grief lest both be drown'd." Anyone
who has ever taken swimming lessons knows that to grab onto a
fellow swimmer is the most dangerous thing one can do: rather than
prevent one from drowning, it actually causes both to drown. What
does Tennyson mean then by saying that Love and Grief should clasp
each other to prevent their being "drown'd"? The answer seems to
lie in the nature of clasping. To clasp something implies unity; clasping or hugging is a way of bringing two things together. But it necessarily implies separateness or division as well: only two distinct or
independent entities can clasp each other. A hand cannot clasp itself
but must clasp a different hand; a raindrop cannot clasp another
raindrop without their melting into each other, because they are not
sufficiently individuated. For Tennyson, both aspects of clasping are
equally important, division as much as unity. He strives in his poem
to reunify what has been fragmented, to achieve a reunion with his
lost friend. At the same time, however, he resists the possibility of
total union; he seeks to clasp his friend—not that they should merge
entirely.

Hence the importance of clasping or embraces in the poem, beginning with the rhyme scheme. A fine example of the unifying power of clasping comes in section LXXXIX; it is the only direct representation we are given of a conversation between Tennyson and Hallam—although they are shown, significantly, disagreeing:

> But if I praised the busy town,
>   He loved to rail against it still,
>   For 'ground in yonder social mill
> We rub each other's angles down,
>
> 'And merge' he said 'in form and gloss
>   The picturesque of man and man.'
>   We talk'd: the stream beneath us ran,
> The wine-flask lying couch'd in moss.
>   (37–44)

It has been pointed out that of these eight lines, Tennyson speaks four and Hallam speaks four; none of Tennyson's lines rhyme together, nor do any of Hallam's. This is the threat, as it were, of the rhyme scheme: divide up the quatrains differently and you are left with four unrhymed lines. But Tennyson takes this memory of a simple prose conversation and, by clasping it within his own words, he turns it into verse.

This seems therefore to exemplify the benefits of clasping, which is able to convert unrhymed fragments into a unified whole. But these same lines also express a fear of unity: Hallam decries the tendency of individuals in society to "merge," to become too much like one another. Love thrives on union, but the poem reminds us that love also requires a certain amount of separation. In section XLVII, for instance, in which he describes his notion of heaven, Tennyson renounces the idea that the souls of the dead all become so equally perfect as to be indistinguishable.

> That each, who seems a separate whole,
>   Should move his rounds, and fusing all
>   The skirts of self again, should fall
> Remerging in the general Soul,
>
> Is faith as vague as all unsweet:
>   Eternal form shall still divide
>   The eternal soul from all beside;
> And I shall know him when we meet.
>   (1–8)

Division, then, has its purpose: how else can those who love recognize each other? Tennyson therefore rejects the notion of spirits who, being all infinitely good, are all alike parts of the "general Soul," and he gives instead his own notion of a homelier heaven.

And we shall sit at endless feast,
    Enjoying each the other's good:
    What vaster dream can hit the mood
Of Love on earth? He seeks at least

Upon the last and sharpest height,
    Before the spirits fade away,
    Some landing-place, to clasp and say,
'Farewell! We lose ourselves in light.'
                                    (XLVII, 9–16)

When Tennyson here asks for the right to "clasp" once more, he is
asking for something mundane: angels presumably are no more capable of hugging each other than raindrops are. But "Love on earth"
(the only love he knows) demands division.

This concern helps explain the difficulty of the earlier image, "Let
Love clasp Grief lest both be drown'd." Tennyson seems to be calling
on love and grief to clasp in the sense of bracketing each other,
limiting each other. Grief must not become infinite, nor must love
grow to become an indistinguishable angel love; both must be kept
earthly and distinct, lest they be "drown'd" in a sea of light and infin-
ity. And this is what the *In Memoriam* stanza manages to do, both
in its shortened lines and in its clasping rhyme scheme: it stresses
its own limits and recognizes the importance of division, even while
the consistency of the rhyme scheme lends unity to the poem as a
whole.

Section I usefully illustrates these effects of the stanza form. It is
not, admittedly, the most captivating section of *In Memoriam*: it contains a rather obscure reference to the German poet Goethe (he is
the one "who sings" in line 1), and its argument is not immediately
clear. But this section boldly introduces the problem of fragmentation or self-division that occupies the whole poem. It begins in apparent self-confidence with the word "I" but then immediately questions
what that "I" might mean. Goethe, it is pointed out, believed that
people leave behind their former lives, their "dead selves," as they
grow older, the way a snake sheds its skin; so "I" is not the same
person from year to year.

Tennyson repudiates this view. There is some continuity, he
insists, between me now and me then, before the death of Hallam.
But the doubt has already been introduced, and it only grows more
acute in the following section. Tennyson may well claim that he is
not completely cut off from his former life, but it is far more difficult
to say the same of Hallam. Having asserted that "I" exists as a continuous, unified self, Tennyson wishes to say the same of "you." As
mentioned above, however, Hallam seems to have become many different selves: Hallam the memory, the corpse, the dream, the angel.

Wishing to address his friend but at a loss where to direct his speech, Tennyson turns to the yew tree in the graveyard:

> Old Yew, which graspest at the stones
> That name the under-lying dead.
>
> (II, 1–2)

Section I began with "I"; section II begins with "Yew," but not the "you" Tennyson wished for. One might call this a pun, but that would be misleading. It is rather an indication of the difficulty of establishing a sense of identity after such a shattering event. The very layout of the poem reinforces the sense of unwanted multiplicity where there ought to be unity. The beginning of the poem looks like an epitaph carved on a headstone: the title is a Latin inscription—*In Memoriam A.H.H. Obiit MDCCCXXXIII*—and there follows a Roman numeral (I) above the opening section. Usually, however, one person gets only one headstone. Here on the other hand the original "epitaph" is followed by another, as if the first were insufficient. Even the Roman numerals seem to suggest something amiss: just after the first section has asserted the unity of "I," we are confronted by "II," as if "I" had divided nevertheless.

"You," meanwhile, is even less stable, more difficult to locate. One of the most moving aspects of the opening sections is the difficulty Tennyson has in finding someone or something to address. He begins with "Old Yew" (II, 1), then turns to "O Sorrow" (III, 1), then "O heart" (IV, 5), "Dark house" (VII, 1), and finally "Fair ship" (IX, 1). When one loses the person one loves best, this is the quandary: the very person you would usually turn to in a time of grief is the one person you cannot find. It could be said that the closest Tennyson comes to locating Hallam in these opening sections is in section I, line 11: "Ah, sweeter to be drunk with loss"—where the very sigh that escapes the speaker ("Ah") contains Hallam's initials. Hallam seems to be both everywhere and nowhere, to be divided into so many different selves as to be irrecoverable. The end of section IX suggests just how fragmented he has become:

> My friend, the brother of my love;
>
> My Arthur, whom I shall not see
>   Till all my widow'd race be run;
>   Dear as the mother to the son,
> More than my brothers are to me.

Hallam is, within the space of five lines, a friend, a brother, a spouse, a mother, a more-than-brother. But none of these will quite do to represent him, nor can the whole of Tennyson's actual family make up for his loss.

And yet for all the division of "I" and "you" that plagues the speaker here, section IX also introduces the first note of comfort and consistency in the poem. After searching vainly for an object to whom, or to which, he can direct his lament, the poet here fixes on the ship, which he continues to address for the following ten sections. This may be a small comfort, but it is a certain one. It gives Tennyson a single point of concentration, and it gives the poem a sense of stability. Just as important, the ship represents a return of some sort: the movement is no longer all outward from the poet; now something is coming back to him, coming home. The newfound (if precarious) stability is evident in the opening stanza of section XVIII, when the ship finally arrives and delivers Hallam's body to his homeland.

> 'Tis well; 'tis something; we may stand
>   Where he in English earth is laid,
>   And from his ashes may be made
> The violet of his native land.

We saw earlier, in discussing the opening of section I, that the eight-syllable line is usually too short to include a complete sentence. Here, however, Tennyson is at last collected enough to fit three complete clauses into the first line. " 'Tis well"—no, not quite that; but at least " 'tis something; we may stand" by his grave. He goes on in line 5 to say, " 'Tis little." It is little, but at least it is more than he had in the beginning; he has begun the process of reassembling the selves shattered by Hallam's sudden death.

Faith, Science, and Other Critical Concerns

At the end of this volume are reprinted a number of essays representing a century of critical reaction to *In Memoriam*. Some of them, including those by Bradley, Ricks, and Peltason, address the question of the poem's unity; others focus on the poem's form, its language, its erotics, or its place in the elegiac tradition. One of the most persistent concerns (evident in the studies by Mattes and Willey) is also the one that most interested the first reviewers of *In Memoriam*: the conflict in the poem between religious faith and doubt, specifically doubt resulting from new scientific theories. The poem's framework is distinctly Christian: its time scheme, for instance—the three years of mourning—is marked out by the recurrence of Christmas at regular intervals (sections XXVIII–XXX, LXXVIII, and CIV–CV). Moreover, the great consolation on which the poem depends and concludes is the immortality of the individual soul, the assurance (as we have seen) that Hallam is in heaven and that "I shall know him when we meet" (XLVII, 8). Within this broad framework, however, there is plenty of room for doubt. Even the Christmas poems seem far more concerned with the loss of Hallam than with possible religious consolations. And Tennyson has little to say for most received doctrine; rather, "There lives more faith in honest doubt," he judges, "than in half the creeds" (XCVI, 11–12). But the profoundest moments of religious questioning come when he considers the evidence of science.

Charles Darwin did not publish his treatise *On the Origin of Species by Means of Natural Selection* until 1859, nine years after *In Memoriam* was published, but there was no dearth of troubling scientific theories earlier in the century. Tennyson was particularly aware of these theories: his poetry reflects a deeper concern with scientific developments than that of any other poet of his time; the allusions to astronomy and geology in *In Memoriam* reveal a sophisticated understanding of current ideas. It might seem odd for a poem of personal grief to refer to complex scientific concepts, but these allusions do not seem out of place, for two reasons. First, science was increasingly depicting both the universe and the human race as doomed to eventual extinction; yet Tennyson's poem is predicated upon an assurance of personal immortality, and such a contradiction could scarcely be ignored. Second, an evolutionary model of development is central to *In Memoriam* from the first section, which speculates whether individuals leave behind their "dead selves" in a constant progression forward. These questions lead naturally to broader speculations about similar evolutions in the natural world.

Doubts about the eternal nature of the world and of the soul had always existed and had been steadily accruing since the eighteenth century; hence there is no single scientist whose work can be said to be the source of the doubts expressed in *In Memoriam*. But we do know that Tennyson was particularly disturbed by reading Charles Lyell's *Principles of Geology* (1830–33) in 1837. Lyell suggested that the earth's surface was constantly changing: natural forces, such as erosion, altered the landscape slowly but eternally. So whereas other scientists had proposed that extinct species had been wiped out by cataclysmic events that would not necessarily be repeated, Lyell reached quite a different conclusion. The same slow but steady forces that had changed the environment and extinguished earlier species were still in operation and would therefore extinguish us as well. This is the pitiless view Tennyson represents in sections LV and LVI, some of the most despairing in the poem. "Nature, red in tooth and claw," tells humankind,

> 'I care for nothing, all shall go.
>
> 'Thou makest thine appeal to me:
> I bring to life, I bring to death:

> The spirit does but mean the breath:
> I know no more.'
>
> (LVI, 4–8)

Such wasteful destruction not only of individuals but of entire species seems irreconcilable with the Christian concept of a God to whom every life is dear for all eternity. If we like every other species are doomed to extinction by impersonal forces, Tennyson concludes, our life is "as futile, then, as frail" (LVI, 25).

And yet there is another way of thinking about this same theory that leads to an opposite conclusion. Lyell, we have noted, disagreed with the catastrophic model of change; rather than a series of cataclysmic breaks with the past, he posited a constant series of small changes. But in that case, nothing is ever left entirely behind, since every stage is part of a continuous progression. So the idea of constant evolution, which posed such a problem, also provides the solution. According to this model, there exists a direct and traceable continuity between earlier stages of life and this one, just as there does between childhood and adulthood. This is exactly the reassurance that Tennyson sought in section I: that what seemed like a catastrophic break with the past—the death of Hallam and, therefore, the death of Tennyson's former self—could be explained in such a way that those former selves would not seem to be wholly extinct. Nothing wholly dies if it gives rise to the next stage of development, and so on infinitely:

> They say,
> The solid earth whereon we tread
>
> In tracts of fluent heat began,
>   And grew to seeming-random forms,
>   The seeming prey of cyclic storms,
> Till at the last arose the man.
>
> (CXVIII, 7–12)

Change is "fluent": the "solid earth" or "the man" can change constantly and yet remain the same, just as a river does. Tennyson returns to this reassurance a few sections later:

> There rolls the deep where grew the tree.
>   O earth, what changes hast thou seen!
>   There where the long street roars, hath been
> The stillness of the central sea.
>
> The hills are shadows, and they flow
>   From form to form, and nothing stands;
>   They melt like mist, the solid lands,
> Like clouds they shape themselves and go.
>
> (CXXIII, 1–8)

There is certainly something melancholy in this vast, almost cinematic sweep through time; Tennyson recognizes the radical instability of the world he depicts. But it has ceased to be terrifying, as it was in section LVI, because at least there is no rupture, no sudden, irretrievable break with the past.

Evolution does not of course hold all the answers; it does not dispel the poet's grief. But it does suggest a way of reconciling parts of a life that seemed to be hopelessly fragmented and also of justifying a God whose workings otherwise seem so careless of individual lives. Evolution therefore features prominently in the "Epilogue"—a section that, like the "Prologue," Tennyson wrote late in the process of composition and left untitled. This final section cannot be taken as a summing-up of all that has gone before: the reader has witnessed too many fluctuations and contradictions along the way to accept any point of view as the final word. Moreover, the Epilogue presents itself more as a coda or counterpoint to the rest of the poem than as a representative piece. It is set on a day nine years after the death of Hallam, at the wedding of one of Tennyson's younger sisters; the poem that begins with a funeral ends, suddenly, with a marriage.

Nevertheless, although the Epilogue is in some ways distinct from the body of the poem, it does present the last word, and it chimes well with the hopefulness that predominates in the sections that immediately precede it. Its final hopeful vision is one of evolution: on this wedding night, Tennyson predicts, a child will be conceived who because the human race is constantly progressing will be slightly more developed than the current generation. But the end point of all this evolution, Tennyson suggests, is a state that Arthur Henry Hallam already achieved when he lived—a form of humanity

> Whereof the man, that with me trod
>   This planet, was a noble type
>   Appearing ere the times were ripe,
> That friend of mine who lives in God,
>
> That God, which ever lives and loves,
>   One God, one law, one element,
>   And one far-off divine event,
> To which the whole creation moves.
>   (Epilogue, 137–144)

The constant progression from one state of being to "higher things" (I, 4), which seems so painful and problematic in earlier sections of the poem, here becomes the source of greatest comfort, because it leads towards an eventual reunion with Hallam.

Yet optimistic though this ending may be—and Tennyson himself is said to have expressed a concern that it was "too hopeful"—it is also disturbing: it comes uncomfortably close to equating Hallam ("That friend") with God ("That God"). We have already seen how much trouble the poet has in finding a fit image to describe his friend: is he a friend, a brother, a parent, or a spouse? A good deal of criticism in recent decades has concentrated on the last of these, the repeated depiction of their relationship as a marriage, and more generally on what one early reviewer called the tone of "amatory tenderness" that pervades the poem (see the studies by Shannon and Nunokawa, herein). The aim of these critics is not to try to determine whether the actual relationship between Tennyson and Hallam involved a homosexual attraction. The aim rather is to understand what it signifies that the poem features phrases Tennyson would not normally use toward a male friend—terms of endearment, expressions of longing, recurrent images of Hallam's body, his hands, his eyes. This line of so-called queer criticism, which has proved very fruitful, is not as different from other schools of criticism as it seems, since it too centers on the difficulty of finding appropriate language. Tennyson responded to objections to his use of terms like "dearest" (LXXIV, 5 and CXXII, 1) by saying, "If any body thinks I ever called him 'dearest' in his life, they are much mistaken, for I never even called him 'dear.' " The comment is interesting not because it suggests that Tennyson had unwittingly revealed himself and was anxious to explain away his slip; if that were true he could easily have changed the text, as he was often willing to do in response to criticism. Instead the comment reveals how conscious Tennyson was of his unusually erotic language: Hallam's death, which changed so much, even altered the nature of the language in which he must be addressed.

Queer criticism also helps remind us that *In Memoriam* is not only an elegy but one of the most beautiful love poems in English. Among its chief glories is the way that Tennyson manages to consider great issues of public import—the latest science and all the questions of faith and doubt to which the contemplation of death leads him—without ever losing the poignancy of an intensely personal lament. Section CXXIX, at the end of the poem, feels the shock and longing of loss as minutely as the opening sections.

> Dear friend, far off, my lost desire,
>   So far, so near in woe and weal;
>   O loved the most, when most I feel
> There is a lower and a higher;
>
> Known and unknown; human, divine;
>   Sweet human hand and lips and eye;

Dear heavenly friend that canst not die,
Mine, mine, for ever, ever mine;

Strange friend, past, present, and to be;
Loved deeplier, darklier understood;
Behold, I dream a dream of good,
And mingle all the world with thee.

Tennyson certainly seems at times to "mingle all the world" with
Hallam; his poem on Hallam looks to be all-encompassing. The word
"all" recurs almost obsessively throughout the poem—157 times in
133 sections. Yet all of those "all"s cannot dispel the underlying
doubt, the sense of something slipping away (the more tentative word
"half" also appears persistently). After all his universal speculations,
Tennyson still dwells with supreme tenderness on the details, the
"sweet human hand and lips and eye." And after so many sections
and so many years, Hallam in the final address remains what he was
at first: "Strange friend." Those we have loved and lost seem "So far,
so near" at once—loved more than ever and yet, at the end of it all,
still a mystery.

It is only appropriate, then, that what is often seen as the climactic
moment of the poem is also described as "strange." In section xcv
Tennyson temporarily achieves the reunion with Hallam for which
he has been longing. Sitting alone outdoors one evening he begins
to read Hallam's old letters:

And strangely on the silence broke
The silent-speaking words, and strange
Was love's dumb cry defying change
To test his worth; and strangely spoke

The faith, the vigour, bold to dwell
On doubts that drive the coward back,
And keen thro' wordy snares to track
Suggestion to her inmost cell.

So word by word, and line by line,
The dead man touch'd me from the past,
And all at once it seem'd at last
The living soul was flash'd on mine.
(25–36)

These stanzas deploy two devices typical of *In Memoriam*. The first
is the immediate repetition of a word: "word by word," "line by line."
Here such repetition suggests the certainty, the undeniability of this
moment of spiritual contact. But this is balanced by the other device,
repetition with a difference: "silence" in the first line becomes
"silent," and "strangely" becomes simply "strange." Such verbal mu-

tation, which occurs often in the poem, here serves as a reminder that the glorious experience Tennyson describes is still unstable, fleeting. This conflict, between the wish to "defy change" and the need to accept it, is the poem's central concern. Its strange and wonderful ability to affirm its faith and yet to alter, to accept the perpetual drift of things, is one reason *In Memoriam* continues to "touch us from the past."

The Text of
IN MEMORIAM

IN MEMORIAM.

LONDON:

EDWARD MOXON, DOVER STREET.

1850.

Facsimile title page of the first edition. Courtesy of The Bodleian Library, Oxford.

PROLOGUE[1]

Strong Son of God, immortal Love,
    Whom we, that have not seen thy face,
    By faith, and faith alone, embrace,
Believing where we cannot prove;

5 Thine are these orbs of light and shade;[2]
    Thou madest Life in man and brute;
    Thou madest Death; and lo, thy foot
Is on the skull which thou hast made.

Thou wilt not leave us in the dust:
10   Thou madest man, he knows not why,
    He thinks he was not made to die;
And thou hast made him: thou art just.

Thou seemest human and divine,
    The highest, holiest manhood, thou:
15   Our wills are ours, we know not how;
Our wills are ours, to make them thine.

Our little systems have their day;[3]
    They have their day and cease to be:
    They are but broken lights of thee,
20 And thou, O Lord, art more than they.

We have but faith: we cannot know;
    For knowledge is of things we see;
    And yet we trust it comes from thee,
A beam in darkness: let it grow.

25 Let knowledge grow from more to more,
    But more of reverence in us dwell;

1. This introductory poem, which Tennyson left untitled, is dated 1849; it was thus composed after the rest of *In Memoriam* was already completed.
2. "Sun and moon" [T.].
3. I.e., our humanly conceived theological, philosophical, and scientific systems.

That mind and soul, according well,
    May make one music as before,[4]

But vaster. We are fools and slight;
30   We mock thee when we do not fear:
        But help thy foolish ones to bear;
Help thy vain worlds to bear thy light.

Forgive what seem'd my sin in me;
        What seem'd my worth since I began;
35   For merit lives from man to man,
And not from man, O Lord, to thee.

Forgive my grief for one removed,
        Thy creature, whom I found so fair.
        I trust he lives in thee, and there
40 I find him worthier to be loved.

Forgive these wild and wandering cries,
        Confusions of a wasted youth;
        Forgive them where they fail in truth,
And in thy wisdom make me wise.

1849

IN MEMORIAM A.H.H.

Obiit MDCCCXXXIII[1]

I

I held it truth, with him who sings
    To one clear harp in divers tones,
    That men may rise on stepping-stones
Of their dead selves to higher things.[2]

4. "As in ages of faith" [T.]. I.e., before the religious doubts that resulted from recent scientific discoveries.
1. "To the memory of A.H.H., died 1833" (Latin). On Tennyson's friendship with Arthur Henry Hallam, see "Tennyson, Hallam, and the Poem," pp. xi–xiv.
2. These lines refer to the German poet Goethe, who wrote in many different styles ("divers tones") and who believed, Tennyson suggests, that individuals should profit from painful experiences and move on. The following stanzas express doubts about this view.

5 But who shall so forecast the years
    And find in loss a gain to match?
    Or reach a hand thro' time to catch
The far-off interest of tears?

    Let Love clasp Grief lest both be drown'd,
10   Let darkness keep her raven gloss:
    Ah, sweeter to be drunk with loss,
To dance with death, to beat the ground,

    Than that the victor Hours should scorn
    The long result of love, and boast,
15   'Behold the man that loved and lost,
But all he was is overworn.'

II

Old Yew, which graspest at the stones
    That name the under-lying dead,
    Thy fibres net the dreamless head,
Thy roots are wrapt about the bones.

5 The seasons bring the flower again,
    And bring the firstling to the flock;
    And in the dusk of thee, the clock
Beats out the little lives of men.[1]

O not for thee the glow, the bloom,
10   Who changest not in any gale,
    Nor branding summer suns avail
To touch thy thousand years of gloom:[2]

And gazing on thee, sullen tree,
    Sick for thy stubborn hardihood,
15   I seem to fail from out my blood
And grow incorporate into thee.

III

O Sorrow, cruel fellowship,
    O Priestess in the vaults of Death,

1. The yew is pictured as growing in the churchyard, the clock as striking the hours from the church tower.
2. The dark green foliage of the English yew, an unusually long-lived tree, does not change color with the seasons.

O sweet and bitter in a breath,
    What whispers from thy lying lip?

5   'The stars,' she whispers, 'blindly run;
        A web is wov'n across the sky;
        From out waste places comes a cry,
    And murmurs from the dying sun:[1]

    'And all the phantom, Nature, stands—
10   With all the music in her tone,
        A hollow echo of my own,—
    'A hollow form with empty hands.'

    And shall I take a thing so blind,
        Embrace her as my natural good;
15   Or crush her, like a vice of blood,
    Upon the threshold of the mind?

IV

To Sleep I give my powers away;
    My will is bondsman to the dark;
    I sit within a helmless bark,[1]
And with my heart I muse and say:

5   O heart, how fares it with thee now,
        That thou should'st fail from thy desire,
        Who scarcely darest to inquire,
    'What is it makes me beat so low?'

    Something it is which thou hast lost,
10   Some pleasure from thine early years.
        Break, thou deep vase of chilling tears,
    That grief hath shaken into frost![2]

    Such clouds of nameless trouble cross
        All night below the darken'd eyes;
15   With morning wakes the will, and cries,
    'Thou shalt not be the fool of loss.'

1. "Sorrow" is referring to the hypothesis, then recently put forth, that the sun was burning down and would eventually be extinguished.
1. Like a passenger in a rudderless boat ("a helmless bark"), the speaker cannot control the direction of his thoughts.
2. "Water can be brought below freezing-point and not turn to ice—if it be kept still; but if it be moved suddenly it turns into ice and may break the vase" [T.].

V[1]

I sometimes hold it half a sin
    To put in words the grief I feel;
    For words, like Nature, half reveal
And half conceal the Soul within.

5   But, for the unquiet heart and brain,
    A use in measured language lies;
    The sad mechanic exercise,
Like dull narcotics, numbing pain.

In words, like weeds,[2] I'll wrap me o'er,
10   Like coarsest clothes against the cold:
    But that large grief which these enfold
Is given in outline and no more.

VI

One writes, that 'Other friends remain,'
    That 'Loss is common to the race'—
    And common is the commonplace,
And vacant chaff well meant for grain.

5   That loss is common would not make
    My own less bitter, rather more:
    Too common! Never morning wore
To evening, but some heart did break.

O father, wheresoe'er thou be,
10   Who pledgest now thy gallant son;
    A shot, ere half thy draught be done,
Hath still'd the life that beat from thee.

O mother, praying God will save
    Thy sailor,—while thy head is bow'd,
15   His heavy-shotted hammock-shroud[1]
Drops in his vast and wandering grave.

Ye know no more than I who wrought
    At that last hour to please him well;

---

1. This is the first of several sections concerning the adequacy or inadequacy of poetry to convey deeply felt human experience. Compare sections XX, XXXVII, XLVIII, LXXV, and XCV.
2. Meaning not only "grass" but also "garments," specifically mourning garments.
1. A sailor buried at sea would be wrapped in his hammock, which would be weighted down with shot to make it sink.

Who mused on all I had to tell,
20   And something written, something thought;[2]

Expecting still his advent home;
    And ever met him on his way
    With wishes, thinking, 'here to-day,'
Or 'here to-morrow will he come.'

25   O somewhere, meek, unconscious dove,
    That sittest ranging[3] golden hair;
    And glad to find thyself so fair,
Poor child, that waitest for thy love!

For now her father's chimney glows
30   In expectation of a guest;
    And thinking 'this will please him best,'
She takes a riband or a rose;

For he will see them on to-night;
    And with the thought her colour burns;
35   And, having left the glass, she turns
Once more to set a ringlet right;

And, even when she turn'd, the curse
    Had fallen, and her future Lord
    Was drown'd in passing thro' the ford,
40   Or kill'd in falling from his horse.

O what to her shall be the end?
    And what to me remains of good?
    To her, perpetual maidenhood,
And unto me no second friend.

VII

Dark house, by which once more I stand
    Here in the long unlovely street,[1]
    Doors, where my heart was used to beat
So quickly, waiting for a hand,

2. According to his son, Tennyson was writing a letter to Hallam at the hour of Hallam's death.
3. Arranging. The young woman addressed in the final five stanzas is a fictitious example, like the father and mother of stanzas 3 and 4.
1. Hallam's house on Wimpole Street, London. This section forms a pair with CXIX, when the speaker returns to the house once more.

5 A hand that can be clasp'd no more—
     Behold me, for I cannot sleep,
     And like a guilty thing I creep
At earliest morning to the door.

He is not here; but far away
10 The noise of life begins again,
     And ghastly thro' the drizzling rain
On the bald street breaks the blank day.

VIII

A happy lover who has come
     To look on her that loves him well,
     Who 'lights and rings the gateway bell,
And learns her gone and far from home;

5 He saddens, all the magic light
     Dies off at once from bower and hall,
     And all the place is dark, and all
The chambers emptied of delight:

So find I every pleasant spot
10 In which we two were wont to meet,
     The field, the chamber and the street,
For all is dark where thou art not.

Yet as that other, wandering there
     In those deserted walks, may find
15 A flower beat with rain and wind,
Which once she fostered up with care;

So seems it in my deep regret,
     O my forsaken heart, with thee
     And this poor flower of poesy
20 Which little cared for fades not yet.

But since it pleased a vanish'd eye,
     I go to plant it on his tomb,
     That if it can it there may bloom,
Or dying, there at least may die.

IX[1]

Fair ship, that from the Italian shore
   Sailest the placid ocean-plains
   With my lost Arthur's loved remains,
Spread thy full wings, and waft him o'er.

5   So draw him home to those that mourn
   In vain; a favourable speed
   Ruffle thy mirror'd mast, and lead
Thro' prosperous floods his holy urn.

All night no ruder air perplex
10   Thy sliding keel, till Phosphor,[2] bright
   As our pure love, thro' early light
Shall glimmer on the dewy decks.

Sphere all your lights around, above;
   Sleep, gentle heavens, before the prow;
15   Sleep, gentle winds, as he sleeps now,
My friend, the brother of my love;

My Arthur, whom I shall not see
   Till all my widow'd race be run;
   Dear as the mother to the son,
20   More than my brothers are to me.

X

I hear the noise about thy keel;
   I hear the bell struck in the night:
   I see the cabin-window bright;
I see the sailor at the wheel.

5   Thou bring'st the sailor to his wife,
   And travell'd men from foreign lands;
   And letters unto trembling hands;
And, thy dark freight, a vanish'd life.

So bring him: we have idle dreams:
10   This look of quiet flatters thus

1. Sections IX to XIX form a unit in which the speaker imagines (and often, as here, addresses) the ship that is bearing Hallam's body back to England. Hallam died in Vienna, and the ship left from Trieste (hence "Italian shore" in line 1). This section is one of the earliest written in the poem, composed while the body was in fact still at sea.
2. The morning star. See section CXXI.

Our home-bred fancies: O to us,
The fools of habit, sweeter seems

To rest beneath the clover sod,
    That takes the sunshine and the rains,
15   Or where the kneeling hamlet drains
The chalice of the grapes of God;

Than if with thee the roaring wells
    Should gulf him fathom-deep in brine;[1]
    And hands so often clasp'd in mine,
20 Should toss with tangle[2] and with shells.

XI

Calm is the morn without a sound,
    Calm as to suit a calmer grief,
    And only thro' the faded leaf
The chestnut pattering to the ground:

5 Calm and deep peace on this high wold,[1]
    And on these dews that drench the furze,
    And all the silvery gossamers[2]
That twinkle into green and gold:

Calm and still light on yon great plain
10   That sweeps with all its autumn bowers,
    And crowded farms and lessening towers,
To mingle with the bounding main:

Calm and deep peace in this wide air,
    These leaves that redden to the fall;
15   And in my heart, if calm at all,
If any calm, a calm despair:

Calm on the seas, and silver sleep,
    And waves that sway themselves in rest,
    And dead calm in that noble breast
20 Which heaves but with the heaving deep.

---

1. Better that Hallam be buried in the churchyard (lines 13–14) or in the church itself, where the congregation receives communion (lines 15–16) than his body be lost at sea.
2. Seaweed.
1. The name for the open, rolling countryside of Tennyson's native Lincolnshire.
2. Spiderwebs. "Furze": a thick shrublike plant.

XII

Lo, as a dove when up she springs
   To bear thro' Heaven a tale of woe,
   Some dolorous message knit below
The wild pulsation of her wings;[1]

5   Like her I go; I cannot stay;
     I leave this mortal ark behind,
     A weight of nerves without a mind,
And leave the cliffs, and haste away

O'er ocean-mirrors rounded large,
10   And reach the glow of southern skies,
     And see the sails at distance rise,
And linger weeping on the marge,

And saying; 'Comes he thus, my friend?
   Is this the end of all my care?'
15   And circle moaning in the air:
'Is this the end? Is this the end?'

And forward dart again, and play
   About the prow, and back return
   To where the body sits, and learn
20   That I have been an hour away.

XIII

Tears of the widower, when he sees
   A late-lost form that sleep reveals,
   And moves his doubtful arms, and feels
Her place is empty, fall like these;

5   Which weep a loss for ever new,
     A void where heart on heart reposed;
     And, where warm hands have prest and closed,
Silence, till I be silent too.

Which weep the comrade of my choice,
10   An awful thought, a life removed,

---

1. The reference is to a carrier pigeon, impatient to deliver a "message" (line 3). But there is also an allusion to the dove that Noah sends forth from the ark in Genesis 8; like the dove, Tennyson's spirit flies forth from his body ("this mortal ark," line 6) but can find no rest and eventually returns.

The human-hearted man I loved,
A Spirit, not a breathing voice.

Come Time, and teach me, many years,[1]
    I do not suffer in a dream;
15   For now so strange do these things seem,
Mine eyes have leisure for their tears;

My fancies time to rise on wing,
    And glance about the approaching sails,
    As tho' they brought but merchants' bales,
20   And not the burthen that they bring.

XIV

If one should bring me this report,
    That thou hadst touch'd the land to-day,
    And I went down unto the quay,
And found thee lying in the port;

5   And standing, muffled round with woe,
    Should see thy passengers in rank
    Come stepping lightly down the plank,
And beckoning unto those they know;

And if along with these should come
10   The man I held as half-divine;
    Should strike a sudden hand in mine,
And ask a thousand things of home;

And I should tell him all my pain,
    And how my life had droop'd of late,
15   And he should sorrow o'er my state
And marvel what possess'd my brain;

And I perceived no touch of change,
    No hint of death in all his frame,
    But found him all in all the same,
20   I should not feel it to be strange.

XV

To-night the winds begin to rise
    And roar from yonder dropping day:[1]

1. "Time" and "many years" are in apposition.
1. I.e., from the setting sun in the west.

The last red leaf is whirl'd away,
    The rooks are blown about the skies;

5   The forest crack'd, the waters curl'd,
        The cattle huddled on the lea;
        And wildly dash'd on tower and tree
    The sunbeam strikes along the world:

    And but for fancies, which aver
10   That all thy motions gently pass
        Athwart a plane of molten glass,
    I scarce could brook the strain and stir

    That makes the barren branches loud;
        And but for fear it is not so,
15   The wild unrest that lives in woe
    Would dote and pore on yonder cloud[2]

    That rises upward always higher,
        And onward drags a labouring breast,
        And topples round the dreary west,
20 A looming bastion fringed with fire.

XVI[1]

What words are these have fall'n from me?
    Can calm despair and wild unrest
    Be tenants of a single breast,
Or sorrow such a changeling be?

5   Or doth she only seem to take
        The touch of change in calm or storm;
        But knows no more of transient form
    In her deep self, than some dead lake

    That holds the shadow of a lark
10   Hung in the shadow of a heaven?
        Or has the shock, so harshly given,
    Confused me like the unhappy bark

2. If I were not able to picture the ship sailing in calm weather, on a sea as smooth as glass, my nerves would not be able to bear the storm I am witnessing. On the other hand, if I were not still so worried about the ship's progress, my grieving spirit would take pleasure in the sublime appearance of the storm cloud (described in the final stanza).

1. Tennyson's son wrote that in this section the speaker "questions himself about these alternations of 'calm despair' and 'wild unrest' [in earlier sections]. Do these changes only pass over the surface of the mind while in the depth still abides his unchanging sorrow? or has his reason been stunned by his grief?"

That strikes by night a craggy shelf,[2]
   And staggers blindly ere she sink?
15   And stunn'd me from my power to think
And all my knowledge of myself;

And made me that delirious man
   Whose fancy fuses old and new,
   And flashes into false and true,
20 And mingles all without a plan?

XVII

Thou comest, much wept for: such a breeze
   Compell'd thy canvas, and my prayer
   Was as the whisper of an air
To breathe thee over lonely seas.

5 For I in spirit saw thee move
   Thro' circles of the bounding sky,
   Week after week: the days go by:
Come quick, thou bringest all I love.

Henceforth, wherever thou may'st roam,
10   My blessing, like a line of light,
   Is on the waters day and night,
And like a beacon guards thee home.

So may whatever tempest mars
   Mid-ocean, spare thee, sacred bark;
15   And balmy drops in summer dark
Slide from the bosom of the stars.

So kind an office hath been done,
   Such precious relics brought by thee;
   The dust of him I shall not see
20 Till all my widow'd race be run.[1]

XVIII

'Tis well; 'tis something; we may stand
   Where he in English earth is laid,[1]
   And from his ashes may be made
The violet of his native land.

---

2. Like a boat ("bark") that strikes a reef ("craggy shelf").
1. Compare section IX, line 18.
1. Hallam was buried in St. Andrew's Church at Clevedon on January 3, 1834. Tennyson did not actually visit Clevedon until many years later.

5   'Tis little; but it looks in truth
    As if the quiet bones were blest
    Among familiar names to rest
And in the places of his youth.

Come then, pure hands, and bear the head
10   That sleeps or wears the mask of sleep,
    And come, whatever loves to weep,
And hear the ritual of the dead.

Ah yet, ev'n yet, if this might be,
    I, falling on his faithful heart,
15   Would breathing thro' his lips impart
The life that almost dies in me;

That dies not, but endures with pain,
    And slowly forms the firmer mind,
    Treasuring the look it cannot find,
20 The words that are not heard again.

XIX

The Danube to the Severn gave[1]
    The darken'd heart that beat no more;
    They laid him by the pleasant shore,
And in the hearing of the wave.

5   There twice a day the Severn fills;
    The salt sea-water passes by,
    And hushes half the babbling Wye,
And makes a silence in the hills.[2]

The Wye is hush'd nor moved along,
10   And hush'd my deepest grief of all,
    When fill'd with tears that cannot fall,
I brim with sorrow drowning song.

The tide flows down, the wave again
    Is vocal in its wooded walls;

---

1. Vienna, where Hallam died, is on the Danube, and Clevedon, where he was buried, is on the Severn.
2. The Wye River feeds into the Severn. Twice a day, at high tide, "the rapids of the Wye are stilled by the incoming sea" [T.].

15   My deeper anguish also falls,
      And I can speak a little then.

XX

The lesser griefs that may be said,
    That breathe a thousand tender vows,
    Are but as servants in a house
Where lies the master newly dead;

5   Who speak their feeling as it is,
      And weep the fulness from the mind:
      'It will be hard,' they say, 'to find
Another service such as this.'

My lighter moods are like to these,
10   That out of words a comfort win;
      But there are other griefs within,
And tears that at their fountain freeze;

For by the hearth the children sit
    Cold in that atmosphere of Death,
15   And scarce endure to draw the breath,
Or like to noiseless phantoms flit:

But open converse is there none,
    So much the vital spirits sink
    To see the vacant chair, and think,
20   'How good! how kind! and he is gone.'

XXI

I sing to him that rests below,
    And, since the grasses round me wave,
    I take the grasses of the grave,
And make them pipes whereon to blow.[1]

5   The traveller hears me now and then,
      And sometimes harshly will he speak:
      'This fellow would make weakness weak,
And melt the waxen hearts of men.'[2]

---

1. Here Tennyson imitates classical pastoral elegy, in which the speaker is imagined to be a
   shepherd or rustic. Where other major English elegies, such as Milton's "Lycidas," adhere
   to pastoral conventions throughout, Tennyson uses them sparingly.
2. In stanzas 2–5 the poet considers the charges that may be brought against him and his

Another answers, 'Let him be,
10   He loves to make parade of pain
        That with his piping he may gain
The praise that comes to constancy.'

A third is wroth: 'Is this an hour
        For private sorrow's barren song,
15   When more and more the people throng
The chairs and thrones of civil power?[3]

'A time to sicken and to swoon,
        When Science reaches forth her arms
        To feel from world to world, and charms
20   Her secret from the latest moon?'[4]

Behold, ye speak an idle thing:
        Ye never knew the sacred dust:
        I do but sing because I must,
And pipe but as the linnets[5] sing:

25   And one is glad; her note is gay,
        For now her little ones have ranged;
        And one is sad; her note is changed,
Because her brood is stol'n away.

XXII

The path by which we twain did go,
        Which led by tracts that pleased us well,
        Thro' four sweet years arose and fell,
From flower to flower, from snow to snow:

5   And we with singing cheer'd the way,
        And, crown'd with all the season lent,
        From April on to April went,
And glad at heart from May to May:

But where the path we walk'd began
10   To slant the fifth autumnal slope,[1]

---

poem: excessive sentimentality (lines 7–8); love of praise (lines 9–12); and selfish, self-imposed isolation from the stirring events of his time (lines 13–20).
3. Perhaps a reference to Chartism, a populist political movement of the 1830s and 1840s.
4. Referring to recent astronomical discoveries, in which Tennyson was keenly interested.
5. A linnet is a songbird.
1. Tennyson met Hallam at Cambridge in the spring of 1829; Hallam died in September, 1833, at the beginning of the fifth autumn of their friendship.

As we descended following Hope,
   There sat the Shadow fear'd of man;

Who broke our fair companionship,
   And spread his mantle dark and cold,
15   And wrapt thee formless in the fold,
And dull'd the murmur on thy lip,

And bore thee where I could not see
   Nor follow, tho' I walk in haste,
   And think, that somewhere in the waste
20   The Shadow sits and waits for me.

XXIII

Now, sometimes in my sorrow shut,
   Or breaking into song by fits;
   Alone, alone, to where he sits,
The Shadow cloak'd from head to foot,

5 Who keeps the keys of all the creeds,[1]
   I wander, often falling lame,
   And looking back to whence I came,
Or on to where the pathway leads;

And crying, How changed from where it ran
10   Thro' lands where not a leaf was dumb;
   But all the lavish hills would hum
The murmur of a happy Pan.[2]

When each by turns was guide to each,
   And Fancy light from Fancy caught,
15   And Thought leapt out to wed with Thought
Ere Thought could wed itself with Speech;

And all we met was fair and good,
   And all was good that Time could bring,
   And all the secret of the Spring
20   Moved in the chambers of the blood;

And many an old philosophy
   On Argive heights divinely sang,

1. This description fits Death ("The Shadow") since "After death we shall learn the truth of
all beliefs" [T.].
2. The Greek god of nature, the patron of shepherds (and hence of pastoral poetry), and the
inventor of the panpipes (see section XXI, line 4).

And round us all the thicket rang
To many a flute of Arcady.[3]

XXIV

And was the day of my delight
    As pure and perfect as I say?
    The very source and fount of Day
Is dash'd with wandering isles of night.[1]

5 If all was good and fair we met,
    This earth had been the Paradise
    It never look'd to human eyes
Since our first Sun arose and set.[2]

  And is it that the haze of grief
10   Makes former gladness loom so great?
    The lowness of the present state,
That sets the past in this relief?

  Or that the past will always win
    A glory from its being far;
15   And orb into the perfect star
We saw not, when we moved therein?

XXV

I know that this was Life,—the track
    Whereon with equal feet we fared;
    And then, as now, the day prepared
The daily burden for the back.

5 But this it was that made me move
    As light as carrier-birds in air;
    I loved the weight I had to bear,
Because it needed help of Love:

  Nor could I weary, heart or limb,
10   When mighty Love would cleave in twain
    The lading of a single pain,
And part it, giving half to him.

3. I.e., Arcadia, the region of Greece that traditionally provides the setting for pastoral poetry. "Argive": Greek. The stanza suggests that Tennyson and Hallam read Greek literature together and also that their own lives echoed the golden age of Greece.
1. I.e., the sun itself is flecked with sunspots.
2. In these stanzas the speaker doubts the recollections of the previous section, since such perfection has not existed on earth since humans were created.

XXVI

Still onward winds the dreary way;
   I with it; for I long to prove
   No lapse of moons can canker Love,[1]
Whatever fickle tongues may say.

5 And if that eye which watches guilt
   And goodness, and hath power to see
   Within the green the moulder'd tree,
And towers fall'n as soon as built—

Oh, if indeed that eye foresee
10 Or see (in Him is no before)
   In more of life true life no more
And Love the indifference to be,[2]

Then might I find, ere yet the morn
   Breaks hither over Indian seas,
15 That Shadow waiting with the keys,
To shroud me from my proper scorn.[3]

XXVII

I envy not in any moods
   The captive void of noble rage,
   The linnet born within the cage,
That never knew the summer woods:

5 I envy not the beast that takes
   His license in the field of time;[1]
   Unfetter'd by the sense of crime,
To whom a conscience never wakes;

Nor, what may count itself as blest,
10 The heart that never plighted troth
   But stagnates in the weeds of sloth;
Nor any want-begotten rest.[2]

I hold it true, what'er befall;
   I feel it, when I sorrow most;

1. I.e., the passage of time cannot destroy love.
2. I.e., if the love I now feel is destined to turn into indifference.
3. My proper scorn: "scorn of myself" [T.], but also with the implication "appropriate."
1. I.e., a man who lives (like a beast) without self-restraint.
2. Rest that springs only from lethargy or dullness.

15   'Tis better to have loved and lost
        Than never to have loved at all.[3]

                        XXVIII[1]

        The time draws near the birth of Christ:
            The moon is hid; the night is still;
            The Christmas bells from hill to hill
        Answer each other in the mist.

5   Four voices of four hamlets round,
            From far and near, on mead and moor,
            Swell out and fail, as if a door
        Were shut between me and the sound:

        Each voice four changes on the wind,[2]
10   That now dilate, and now decrease,
            Peace and goodwill, goodwill and peace,
        Peace and goodwill, to all mankind.

        This year I slept and woke with pain,
            I almost wish'd no more to wake,
15   And that my hold on life would break
        Before I heard those bells again:

        But they my troubled spirit rule,
            For they controll'd me when a boy;
            They bring me sorrow touch'd with joy,
20   The merry merry bells of Yule.

                        XXIX

        With such compelling cause to grieve
            As daily vexes household peace,
            And chains regret to his decease,
        How dare we keep our Christmas-eve;

5   Which brings no more a welcome guest
            To enrich the threshold of the night
            With shower'd largess of delight
        In dance and song and game and jest?

3. These lines are repeated in section LXXXV, lines 2–4; compare also Section I, lines 11–16.
1. Sections XXVIII–XXX describe the first Christmas after Hallam's death (1833). This is the first of three Christmases (the others occurring at LXXVIII and CV), that according to Tennyson mark the major divisions in the poem.
2. Sets of bells are pealed in varying sequences, or changes.

    Yet go, and while the holly boughs
10   Entwine the cold baptismal font,
      Make one wreath more for Use and Wont,
    That guard the portals of the house,

    Old sisters of a day gone by,
      Gray nurses, loving nothing new;[1]
15   Why should they miss their yearly due
    Before their time? They too will die.

XXX

    With trembling fingers did we weave
      The holly round the Christmas hearth;
      A rainy cloud possess'd the earth,
    And sadly fell our Christmas-eve.

5   At our old pastimes in the hall
      We gambol'd, making vain pretence
      Of gladness, with an awful sense
    Of one mute Shadow watching all.[1]

    We paused: the winds were in the beech:
10   We heard them sweep the winter land;
      And in a circle hand-in-hand
    Sat silent, looking each at each.

    Then echo-like our voices rang;
      We sung, tho' every eye was dim,
15   A merry song we sang with him
    Last year: impetuously we sang:

    We ceased: a gentler feeling crept
      Upon us: surely rest is meet:
      'They rest,' we said, 'their sleep is sweet,'
20   And silence follow'd, and we wept.

    Our voices took a higher range;
      Once more we sang: 'They do not die
      Nor lose their mortal sympathy,
    Nor change to us, although they change;

1. Both "sisters" and "nurses" refer to "Use and Wont" (line 11), i.e., custom and tradition.
1. The "Shadow" is Hallam, who had spent the previous Christmas with the Tennysons. "Awful": literally, "full of awe."

25 'Rapt from the fickle and the frail
    With gather'd power, yet the same,
    Pierces the keen seraphic flame
From orb to orb, from veil to veil.'[2]

    Rise, happy morn, rise, holy morn,
30   Draw forth the cheerful day from night:
    O Father, touch the east, and light
The light that shone when Hope was born.

XXXI[1]

When Lazarus left his charnel-cave,
    And home to Mary's house return'd,
    Was this demanded—if he yearn'd
To hear her weeping by his grave?

5 'Where wert thou, brother, those four days?'
    There lives no record of reply,
    Which telling what it is to die
Had surely added praise to praise.

From every house the neighbours met,
10   The streets were fill'd with joyful sound,
    A solemn gladness even crown'd
The purple brows of Olivet.[2]

Behold a man raised up by Christ!
    The rest remaineth unreveal'd;
15   He told it not; or something seal'd
The lips of that Evangelist.

XXXII[1]

Her eyes are homes of silent prayer,
    Nor other thought her mind admits

---

2. The spirit of the deceased (the "seraphic flame"), removed from this frail world, penetrates into ever higher reaches of heaven.
1. Sections XXXI and XXXII refer to the Gospel of John 11–12; John is the "Evangelist" of line 16. Lazarus, the brother of Mary and Martha, all of them followers of Jesus, dies and is buried. After four days Jesus visits the grave (the "charnel-cave") and raises Lazarus from death. Tennyson is intrigued by this episode because it implies a state after death but purposely does not describe it.
2. The Mount of Olives, near Jerusalem.
1. Tennyson pictures the scene in Mary's house after her brother Lazarus has returned. Stanza 3 refers to John 12:3 ("Then took Mary a pound of ointment of spikenard, very costly, and anointed the feet of Jesus, and wiped his feet with her hair").

But, he was dead, and there he sits,
And he that brought him back is there.

5   Then one deep love doth supersede
        All other, when her ardent gaze
        Roves from the living brother's face,
And rests upon the Life indeed.

All subtle thought, all curious fears,
10   Borne down by gladness so complete,
        She bows, she bathes the Saviour's feet
With costly spikenard and with tears.

Thrice blest whose lives are faithful prayers,
        Whose loves in higher love endure;
15   What souls possess themselves so pure,
Or is there blessedness like theirs?

XXXIII[1]

O thou that after toil and storm
        Mayst seem to have reach'd a purer air,
        Whose faith has centre everywhere,
Nor cares to fix itself to form,

5   Leave thou thy sister when she prays,
        Her early Heaven, her happy views;
        Nor thou with shadow'd hint confuse
A life that leads melodious days.

Her faith thro' form is pure as thine,
10   Her hands are quicker unto good:
        Oh, sacred be the flesh and blood
To which she links a truth divine!

See thou, that countest reason ripe
        In holding by the law within,[2]
15   Thou fail not in a world of sin,
And ev'n for want of such a type.

1. With the Lazarus story still in mind, Tennyson here imagines a brother and sister of his
   own day. The brother ("thou") has been through the "toil and storm" of doubt and developed his own faith, unattached to "form," i.e., any particular religious denomination. The
   sister retains the more formal doctrines she learned in childhood ("her early Heaven").
   The speaker warns the brother that such faith is just as "pure" and true as his own and
   should not be needlessly disturbed.
2. I.e., who consider it more rational to develop one's own understanding of faith.

XXXIV

My own dim life should teach me this,
　　That life shall live for evermore,
　　Else earth is darkness at the core,
And dust and ashes all that is;

5　This round of green, this orb of flame,
　　Fantastic beauty; such as lurks
　　In some wild Poet, when he works
Without a conscience or an aim.[1]

What then were God to such as I?
10　　'Twere hardly worth my while to choose
　　Of things all mortal, or to use
A little patience ere I die;

'Twere best at once to sink to peace,
　　Like birds the charming serpent draws,[2]
15　　To drop head-foremost in the jaws
Of vacant darkness and to cease.

XXXV

Yet if some voice that man could trust
　　Should murmur from the narrow house,[1]
　　'The cheeks drop in; the body bows;
Man dies: nor is there hope in dust:'

5　Might I not say? 'Yet even here,
　　But for one hour, O Love, I strive
　　To keep so sweet a thing alive:'
But I should turn mine ears and hear

The moanings of the homeless sea,
10　　The sound of streams that swift or slow
　　Draw down Aeonian hills, and sow
The dust of continents to be;[2]

---

1. If there is no life after death (stanza 1), then even the beauty of the earth and the sun are "fantastic," i.e., meaningless, like an artistic accident.
2. Certain snakes are said to be able to charm birds to fall out of trees.
1. I.e., the grave.
2. "Aeonian": everlasting. "The vastness of the Ages to come may seem to militate against . . . Love" [T.]. Compare section CXXIII, which also considers how the latest theories of geological change undermine faith.

And Love would answer with a sigh,
    'The sound of that forgetful shore[3]
15   Will change my sweetness more and more,
Half-dead to know that I shall die.'

O me, what profits it to put
    An idle case? If Death were seen
    At first as Death, Love had not been,
20   Or been in narrowest working shut,

Mere fellowship of sluggish moods,
    Or in his coarsest Satyr-shape
    Had bruised the herb and crush'd the grape,
And bask'd and batten'd in the woods.[4]

XXXVI

Tho' truths in manhood darkly join,
    Deep-seated in our mystic frame,
    We yield all blessing to the name
Of Him that made them current coin;[1]

5   For Wisdom dealt with mortal powers,
    Where truth in closest words shall fail,
    When truth embodied in a tale
Shall enter in at lowly doors.[2]

And so the Word had breath, and wrought
10   With human hands the creed of creeds
    In loveliness of perfect deeds,
More strong than all poetic thought;

Which he may read that binds the sheaf,
    Or builds the house, or digs the grave,
15   And those wild eyes that watch the wave
In roarings round the coral reef.[3]

3. The shore of the river Lethe, the boundary of the underworld, the waters of which cause the dead to forget their former lives.
4. I.e., if we were always conscious of death, no one would ever have bothered to love beyond mere animal love. "Batten'd": fed.
1. Tennyson audaciously suggests that the truths of Christianity are intuitively though "darkly" understood by everyone (lines 1–2), but that Christ deserves blessing for having made them clearly, generally known (lines 3–4).
2. "For divine Wisdom had to deal with the limited powers of humanity, to which truth logically argued out would be ineffectual, whereas truth coming in the story of the Gospel can influence the poorest"[T].
3. Christ, as the word of God made flesh (line 9), is accessible to everyone. Lines 15–16 refer to "Pacific Islanders" [T.].

XXXVII

Urania speaks with darken'd brow:[1]
　　'Thou pratest here where thou art least;
　　This faith has many a purer priest,
And many an abler voice than thou.

5　　'Go down beside thy native rill,
　　　On thy Parnassus set thy feet,
　　　And hear thy laurel whisper sweet
About the ledges of the hill.'[2]

And my Melpomene[3] replies,
10　　A touch of shame upon her cheek:
　　　'I am not worthy ev'n to speak
Of thy prevailing mysteries;

'For I am but an earthly Muse,
　　And owning but a little art
15　　To lull with song an aching heart,
And render human love his dues;

'But brooding on the dear one dead,
　　And all he said of things divine,[4]
　　(And dear to me as sacred wine
20　　To dying lips is all he said),

'I murmur'd, as I came along,
　　Of comfort clasp'd in truth reveal'd:
　　And loiter'd in the master's field,[5]
And darken'd sanctities with song.'

XXXVIII

With weary steps I loiter on,
　　Tho' always under alter'd skies
　　The purple from the distance dies,
My prospect and horizon gone.

1. Urania was the classical muse of astronomy, but in *Paradise Lost* Milton makes her the muse of heavenly or religious poetry. Here she berates the poet for dealing with matters of religion in which he is not skilled.
2. In other words, keep to your own type of poetry. "Parnassus": Greek mountain sacred to the Muses. "Laurel": traditional symbol of the classical poet.
3. Muse of tragic or elegiac poetry.
4. Tennyson greatly admired Hallam's writings about theology.
5. The master is God; hence "the province of Christianity" [T.].

5 No joy the blowing[1] season gives,
     The herald melodies of spring,
     But in the songs I love to sing
  A doubtful gleam of solace lives.

    If any care for what is here
10   Survive in spirits render'd free,
     Then are these songs I sing of thee
  Not all ungrateful to thine ear.

XXXIX[1]

Old warder of these buried bones,
    And answering now my random stroke
    With fruitful cloud and living smoke,[2]
Dark yew, that graspest at the stones

5 And dippest toward the dreamless head,
    To thee too comes the golden hour
    When flower is feeling after flower;
But Sorrow—fixt upon the dead,

And darkening the dark graves of men,—
10   What whisper'd from her lying lips?
    Thy gloom is kindled at the tips,
And passes into gloom again.

XL

Could we forget the widow'd hour
    And look on Spirits breathed away,
    As on a maiden in the day
When first she wears her orange-flower![1]

5 When crown'd with blessing she doth rise
    To take her latest leave of home,
    And hopes and light regrets that come
Make April of her tender eyes;

And doubtful joys the father move,
10   And tears are on the mother's face,

1. "Blossoming" [T.].
1. Written in 1868 and added to *In Memoriam* in 1870, this poem closely echoes sections II and III.
2. "The yew, when flowering, in a wind or if struck sends up its pollen like smoke." [T.].
1. An orange blossom was worn by a bride on her wedding day.

As parting with a long embrace
She enters other realms of love;

Her office there to rear, to teach,
    Becoming as is meet and fit
15   A link among the days, to knit
The generations each with each;

And, doubtless, unto thee² is given
    A life that bears immortal fruit
    In those great offices that suit
20   The full-grown energies of heaven.

Ay me, the difference I discern!
    How often shall her old fireside
    Be cheer'd with tidings of the bride,
How often she herself return,

25   And tell them all they would have told,³
    And bring her babe, and make her boast,
    Till even those that miss'd her most
Shall count new things as dear as old:

But thou and I have shaken hands,
30   Till growing winters lay me low;
    My paths are in the fields I know.
And thine in undiscover'd lands.

XLI

Thy spirit ere our fatal loss
    Did ever rise from high to higher;
    As mounts the heavenward altar-fire,
As flies the lighter thro' the gross.

5   But thou art turn'd to something strange,
    And I have lost the links that bound
    Thy changes; here upon the ground,
No more partaker of thy change.

Deep folly! yet that this could be—
10   That I could wing my will with might

2. Hallam.
3. I.e., all they wish to be told.

To leap the grades of life and light,
And flash at once, my friend, to thee.

For tho' my nature rarely yields
    To that vague fear implied in death;
15   Nor shudders at the gulfs beneath,
The howlings from forgotten fields;[1]

Yet oft when sundown skirts the moor
    An inner trouble I behold,
    A spectral doubt which makes me cold,
20 That I shall be thy mate no more,

Tho' following with an upward mind
    The wonders that have come to thee,
    Thro' all the secular to-be,[2]
But evermore a life behind.

XLII

I vex my heart with fancies dim:
    He still outstript me in the race;
    It was but unity of place
That made me dream I rank'd with him.

5   And so may Place retain us still,
    And he the much-beloved again,
    A lord of large experience, train
To riper growth the mind and will:

And what delights can equal those
10   That stir the spirit's inner deeps,
    When one that loves but knows not, reaps
A truth from one that loves and knows?

XLIII

If Sleep and Death be truly one,
    And every spirit's folded bloom
    Thro' all its intervital gloom
In some long trance should slumber on;[1]

1. Refers to "the eternal miseries of [Dante's] Inferno" [T.].
2. The "aeons of the future" [T.].
1. "Intervital gloom": "the passage between this life and the next" [T.]. Tennyson speculates
   that the souls of the deceased, rather than going straight to heaven, enter a state like sleep,
   until all souls awaken simultaneously at the end of time.

5   Unconscious of the sliding hour,
      Bare of the body, might it last,
      And silent traces of the past
   Be all the colour of the flower:[2]

   So then were nothing lost to man;
10   So that still garden of the souls
      In many a figured leaf enrolls
   The total world since life began;

   And love will last as pure and whole
      As when he loved me here in Time,
15   And at the spiritual prime
   Rewaken with the dawning soul.[3]

XLIV

   How fares it with the happy dead?
      For here the man is more and more;
      But he forgets the days before
   God shut the doorways of his head.[1]

5   The days have vanish'd, tone and tint,
      And yet perhaps the hoarding sense
      Gives out at times (he knows not whence)
   A little flash, a mystic hint;

   And in the long harmonious years
10   (If Death so taste Lethean springs),[2]
      May some dim touch of earthly things
   Surprise thee ranging with thy peers.

   If such a dreamy touch should fall,
      O turn thee round, resolve the doubt;
15   My guardian angel will speak out
   In that high place, and tell thee all.

2. "If . . . the spirit between this life and the next should be folded like a flower in a night slumber, then the remembrance of the past might remain, as the smell and colour do in the sleeping flower" [T.].

3. "Spiritual prime": dawn of the afterlife. "In that case the memory of our love would last as true, and would live pure and whole within the spirit of my friend until it was unfolded at the breaking of the morn" [T.].

1. "Closing of the skull after babyhood. The dead after this life may have no remembrance of life, like the living babe who forgets the time before the sutures of the skull are closed, yet . . . though the remembrance of his earliest days are vanished, . . . there comes a dreamy vision of what has been; it may be so with the dead" [T.].

2. I.e., if the dead do indeed forget; see n. 3, p. 29.

XLV

The baby new to earth and sky,
  What time his tender palm is prest
  Against the circle of the breast,
Has never thought that 'this is I:'

5 But as he grows he gathers much,
    And learns the use of 'I,' and 'me,'
    And finds 'I am not what I see,
  And other than the things I touch.'

So rounds he to a separate mind
10   From whence clear memory may begin,
    As thro' the frame that binds him in
  His isolation grows defined.

This use may lie in blood and breath,
    Which else were fruitless of their due,
15   Had man to learn himself anew
  Beyond the second birth of Death.[1]

XLVI

We ranging down this lower track,
    The path we came by, thorn and flower,
    Is shadow'd by the growing hour,
  Lest life should fail in looking back.

5 So be it: there no shade can last
    In that deep dawn behind the tomb,
    But clear from marge to marge shall bloom
  The eternal landscape of the past;

A lifelong tract of time reveal'd;
10   The fruitful hours of still increase;
    Days order'd in a wealthy peace,
  And those five years its richest field.[1]

---

1. The final stanza suggests that "the purpose of the life here [on earth] may be to realise personal consciousness" [T.], as described in the first three stanzas. In that case, the dead must surely retain some memory of their earthly life; otherwise the individual would have to "learn himself anew" after death, and the whole of this life would have been "fruitless."
1. On earth the past is not clearly remembered (stanza 1), but in heaven it will be (stanza 2), and "those five years" of Tennyson's friendship with Hallam will then be clearly seen as the "richest field" in the landscape of his life.

O Love, thy province were not large,
  A bounded field, nor stretching far;[2]
15   Look also, Love, a brooding star,
A rosy warmth from marge to marge.

XLVII[1]

That each, who seems a separate whole,
  Should move his rounds, and fusing all
  The skirts of self again, should fall
Remerging in the general Soul,

5 Is faith as vague as all unsweet:
  Eternal form shall still divide
  The eternal soul from all beside;
And I shall know him when we meet:

And we shall sit at endless feast,
10   Enjoying each the other's good:
  What vaster dream can hit the mood
Of Love on earth? He seeks at least

Upon the last and sharpest height,
  Before the spirits fade away,
15   Some landing-place, to clasp and say,
'Farewell! We lose ourselves in light.'

XLVIII

If these brief lays, of Sorrow born,
  Were taken to be such as closed
  Grave doubts and answers here proposed,
Then these were such as men might scorn:

5 Her care is not to part[1] and prove;
  She takes, when harsher moods remit,
  What slender shade of doubt may flit,
And makes it vassal unto love:

And hence, indeed, she sports with words,
10   But better serves a wholesome law,

2. I.e., but if Love shone only over those five years, its "province" would be restricted; therefore, "Look also."
1. Tennyson resists the notion that the soul loses its personal identity in heaven. "Individuality lasts after death, and we are not utterly absorbed in the Godhead. If we are to be finally merged in the Universal Soul, Love asks [in stanza 4] to have at least one more parting before we lose ourselves" [T.].
1. To analyze. "Her": refers to Sorrow.

And holds it sin and shame to draw
The deepest measure from the chords:

Nor dare she trust a larger lay,
    But rather loosens from the lip
15   Short swallow-flights of song, that dip
Their wings in tears, and skim away.

XLIX

From art, from nature, from the schools[1]
    Let random influences glance,
    Like light in many a shiver'd lance
That breaks about the dappled pools:

5 The lightest wave of thought shall lisp,
    The fancy's tenderest eddy wreathe,
    The slightest air of song shall breathe
To make the sullen surface crisp.[2]

And look thy look, and go thy way[3]
10   But blame not thou the winds that make
    The seeming-wanton ripple break,
The tender-pencil'd shadow play.

Beneath all fancied hopes and fears
    Ay me, the sorrow deepens down,
15   Whose muffled motions blindly drown
The bases of my life in tears.

L

Be near me when my light is low,
    When the blood creeps, and the nerves prick
    And tingle; and the heart is sick,
And all the wheels of Being slow.

5 Be near me when the sensuous frame
    Is rack'd with pangs that conquer trust;
    And Time, a maniac scattering dust,
And Life, a Fury slinging flame.

1. I.e., schools of thought.
2. Ripple. As in the previous section, the speaker says that his poetry will respond to all sorts of hopes and doubts; but it does not pretend to answer them or to resolve grief entirely (stanza 4).
3. Addressed to the reader, according to Tennyson.

Be near me when my faith is dry,
10   And men the flies of latter spring
        That lay their eggs, and sting and sing
And weave their petty cells and die.

Be near me when I fade away,
        To point the term[1] of human strife,
15   And on the low dark verge of life
The twilight of eternal day.

LI

Do we indeed desire the dead
        Should still be near us at our side?
        Is there no baseness we would hide?
No inner vileness that we dread?

5   Shall he for whose applause I strove,
        I had such reverence for his blame,
        See with clear eye some hidden shame
And I be lessen'd in his love?

I wrong the grave with fears untrue:
10   Shall love be blamed for want of faith?
        There must be wisdom with great Death:
The dead shall look me thro' and thro'.

Be near us when we climb or fall:
        Ye watch, like God, the rolling hours
15   With larger other eyes than ours,
To make allowance for us all.

LII

I cannot love thee as I ought,
        For love reflects the thing beloved;
        My words are only words, and moved
Upon the topmost froth of thought.[1]

5   'Yet blame not thou thy plaintive song,'
        The Spirit of true love replied;
        'Thou canst not move me from thy side,
Nor human frailty do me wrong.

1. Show the end.
1. Tennyson explained this: "There is so much evil in me that I don't really reflect you and all my talk is only *words*."

'What keeps a spirit wholly true
    To that ideal which he bears?
    What record? not the sinless years
That breathed beneath the Syrian blue:[2]

'So fret not, like an idle girl,
    That life is dash'd with flecks of sin.
    Abide: thy wealth is gather'd in,
When Time hath sunder'd shell from pearl.'

LIII

How many a father have I seen,
    A sober man, among his boys,
    Whose youth was full of foolish noise,
Who wears his manhood hale and green:

And dare we to this fancy give,[1]
    That had the wild oat not been sown,
    That soil, left barren, scarce had grown
The grain by which a man may live?

Or, if we held the doctrine sound
    For life outliving heats of youth,
    Yet who would preach it as a truth
To those that eddy round and round?[2]

Hold thou the good: define it well:
    For fear divine Philosophy
    Should push beyond her mark, and be
Procuress to the Lords of Hell.

LIV[1]

Oh yet we trust that somehow good
    Will be the final goal of ill,
    To pangs of nature, sins of will,
Defects of doubt, and taints of blood;

2. I.e., not even the story of the life of Christ (the "record" of the "sinless years") is enough to keep frail humans from occasionally sinning. The "Spirit of true love" (line 6) therefore encourages the speaker not to "fret" about falling short of his ideal of Hallam.

1. I.e., can we dare believe the following proposition?

2. Even if we believe that sowing wild oats sometimes proves beneficial for some, who would be so bold as to prescribe it to heedless young people?

1. Here Tennyson takes up the theme of the previous section, that good will arise from ill or from suffering. This then leads into the two following sections, in which he looks for confirmation of this doctrine in nature but does not find it.

5   That nothing walks with aimless feet;
    That not one life shall be destroy'd,
    Or cast as rubbish to the void,
When God hath made the pile complete;

    That not a worm is cloven in vain;
10   That not a moth with vain desire
    Is shrivell'd in a fruitless fire,
Or but subserves another's gain.

Behold, we know not anything;
    I can but trust that good shall fall
15   At last—far off—at last, to all,
And every winter change to spring.

So runs my dream: but what am I?
    An infant crying in the night:
    An infant crying for the light:
20 And with no language but a cry.

LV

The wish, that of the living whole
    No life may fail beyond the grave,
    Derives it not from what we have
The likest God within the soul?[1]

5   Are God and Nature then at strife,
    That Nature lends such evil dreams?
    So careful of the type she seems,
So careless of the single life;[2]

That I, considering everywhere
10   Her secret meaning in her deeds,
    And finding that of fifty seeds
She often brings but one to bear,[3]

I falter where I firmly trod,
    And falling with my weight of cares

1. "The divine in man" [T.].
2. Nature cares only for the continuation of the species ("the type"), not for individual lives. Hence Nature seems to be "at strife" with a God for whom each life is so precious that it survives forever.
3. " 'Fifty' should be 'myriad' " [T.]. Tennyson was familiar with contemporary scientific treatises, which noted the ruthlessness of the struggle for survival in nature well before Darwin put forward his theory of natural selection in 1859.

15   Upon the great world's altar-stairs
       That slope thro' darkness up to God,

       I stretch lame hands of faith, and grope,
          And gather dust and chaff, and call
          To what I feel is Lord of all,
20   And faintly trust the larger hope.

                         LVI

       'So careful of the type?' but no.
          From scarped cliff and quarried stone
          She cries, 'A thousand types are gone:
       I care for nothing, all shall go.[1]

5   'Thou makest thine appeal to me:
          I bring to life, I bring to death:
          The spirit does but mean the breath.[2]
       I know no more.' And he, shall he,

       Man, her last work, who seem'd so fair,
10   Such splendid purpose in his eyes,
          Who roll'd the psalm to wintry skies,
       Who built him fanes[3] of fruitless prayer,

       Who trusted God was love indeed
          And love Creation's final law—
15   Tho' Nature, red in tooth and claw
       With ravine, shriek'd against his creed—

       Who loved, who suffer'd countless ills,
          Who battled for the True, the Just,
          Be blown about the desert dust,
20   Or seal'd within the iron hills?

       No more? A monster then, a dream,
          A discord. Dragons of the prime,
          That tare each other in their slime,
       Were mellow music match'd with him.[4]

---

1. From the evidence of fossils found in quarried stone and cliffs cut away so that rock strata are exposed ("scarped"), we know that not only individuals but entire species have become extinct.
2. In Latin *spiritus* means "breath."
3. Temples.
4. If the true order of Nature is destruction and not love, then dinosaurs (the primordial

25   O life as futile, then, as frail!
      O for thy voice to soothe and bless!
      What hope of answer, or redress?
   Behind the veil, behind the veil.

LVII[1]

Peace; come away: the song of woe
   Is after all an earthly song:
   Peace; come away: we do him wrong
To sing so wildly: let us go.

5   Come; let us go: your cheeks are pale;
     But half my life I leave behind:
     Methinks my friend is richly shrined;
   But I shall pass; my work will fail.

Yet in these ears, till hearing dies,
10   One set slow bell will seem to toll
     The passing of the sweetest soul
   That ever look'd with human eyes.

I hear it now, and o'er and o'er,
   Eternal greetings to the dead;
15   And 'Ave, Ave, Ave,' said,
   'Adieu, adieu' for evermore.[2]

LVIII[1]

In those sad words I took farewell:
   Like echoes in sepulchral halls,
   As drop by drop the water falls
In vaults and catacombs, they fell;

5   And, falling, idly broke the peace
     Of hearts that beat from day to day,

"Dragons" who "tare [i.e., tore] each other in their slime") were more in harmony with
Nature than self-deluded humankind.

1. These lines are addressed to an unspecified auditor, clearly a fellow mourner.
2. "Ave": hail! (Latin). Tennyson noted that these lines echo the elegy by the Roman poet
Catullus for his brother (Catullus 101), which concludes with the words "ave atque vale,"
"hail and farewell." According to Tennyson, Catullus's lament is particularly poignant
because he did not believe in the afterlife; this allusion comes at a point in the poem when
the speaker's own faith in eternal life is at its lowest.
1. Tennyson said of the previous section that although it sounds like a conclusion, it was
"too sad for an ending." Here the speaker declares his intention to continue in a different
vein. The "high Muse" (line 9) is again Urania, as in section XXXVII.

Half-conscious of their dying clay,
And those cold crypts where they shall cease.

The high Muse answer'd: 'Wherefore grieve
10   Thy brethren with a fruitless tear?
      Abide a little longer here,
And thou shalt take a nobler leave.'

LIX[1]

O Sorrow, wilt thou live with me
      No casual mistress, but a wife,
      My bosom-friend and half of life;
As I confess it needs must be;

5   O Sorrow, wilt thou rule my blood,
      Be sometimes lovely like a bride,
      And put thy harsher moods aside,
If thou wilt have me wise and good.

My centred passion cannot move,
10   Nor will it lessen from to-day;
      But I'll have leave at times to play
As with the creature of my love;

And set thee forth, for thou art mine,
      With so much hope for years to come,
15   That, howsoe'er I know thee, some
Could hardly tell what name were thine.[2]

LX[1]

He past; a soul of nobler tone:
      My spirit loved and loves him yet,
      Like some poor girl whose heart is set
On one whose rank exceeds her own.

---

1. This section was added in the fourth edition of *In Memoriam* (1851) as the "pendant," or pair, to section III, just as section XXXIX is paired with section II.
2. My love for Hallam will never waver (lines 9–10), but my sorrow, the result or "creature" of that love (line 12), will take different forms, to the point that others may scarcely recognize it as sorrow at all.
1. Sections LX–LXV form one of the most tightly connected groups in the poem, being linked not only thematically but sometimes syntactically as well. The metaphor of this section is particularly poignant, since Tennyson's sister Emily was engaged to Hallam; their wedding was delayed because of the disparity in their social status.

5 He mixing with his proper sphere,
    She finds the baseness of her lot,
    Half jealous of she knows not what,
And envying all that meet him there.

    The little village looks for forlorn;
10   She sighs amid her narrow days,
    Moving about the household ways,
In that dark house where she was born.

    The foolish neighbours come and go,
    And tease her till the day draws by:
15   At night she weeps, 'How vain am I!
How should he love a thing so low?'

LXI

If, in thy second state sublime,
    Thy ransom'd reason change replies
    With all the circle of the wise,
The perfect flower of human time;[1]

5 And if thou cast thine eyes below,
    How dimly character'd and slight,
    How dwarf'd a growth of cold and night,
How blanch'd with darkness must I grow!

    Yet turn thee to the doubtful shore,
10   Where thy first form was made a man;[2]
    I loved thee, Spirit, and love, nor can
The soul of Shakspeare love thee more.[3]

LXII

Tho' if an eye that's downward cast
    Could make thee somewhat blench or fail,[1]
    Then be my love an idle tale,
And fading legend of the past;

1. If you in heaven, with your now higher understanding ("ransom'd reason"), hold conversation with all the wise people who ever lived on earth. "Change": exchange.
2. I.e., this world, now almost indiscernible to you ("doubtful").
3. Shakespeare is specifically cited because he too addressed a series of poems (the Sonnets) to a beloved friend. Both this section and the next contain echoes of Sonnet 116.
1. Balk or falter.

5   And thou, as one that once declined,[2]
      When he was little more than boy,
      On some unworthy heart with joy,
    But lives to wed an equal mind;

    And breathes a novel world, the while
10   His other passion wholly dies,
      Or in the light of deeper eyes
    Is matter for a flying smile.

LXIII

    Yet pity for a horse o'er-driven,
      And love in which my hound has part,
      Can hang no weight upon my heart
    In its assumptions up to heaven;

5   And I am so much more than these,
      As thou, perchance, art more than I,
      And yet I spare them sympathy,
    And I would set their pains at ease.

    So mayst thou watch me where I weep,
10   As, unto vaster motions bound,
      The circuits of thine orbit round
    A higher height, a deeper deep.

LXIV

    Dost thou look back on what hath been,
      As some divinely gifted man,
      Whose life in low estate began
    And on a simple village green;

5   Who breaks his birth's invidious bar,
      And grasps the skirts of happy chance,
      And breasts the blows of circumstance,
    And grapples with his evil star;[1]

    Who makes by force his merit known
10   And lives to clutch the golden keys,[2]
      To mould a mighty state's decrees,
    And shape the whisper of the throne;

2. I.e., stooped to love.
1. Bad fortune (of being born "in low estate").
2. Symbols of public office.

And moving up from high to higher,
　　Becomes on Fortune's crowning slope
15　　The pillar of a people's hope,
The centre of a world's desire;

Yet feels, as in a pensive dream,
　　When all his active powers are still,
　　A distant dearness in the hill,
20　A secret sweetness in the stream,

The limit of his narrower fate,
　　While yet beside its vocal springs
　　He play'd at counsellors and kings,
With one that was his earliest mate;

25　Who ploughs with pain his native lea
　　And reaps the labour of his hands,
　　Or in the furrow musing stands;
'Does my old friend remember me?'

LXV

Sweet soul, do with me as thou wilt;
　　I lull a fancy trouble-tost
　　With 'Love's too precious to be lost,
A little grain shall not be spilt.'[1]

5　And in that solace can I sing,
　　Till out of painful phases wrought
　　There flutters up a happy thought,
Self-balanced on a lightsome wing:

Since we deserved the name of friends,
10　　And thine effect so lives in me,
　　A part of mine may live in thee
And move thee on to noble ends.

LXVI

You thought my heart too far diseased;[1]
　　You wonder when my fancies play
　　To find me gay among the gay,
Like one with any trifle pleased.

1. This phrase (which is not a direct quotation from any known source) looks back to section
LV, lines 11–12, and forward to section LXXXI.
1. Addressed, like Section LVII, to an unspecified auditor.

5   The shade by which my life was crost,
           Which makes a desert in the mind,
           Has made me kindly with my kind,
       And like to him whose sight is lost;

       Whose feet are guided thro' the land,
10   Whose jest among his friends is free,
           Who takes the children on his knee,
       And winds their curls about his hand:

       He plays with threads,[2] he beats his chair
           For pastime, dreaming of the sky;
15   His inner day can never die,
       His night of loss is always there.

                        LXVII

       When on my bed the moonlight falls,
           I know that in thy place of rest
           By that broad water of the west,[1]
       There comes a glory on the walls;

5   Thy marble bright in dark appears,
           As slowly steals a silver flame
           Along the letters of thy name,
       And o'er the number of thy years.

       The mystic glory swims away;
10   From off my bed the moonlight dies;
           And closing eaves of wearied eyes
       I sleep till dusk is dipt in gray:

       And then I know the mist is drawn
           A lucid veil from coast to coast,
15   And in the dark church like a ghost
       Thy tablet glimmers to the dawn.[2]

                        LXVIII

       When in the down I sink my head,
           Sleep, Death's twin-brother, times my breath;

---

2. Makes cat's cradles to amuse children.
1. "The Severn" [T.].
2. "I myself did not see Clevedon until years after the burial of A.H.H" [T.]; for this reason,
   the earliest editions of In Memoriam mistake the position in the church of Hallam's com-
   memorative "tablet."

Sleep, Death's twin-brother, knows not Death,
Nor can I dream of thee as dead:

5   I walk as ere I walk'd forlorn,
        When all our path was fresh with dew,
        And all the bugle breezes blew
Reveillée to the breaking morn.

But what is this? I turn about,
10   I find a trouble in thine eye,
        Which makes me sad I know not why,
Nor can my dream resolve the doubt:

But ere the lark hath left the lea
        I wake, and I discern the truth;
15   It is the trouble of my youth
That foolish sleep transfers to thee.

LXIX

I dream'd there would be Spring no more,
        That Nature's ancient power was lost:
        The streets were black with smoke and frost,
They chatter'd trifles at the door:

5   I wander'd from the noisy town,
        I found a wood with thorny boughs:
        I took the thorns to bind my brows,
I wore them like a civic crown:

I met with scoffs, I met with scorns
10   From youth and babe and hoary hairs:
        They call'd me in the public squares
The fool that wears a crown of thorns:[1]

They call'd me fool, they call'd me child:
        I found an angel of the night;
15   The voice was low, the look was bright;
He look'd upon my crown and smiled:

He reach'd the glory of a hand,
        That seem'd to touch it into leaf:

1. "To write poems about death and grief is 'to wear a crown of thorns,' which the people
say ought to be laid aside" [T.]. Compare Jesus' crown of thorns (Matthew 27:29).

The voice was not the voice of grief,
20   The words were hard to understand.

LXX

I cannot see the features right,
    When on the gloom I strive to paint
    The face I know; the hues are faint
And mix with hollow masks of night;

5   Cloud-towers by ghostly masons wrought,
    A gulf that ever shuts and gapes,
    A hand that points, and palled[1] shapes
In shadowy thoroughfares of thought;

And crowds that stream from yawning doors,
10   And shoals of pucker'd faces drive;
    Dark bulks that tumble half alive,
And lazy lengths on boundless shores;

Till all at once beyond the will
    I hear a wizard[2] music roll,
15   And thro' a lattice on the soul
Looks thy fair face and makes it still

LXXI

Sleep, kinsman thou to death and trance
    And madness, thou hast forged at last
    A night-long Present of the Past
In which we went thro' summer France.[1]

5   Hadst thou such credit with the soul?
    Then bring an opiate trebly strong,
    Drug down the blindfold sense of wrong
That so my pleasure may be whole;[2]

While now we talk as once we talk'd
10   Of men and minds, the dust of change,
    The days that grow to something strange,
In walking as of old we walk'd

1. Shrouded.
2. Magic.
1. Tennyson has dreamed of the trip he took with Hallam to the Pyrenees in the summer of 1830.
2. I.e., if sleep can revive the past, let it also obliterate the grievous sense of injury.

Beside the river's wooded reach,
 The fortress, and the mountain ridge,
15 The cataract flashing from the bridge,
The breaker breaking on the beach.

LXXII

Risest thou thus, dim dawn, again,[1]
 And howlest, issuing out of night,
 With blasts that blow the poplar white,[2]
And lash with storm the streaming pane?

5 Day, when my crown'd estate begun
 To pine in that reverse of doom,
 Which sicken'd every living bloom,
And blurr'd the splendour of the sun;

Who usherest in the dolorous hour
10 With thy quick tears that make the rose
 Pull sideways, and the daisy close
Her crimson fringes to the shower;

Who might'st have heaved a windless flame[3]
 Up the deep East, or, whispering, play'd
15 A chequer-work of beam and shade
Along the hills, yet look'd the same,

As wan, as chill, as wild as now;
 Day, mark'd as with some hideous crime,
 When the dark hand struck down thro' time,
20 And cancell'd nature's best: but thou,

Lift as thou may'st thy burthen'd brows
 Thro' clouds that drench the morning star,
 And whirl the ungarner'd sheaf afar,
And sow the sky with flying boughs,

25 And up thy vault with roaring sound
 Climb thy thick noon, disastrous day;
 Touch thy dull goal of joyless gray,
And hide thy shame beneath the ground.

---

1. "Hallam's death-day, September the 15th" [T.]. The first anniversary (1834); the second is commemorated in section XCIX.
2. I.e., the wind exposes the white undersides of the poplar leaves.
3. I.e., a calm, sunny day.

LXXIII

So many worlds; so much to do,
   So little done, such things to be,
   How know I what had need of thee,
For thou wert strong as thou wert true?

5   The fame is quench'd that I foresaw,
   The head hath miss'd an earthly wreath:
   I curse not nature, no, nor death;
For nothing is that errs from law.

We pass; the path that each man trod
10   Is dim, or will be dim, with weeds:
   What fame is left for human deeds
In endless age? It rests with God.

O hollow wraith of dying fame,
   Fade wholly, while the soul exults,
15   And self-infolds the large results
Of force that would have forged a name.[1]

LXXIV

As sometimes in a dead man's face,
   To those that watch it more and more,
   A likeness, hardly seen before,
Comes out—to some one of his race:

5   So, dearest, now thy brows are cold,[1]
   I see thee what thou art, and know
   Thy likeness to the wise below,
Thy kindred with the great of old.

But there is more than I can see,
10   And what I see I leave unsaid,
   Nor speak it, knowing Death has made
His darkness beautiful with thee.

LXXV

I leave thy praises unexpress'd
   In verse that brings myself relief,

1. I.e., Hallam's soul in heaven still reaps the benefits of talents that would have made him famous on earth.
1. In response to a reviewer's remarks on these lines, Tennyson commented, "If anybody thinks I ever called him 'dearest' in his life they are much mistaken, for I never even called him 'dear.' "

And by the measure of my grief
I leave thy greatness to be guess'd;

5   What practice howsoe'er expert
      In fitting aptest words to things,
      Or voice the richest-toned that sings,
Hath power to give thee as thou wert?

I care not in these fading days
10   To raise a cry that lasts not long,
      And round thee with the breeze of song
To stir a little dust of praise.

Thy leaf has perish'd in the green,
      And, while we breathe beneath the sun,
15   The world which credits what is done
Is cold to all that might have been.

So here shall silence guard thy fame;
      But somewhere, out of human view,
      Whate'er thy hands are set to do
20 Is wrought with tumult of acclaim.

LXXVI

Take wings of fancy, and ascend,
      And in a moment set thy face
      Where all the starry heavens of space
Are sharpen'd to a needle's end;[1]

5   Take wings of foresight; lighten thro'
      The secular abyss to come,[2]
      And lo, thy deepest lays are dumb
Before the mouldering of a yew;

And if the matin songs,[3] that woke
10   The darkness of our planet, last,
      Thine own shall wither in the vast,
Ere half the lifetime of an oak.

Ere these have clothed their branchy bowers
      With fifty Mays, thy songs are vain;

1. Imagine yourself "so distant in void space that all our firmament would appear to be a needle-point thence" [T.]. The poet addresses an auditor, or perhaps himself.
2. "The ages upon ages to be" [T.].
3. "The great early poets" [T.].

15   And what are they when these remain
        The ruin'd shells of hollow towers?

LXXVII

What hope is here for modern rhyme
        To him, who turns a musing eye
        On songs, and deeds, and lives, that lie
Foreshorten'd in the tract of time?

5   These mortal lullabies of pain
        May bind a book, may line a box,
        May serve to curl a maiden's locks;
Or when a thousand moons shall wane

A man upon a stall may find,
10   And, passing, turn the page that tells
        A grief, then changed to something else
Sung by a long-forgotten mind.

But what of that? My darken'd ways
        Shall ring with music all the same;
15   To breathe my loss is more than fame,
To utter love more sweet than praise.

LXXVIII

Again at Christmas did we weave
        The holly round the Christmas hearth;
        The silent snow possess'd the earth,
And calmly fell our Christmas eve:[1]

5   The yule-clog[2] sparkled keen with frost,
        No wing of wind the region swept,
        But over all things brooding slept
The quiet sense of something lost.

As in the winters left behind,
10   Again our ancient games had place,
        The mimic picture's breathing grace,[3]
And dance and song and hoodman-blind.[4]

1. Compare the opening of the two other Christmas sections (XXX and CV).
2. Yule log (Lincolnshire dialect).
3. "Tableaux vivants" [T.]; a parlor game like charades.
4. Blind man's bluff, another parlor game.

Who show'd a token of distress?
 No single tear, no mark of pain:
15 O sorrow, then can sorrow wane?
O grief, can grief be changed to less?

 O last regret, regret can die!
  No—mixt with all this mystic frame,
  Her deep relations are the same
20 But with long use her tears are dry.[5]

LXXIX

'More than my brothers are to me,'—
 Let this not vex thee, noble heart![1]
 I know thee of what force thou art
To hold the costliest love in fee.[2]

5 But thou and I are one in kind,
  As moulded like in Nature's mint;
  And hill and wood and field did print
The same sweet forms in either mind.

 For us the same cold streamlet curl'd
10 Thro' all his eddying coves; the same
  All winds that roam the twilight came
In whispers of the beauteous world.

 At one dear knee we proffer'd vows,
  One lesson from one book we learn'd,
15 Ere childhood's flaxen ringlet turn'd
To black and brown on kindred brows.

 And so my wealth resembles thine,
  But he was rich where I was poor,
  And he supplied my want the more
20 As his unlikeness fitted mine.

LXXX

If any vague desire should rise,
 That holy Death ere Arthur died

---

5. Regret remains diffused throughout the deepest parts of the spirit, though no longer out-
wardly visible.
1. "The section is addressed to my brother Charles" [T.]. Line 1 quotes section IX, line 20.
2. In possession.

Had moved me kindly from his side,
And dropt the dust on tearless eyes;[1]

5   Then fancy shapes, as fancy can,
        The grief my loss in him had wrought,
        A grief as deep as life or thought,
     But stay'd in peace with God and man.

     I make a picture in the brain;
10   I hear the sentence that he speaks;
        He bears the burthen of the weeks
     But turns his burthen into gain.

     His credit thus shall set me free;
        And, influence-rich to soothe and save,
15   Unused example from the grave
     Reach out dead hands to comfort me.

LXXXI

     Could I have said while he was here,[1]
        'My love shall now no further range;
        There cannot come a mellower change,
     For now is love mature in ear.'

5   Love, then, had hope of richer store:
        What end is here to my complaint?
        This haunting whisper makes me faint,
     'More years had made me love thee more.'

     But Death returns an answer sweet:
10   'My sudden frost was sudden gain,
        And gave all ripeness to the grain,
     It might have drawn from after-heat.'

LXXXII

     I wage not any feud with Death
        For changes wrought on form and face;
        No lower life that earth's embrace
     May breed with him, can fright my faith.

---

1. I.e., that I had died before Arthur did (and so been buried with "tearless eyes").
1. I.e., "I wish I could have said."

5   Eternal process moving on,
        From state to state the spirit walks;
        And these are but the shatter'd stalks,
    Or ruin'd chrysalis of one.[1]

    Nor blame I Death, because he bare[2]
10   The use of virtue out of earth:
        I know transplanted human worth
    Will bloom to profit, otherwise.

    For this alone on Death I wreak
        The wrath that garners[3] in my heart;
15   He put our lives so far apart
    We cannot hear each other speak.

LXXXIII[1]

    Dip down upon the northern shore,
        O sweet new-year delaying long;
        Thou doest expectant nature wrong;
    Delaying long, delay no more.

5   What stays thee from the clouded noons,
        Thy sweetness from its proper place?
        Can trouble live with April days,
    Or sadness in the summer moons?

    Bring orchis, bring the foxglove spire,
10   The little speedwell's darling blue,
        Deep tulips dash'd with fiery dew,
    Laburnums, dropping-wells of fire.

    O thou, new-year, delaying long,
        Delayest the sorrow in my blood,
15   That longs to burst a frozen bud
    And flood a fresher throat with song.

---

1. "These" (i.e., the stages of decomposition, described in lines 2–4) merely represent the worn-out husks discarded by the developing soul, as a butterfly discards its "chrysalis" or cocoon.
2. Bore.
3. Gathers (used especially of grain).
1. This lyric marks the beginning of the second spring since Hallam's death; compare the other springs (sections XXXVIII and CXV).

LXXXIV

When I contemplate all alone
    The life that had been[1] thine below,
    And fix my thoughts on all the glow
To which thy crescent would have grown;

5   I see thee sitting crown'd with good,
    A central warmth diffusing bliss
    In glance and smile, and clasp and kiss,
On all the branches of thy blood;

Thy blood, my friend, and partly mine;
10   For now the day was drawning on,
    When thou should'st link thy life with one
Of mine own house,[2] and boys of thine

Had babbled 'Uncle' on my knee;
    But that remorseless iron hour
15   Made cypress of her orange flower,[3]
Despair of Hope, and earth of thee.

I seem to meet their least desire,
    To clap their cheeks, to call them mine.
    I see their unborn faces shine
20 Beside the never-lighted fire.

I see myself an honour'd guest,
    Thy partner in the flowery walk
    Of letters, genial table-talk,
Or deep dispute, and graceful jest;

25 While now thy prosperous labour fills
    The lips of men with honest praise,
    And sun by sun the happy days
Descend below the golden hills

With promise of a morn as fair;
30   And all the train of bounteous hours
    Conduct by paths of growing powers,
To reverence and the silver hair;

1. I.e., would have been.
2. "The projected marriage of A.H.H. with Emily Tennyson" [T.]. Hallam was engaged to Tennyson's younger sister.
3. The cypress is a symbol of mourning, the orange blossom of a bride.

Till slowly worn her earthly robe,
     Her lavish mission richly wrought,
35   Leaving great legacies of thought,
Thy spirit should fail from off the globe;

What time mine own might also flee,
     As link'd with thine in love and fate,
     And, hovering o'er the dolorous strait
40 To the other shore, involved in thee,

Arrive at last the blessed goal,
     And He that died in Holy Land
     Would reach us out the shining hand,
And take us as a single soul.

45 What reed was that on which I leant?
     Ah, backward fancy, wherefore wake
     The old bitterness again, and break
The low beginnings of content.

LXXXV

This truth came borne with bier and pall,
     I felt it, when I sorrow'd most,
     'Tis better to have loved and lost,
Than never to have loved at all[1]—

5 O true in word, and tried in deed,[2]
     Demanding, so to bring relief
     To this which is our common grief,
What kind of life is that I lead;

And whether trust in things above
10   Be dimm'd of sorrow, or sustain'd;
     And whether love for him have drain'd
My capabilities of love;

Your words have virtue such as draws
     A faithful answer from the breast,
15   Thro' light reproaches, half exprest,
And loyal unto kindly laws.

1. Compare section XXVII, lines 13–16.
2. This whole section is addressed, according to Tennyson, to Edmund Lushington, a close
friend who later (1842) married Tennyson's sister Cecilia; their wedding is described in
the Epilogue.

My blood an even tenor kept,
 Till on mine ear this message falls,
 That in Vienna's fatal walls
20 God's finger touch'd him, and he slept.

 The great Intelligences fair
  That range above our mortal state,
  In circle round the blessed gate,
 Received and gave him welcome there;

25 And led him thro' the blissful climes,
  And show'd him in the fountain fresh
  All knowledge that the sons of flesh
 Shall gather in the cycled times.[3]

 But I remain'd, whose hopes were dim,
30 Whose life, whose thoughts were little worth,
  To wander on a darken'd earth,
 Where all things round me breathed of him.

 O friendship, equal-poised control,
  O heart, with kindliest motion warm,
35 O sacred essence, other form,
 O solemn ghost, O crowned soul!

 Yet none could better know than I,
  How much of act at human hands
  The sense of human will demands[4]
40 By which we dare to live or die.

 Whatever way my days decline,
  I felt and feel, tho' left alone,
  His being working in mine own,
 The footsteps of his life in mine;

45 A life that all the Muses deck'd
  With gifts of grace, that might express
  All-comprehensive tenderness,
 All-subtilising intellect:

3. The angels or "Intelligences" (line 21) showed Hallam all the knowledge that will be gathered on earth in ages to come ("the cycled times").
4. Although bereft (as the two previous stanzas express), the speaker admits "that the knowledge that we have free will demands from us action" [T.].

And so my passion hath not swerved
50 To works of weakness, but I find
  An image comforting the mind,
And in my grief a strength reserved.

Likewise the imaginative woe,[5]
  That loved to handle spiritual strife,
55 Diffused the shock thro' all my life,
But in the present broke the blow.

My pulses therefore beat again
  For other friends that once I met;
  Nor can it suit me to forget
60 The mighty hopes that make us men.

I woo your love: I count it crime
  To mourn for any overmuch;
  I, the divided half of such
A friendship as had master'd Time;

65 Which masters Time indeed, and is
  Eternal, separate from fears:
  The all-assuming months and years
Can take no part away from this:

But Summer on the steaming floods,
70 And Spring that swells the narrow brooks,
  And Autumn, with a noise of rooks,
That gather in the waning woods,

And every pulse of wind and wave
  Recalls, in change of light or gloom,
75 My old affection of the tomb,
And my prime passion in the grave:

My old affection of the tomb,
  A part of stillness, yearns to speak:
  'Arise, and get thee forth and seek
80 A friendship for the years to come.

'I watch thee from the quiet shore;
  Thy spirit up to mine can reach;

---

5. I.e., the ability and tendency to sympathize with grief.

But in dear words of human speech
We two communicate no more.'

85   And I, 'Can clouds of nature stain
The starry clearness of the free?
How is it? Canst thou feel for me
Some painless sympathy with pain?'

And lightly does the whisper fall;
90   ' 'Tis hard for thee to fathom this;
I triumph in conclusive bliss,
And that serene result of all.'

So hold I commerce with the dead;
Or so methinks the dead would say;
95   Or so shall grief with symbols play
And pining life be fancy-fed.

Now looking to some settled end,
That these things pass, and I shall prove[6]
A meeting somewhere, love with love,
100   I crave your pardon, O my friend;

If not so fresh, with love as true,
I, clasping brother-hands, aver
I could not, if I would, transfer
The whole I felt for him to you.

105   For which be they that hold apart
The promise of the golden hours?[7]
First love, first friendship, equal powers,
That marry with the virgin heart.

Still mine, that cannot but deplore,
110   That beats within a lonely place,
That yet remembers his embrace,
But at his footstep leaps no more,

My heart, tho' widow'd may not rest
Quite in the love of what is gone,
115   But seeks to beat in time with one
That warms another living breast.

6. Experience.
7. For what are the things that make youth a time "apart" from all others?

Ah, take the imperfect gift I bring,
    Knowing the primrose yet is dear,
    The primrose of the later year,
120 As not unlike to that of Spring.

LXXXVI

Sweet after showers, ambrosial air,
    That rollest from the gorgeous gloom
    Of evening over brake[1] and bloom
And meadow, slowly breathing bare

5 The round of space, and rapt below
    Thro' all the dewy-tassell'd wood,
    And shadowing down the horned flood[2]
In ripples, fan my brows and blow

The fever from my cheek, and sigh
10   The full new life that feeds thy breath
    Throughout my frame, till Doubt and Death,
Ill brethren, let the fancy fly

From belt to belt of crimson seas
    On leagues of odour streaming far,
15   To where in yonder orient[3] star
A hundred spirits whisper 'Peace.'

LXXXVII

I past beside the reverend walls
    In which of old I wore the gown;[1]
    I roved at random thro' the town,
And saw the tumult of the halls;

5 And heard once more in college fanes
    The storm their high-built organs make,
    And thunder-music, rolling, shake
The prophet blazon'd on the panes;[2]

And caught once more the distant shout,
10   The measured pulse of racing oars

1. Bush or thicket. The "air" (line 1) is meant to be "a west wind" [T.].
2. A river "between two promontories" [T.].
3. Rising. "Any rising star is here intended" [T.].
1. "Trinity College, Cambridge" [T.], where Tennyson and Hallam met as undergraduates.
2. I.e., the organ music rattles the stained glass of the college chapels ("fanes").

Among the willows; paced the shores
And many a bridge, and all about

The same gray flats again, and felt
    The same, but not the same; and last
15   Up that long walk of limes I past
To see the rooms in which he dwelt.[3]

Another name was on the door:
    I linger'd; all within was noise
    Of songs, and clapping hands, and boys
20   That crash'd the glass and beat the floor;

Where once we held debate, a band
    Of youthful friends, on mind and art,
    And labour, and the changing mart,
And all the framework of the land;[4]

25   When one would aim an arrow fair,
    But send it slackly from the string;
    And one would pierce an outer ring,
And one an inner, here and there;

And last the master-bowman, he,
30   Would cleave the mark. A willing ear
    We lent him. Who, but hung to hear
The rapt oration flowing free

From point to point, with power and grace
    And music in the bounds of law,
35   To those conclusions when we saw
The God within him light his face,

And seem to lift the form, and glow
    In azure orbits heavenly-wise;
    And over those ethereal eyes
40   The bar of Michael Angelo.[5]

LXXXVIII

Wild bird, whose warble, liquid sweet,
    Rings Eden thro' the budded quicks,[1]

3. Hallam's rooms "were in New Court" [T.], at the end of Trinity Avenue ("that long walk").
4. Hallam and Tennyson were members of the Apostles, a society for intellectual discussion.
5. Like Michelangelo, Hallam had "a broad bar of frontal bone over the eyes" [T.].
1. Hedgerows. The bird addressed is "the Nightingale" [T.].

O tell me where the senses mix,
O tell me where the passions meet,

5   Whence radiate: fierce extremes employ
    Thy spirits in the darkening leaf,
    And in the midmost heart of grief
Thy passion clasps a secret joy:

And I—my harp would prelude woe—
10   I cannot all command the strings;
    The glory of the sum of things
Will flash along the chords and go.

LXXXIX

Witch-elms that counterchange the floor
    Of this flat lawn with dusk and bright;[1]
    And thou, with all they breadth and height
Of foliage, towering sycamore;

5   How often, hither wandering down,
    My Arthur found your shadows fair,
    And shook to all the liberal air
The dust and din and steam of town:

He brought an eye for all he saw;
10   He mixt in all our simple sports;
    They pleased him, fresh from brawling courts
And dusty purlieus of the law.[2]

O joy to him in this retreat,
    Immantled in ambrosial dark,
15   To drink the cooler air, and mark
The landscape winking thro' the heat:

O sound to rout the brood of cares,
    The sweep of scythe in morning dew,
    The gust that round the garden flew,
20 And tumbled half the mellowing pears!

O bliss, when all in circle drawn
    About him, heart and ear were fed

1. The setting is Tennyson's family's home in Somersby, Lincolnshire, where the wych elms checker ("counterchange") the lawn with shade.
2. After leaving Cambridge Hallam studied law in London.

To hear him, as he lay and read
The Tuscan poets[3] on the lawn:

25   Or in the all-golden afternoon
        A guest, or happy sister, sung,
        Or here she brought the harp and flung
A ballad to the brightening moon:

Nor less it pleased in livelier moods,
30   Beyond the bounding hill to stray,
        And break the livelong summer day
With banquet in the distant woods;

Whereat we glanced from theme to theme,
        Discuss'd the books to love or hate,
35   Or touch'd the changes of the state,
Or threaded some Socratic dream;[4]

But if I praised the busy town,
        He loved to rail against it still,
        For 'ground in yonder social mill
40   We rub each other's angles down,

'And merge' he said 'in form and gloss
        The picturesque of man and man.'
        We talk'd: the stream beneath us ran,
The wine-flask lying couch'd in moss,

45   Or cool'd within the glooming wave;
        And last, returning from afar,
        Before the crimson-circled star
Had fall'n into her father's grave,[5]

And brushing ankle-deep in flowers,
50   We heard behind the woodbine veil
        The milk that bubbled in the pail,
And buzzings of the honied hours.

3. Dante and Petrarch, Hallam's favorites among the Italian poets.
4. I.e., discussed idealist philosophy.
5. "Before Venus, the evening star, had dipt into the sunset" [T.]. The sun is "father" to
    Venus because "according to Laplace," an early-nineteenth-century astronomer, the plan-
    ets "were evolved from the sun" [T.].

XC

He tasted love with half his mind,
    Nor ever drank the inviolate spring
    Where nighest heaven, who first could fling
This bitter seed among mankind;

5   That could the dead, whose dying eyes
    Were closed with wail, resume their life,
    They would but find in child and wife
An iron welcome when they rise:[1]

'Twas well, indeed, when warm with wine,
10   To pledge them with a kindly tear,
    To talk them o'er, to wish them here,
To count their memories half divine;

But if they came who past away,
    Behold their brides in other hands;
15   The hard heir strides about their lands,
And will not yield them for a day.

Yea, tho' their sons were none of these,
    Not less the yet-loved sire would make
    Confusion worse than death, and shake
20   The pillars of domestic peace.

Ah dear, but come thou back to me:
    Whatever change the years have wrought,
    I find not yet one lonely thought
That cries against my wish for thee.

XCI

When rosy plumelets tuft the larch,
    And rarely pipes the mounted thrush;
    Or underneath the barren bush
Flits by the sea-blue bird of March;

5   Come, wear the form by which I know
    Thy spirit in time among they peers;[1]
    The hope of unaccomplish'd years
Be large and lucid round thy brow.

1. Tennyson's son paraphrases the opening stanzas: "He who first suggested that the dead would not be welcome if they came to life again knew not the highest love."
1. I.e., appear to me in the form I remember on earth.

When summer's hourly-mellowing change
10   May breathe, with many roses sweet,
      Upon the thousand waves of wheat,
That ripple round the lonely grange;

Come: not in watches of the night,
      But where the sunbeam broodeth warm,
15   Come, beauteous in thine after form,
And like a finer light in light.

XCII

If any vision should reveal
      Thy likeness, I might count it vain
      As but the canker of the brain;
Yea, tho' it spake and made appeal

5   To chances where our lots were cast
      Together in the days behind,
      I might but say, I hear a wind
Of memory murmuring the past.

Yea, tho' it spake and bared to view
10   A fact within the coming year;
      And tho' the months, revolving near,
Should prove the phantom-warning true,

They might not seem thy prophecies,
      But spiritual presentiments,
15   And such refraction of events
As often rises ere they rise.[1]

XCIII

I shall not see thee. Dare I say
      No spirit ever brake the band
      That stays him from the native land
Where first he walk'd when claspt in clay?

5   No visual shade of some one lost,
      But he, the Spirit himself, may come
      Where all the nerve of sense is numb;
Spirit to Spirit, Ghost to Ghost.

1. "The heavenly bodies are seen above the horizon, by refraction, before they actually rise" [T.]. The same might be true of "events"; hence even a correct prediction of the future would not prove that the "vision" (line 1) was really a ghost.

O, therefore from thy sightless range
10   With gods in unconjectured bliss,
      O, from the distance of the abyss
Of tenfold-complicated change,[1]

Descend, and touch, and enter; hear
      The wish too strong for words to name;
15   That in this blindness of the frame
My Ghost may feel that thine is near.

XCIV

How pure at heart and sound in head,
      With what divine affections bold
      Should be the man whose thought would hold
An hour's communion with the dead.

5   In vain shalt thou, or any, call
      The spirits from their golden day,
      Except, like them, thou too canst say,
My spirit is at peace with all.

They haunt the silence of the breast,
10   Imaginations calm and fair,
      The memory like a cloudless air,
The conscience as a sea at rest:

But when the heart is full of din,
      And doubt beside the portal waits,
15   They can but listen at the gates,
And hear the household jar within.

XCV[1]

By night we linger'd on the lawn,
      For underfoot the herb was dry;
      And genial warmth; and o'er the sky
The silvery haze of summer drawn;

5   And calm that let the tapers burn
      Unwavering: not a cricket chirr'd:

1. In Dante's *Divine Comedy*, Heaven has ten levels or spheres. "Sightless": invisible.
1. The spiritual reunion with Hallam in this section not only represents a culmination to the speculations of the previous five sections but has often been seen as a climax (if not *the* climax) of the poem as a whole.

The brook alone far off was heard,
And on the board the fluttering urn:[2]

And bats went round in fragrant skies,
10   And wheel'd or lit the filmy shapes
        That haunt the dusk, with ermine capes
And woolly breasts and beaded eyes;[3]

While now we sang old songs that peal'd
        From knoll to knoll, where, couch'd at ease,
15   The white kine glimmer'd, and the trees
Laid their dark arms about the field.

But when those others, one by one,
        Withdrew themselves from me and night,
        And in the house light after light
20   Went out, and I was all alone,

A hunger seized my heart; I read
        Of that glad year which once had been,[4]
        In those fall'n leaves which kept their green,
The noble letters of the dead:

25   And strangely on the silence broke
        The silent-speaking words, and strange
        Was love's dumb cry defying change
To test his worth; and strangely spoke

The faith, the vigour, bold to dwell
30   On doubts that drive the coward back,
        And keen thro' wordy snares to track
Suggestion to her inmost cell.

So word by word, and line by line,
        The dead man touch'd me from the past,
35   And all at once it seem'd at last
The living soul was flash'd on mine,

And mine in this was wound,[5] and whirl'd
        About empyreal heights of thought,

2. Tea urn. "It was a marvellously still night, and I asked my brother Charles to listen to the brook, which we had never heard so far off before" [T.]. The setting is the lawn at Somersby (compare section LXXXIX).
3. "Moths" [T.]. "Lit": alighted.
4. The whole time of their friendship.
5. In early editions, these two lines read: "His living soul was flash'd on mine, / And mine in

And came on that which is, and caught
40   The deep pulsations of the world,

Aeonian music measuring out
     The steps of Time—the shocks of Chance—
     The blows of Death. At length my trance
Was cancell'd, stricken thro' with doubt.[6]

45   Vague words! but ah, how hard to frame
     In matter-moulded forms of speech,
     Or ev'n for intellect to reach
Thro' memory that which I became:

Till now the doubtful dusk reveal'd
50   The knolls once more where, couch'd at ease,
     The white kine glimmer'd, and the trees
Laid their dark arms about the field:

And suck'd from out the distant gloom
     A breeze began to tremble o'er
55   The large leaves of the sycamore,
And fluctuate all the still perfume,

And gathering freshlier overhead,
     Rock'd the full-foliaged elms, and swung
     The heavy-folded rose, and flung
60   The lilies to and fro, and said

'The dawn, the dawn,' and died away;
     And East and West, without a breath,
     Mixt their dim lights, like life and death,
To broaden into boundless day.

XCVI

You[1] say, but with no touch of scorn,
     Sweet-hearted, you, whose light-blue eyes

---

his was wound." Tennyson changed to the more impersonal reading only in 1872 and later commented, enigmatically, "The first reading . . . troubled me, as perhaps giving a wrong impression."
6. "The trance came to an end in a moment of critical doubt, but the doubt was dispelled by the glory of the dawn of the 'boundless day' [line 64]" [T.]. "Empyreal": celestial. "Aeonian": of the eons, everlasting.
1. The addressee is a woman—perhaps Emily Sellwood, Tennyson's future wife, who was troubled by Tennyson's apparent lapses of faith.

Are tender over drowning flies,
You tell me, doubt is Devil-born.

5   I know not: one indeed I knew[2]
        In many a subtle question versed,
        Who touch'd a jarring lyre at first,
    But ever strove to make it true:

    Perplext in faith, but pure in deeds,
10   At last he beat his music out.
        There lives more faith in honest doubt,
    Believe me, than in half the creeds.

    He fought his doubts and gather'd strength,
        He would not make his judgment blind,
15   He faced the spectres of the mind
    And laid them: thus he came at length

    To find a stronger faith his own;
        And Power was with him in the night,
        Which makes the darkness and the light,
20 And dwells not in the light alone,

    But in the darkness and the cloud,
        As over Sinaï's peaks of old,
        While Israel made their gods of gold,
    Altho' the trumpet blew so loud.[3]

XCVII

    My love has talk'd with rocks and trees;
        He finds on misty mountain-ground
        His own vast shadow glory-crown'd;
    He sees himself in all he sees.[1]

5   Two partners of a married life—
        I look'd on these and thought of thee
        In vastness and in mystery,
    And of my spirit as of a wife.[2]

2. "A.H.H." [T.]. Compare the two figures in this section to those in section XXXIII.
3. Tennyson cites Exodus 19, in which God appears "in a thick cloud upon the mount [Mount Sinai], and the voice of the trumpet exceeding loud" [T.]. But the stanza also alludes to a later episode (Exodus 32) in which the Israelites build themselves a golden idol to worship while Moses is on the mountain.
1. The speaker's love (here personified) finds a reflection of itself everywhere.
2. This extended metaphor illustrates "the relation of one on earth to one in the other and

These two—they dwelt with eye on eye,
10   Their hearts of old have beat in tune,
     Their meetings made December June,
Their every parting was to die.

Their love has never past away;
     The days she never can forget
15   Are earnest that he loves her yet,
Whate'er the faithless people say.

Her life is lone, he sits apart,
     He loves her yet, she will not weep,
     Tho' rapt in matters dark and deep
20   He seems to slight her simple heart.

He thrids the labyrinth of the mind,
     He reads the secret of the star,
     He seems so near and yet so far,
He looks so cold: she thinks him kind.

25   She keeps the gift of years before,
     A wither'd violet is her bliss:
     She knows not what his greatness is,
For that, for all, she loves him more.

For him she plays, to him she sings
30   Of early faith and plighted vows;
     She knows but matters of the house,
And he, he knows a thousand things.

Her faith is fixt and cannot move,
     She darkly feels him great and wise,
35   She dwells on him with faithful eyes,
'I cannot understand: I love.'

XCVIII[1]

You leave us: you will see the Rhine,
     And those fair hills I sail'd below,

---

higher world. Not my relation to him here. He looked up to me as I looked up to him"
[T.].

1. Although Tennyson noted that the "You" of line 1 "is imaginary," he elsewhere said that
it referred to his brother Charles, who traveled on the Rhine during his honeymoon in
1836. Hallam and Tennyson had taken a similar voyage in 1832 (lines 2–3). It was on a
trip to Vienna ("That City," line 6) that Hallam died in 1833.

When I was there with him; and go
By summer belts of wheat and vine

5   To where he breathed his latest breath,
         That City. All her splendour seems
         No livelier than the wisp that gleams
On Lethe in the eyes of Death.[2]

Let her great Danube rolling fair
10   Enwind her isles, unmark'd of me:
         I have not seen, I will not see
Vienna; rather dream that there,

A treble darkness, Evil haunts
         The birth, the bridal; friend from friend
15   Is oftener parted, fathers bend
Above more graves, a thousand wants

Gnarr[3] at the heels of men, and prey
         By each cold hearth, and sadness flings
         Her shadow on the blaze of kings:
20   And yet myself have heard him say,

That not in any mother town
         With statelier progress to and fro
         The double tides of chariots flow
By park and suburb under brown[4]

25   Of lustier leaves; nor more content,
         He told me, lives in any crowd,
         When all is gay with lamps, and loud
With sport and song, in booth and tent,

Imperial halls, or open plain;
30   And wheels the circled dance, and breaks
         The rocket molten into flakes[5]
Of crimson or in emerald rain.

2. "Lethe": the river of the underworld. "Wisp": "ignis-fatuus" [T.].
3. "Snarl" [T.].
4. I.e., shadow. "Mother town": "metropolis" [T.].
5. Fireworks.

XCIX

Risest thou thus, dim dawn, again,[1]
　　So loud with voices of the birds,
　　So thick with lowings of the herds,
Day, when I lost the flower of men;

5　Who tremblest thro' thy darkling red
　　On yon swoll'n brook that bubbles fast
　　By meadows breathing of the past,
And woodlands holy to the dead;

Who murmurest in the foliaged eaves
10　A song that slights the coming care,[2]
　　And Autumn laying here and there
A fiery finger on the leaves;

Who wakenest with thy balmy breath
　　To myriads on the genial earth,
15　Memories of bridal, or of birth,
And unto myriads more, of death.

O wheresoever those may be,
　　Betwixt the slumber of the poles,[3]
　　To-day they count as kindred souls;
20　They know me not, but mourn with me.

C[1]

I climb the hill: from end to end
　　Of all the landscape underneath,
　　I find no place that does not breathe
Some gracious memory of my friend;

5　No gray old grange, or lonely fold,
　　Or low morass and whispering reed,
　　Or simple stile from mead to mead,
Or sheepwalk up the windy wold;

1. The second anniversary of Hallam's death, September 15; compare section LXXII, line 1.
2. I.e., the hardships of winter.
3. "The ends of the axis of the earth, which move so slowly that they seem not to move, but slumber"[T.].
1. This and the following sections concern the Tennyson family's departure from their home at Somersby to the unfamiliar surroundings of High Beech, north of London. The move took place in 1837, four years after Hallam's death, but the chronology has been altered to fit the poem.

Nor hoary knoll of ash and haw
10   That hears the latest linnet trill,
         Nor quarry trench'd along the hill
And haunted by the wrangling daw;

Nor runlet tinkling from the rock;
         Nor pastoral rivulet that swerves
15   To left and right thro' meadowy curves,
That feed the mothers of the flock;

But each has pleased a kindred eye,
         And each reflects a kindlier day;
         And, leaving these, to pass away,
20   I think once more he seems to die.

CI

Unwatch'd, the garden bough shall sway,
         The tender blossom flutter down,
         Unloved, that beech will gather brown,
This maple burn itself away;

5   Unloved, the sun-flower, shining fair,
         Ray round with flames her disk of seed,
         And many a rose carnation feed
With summer spice the humming air;

Unloved, by many a sandy bar,
10   The brook shall babble down the plain,
         At noon or when the lesser wain[1]
Is twisting round the polar star;

Uncared for, gird the windy grove,
         And flood the haunts of hern and crake;[2]
15   Or into silver arrows break
The sailing moon in creek and cove;

Till from the garden and the wild
         A fresh association blow,
         And year by year the landscape grow
20   Familiar to the stranger's child;

1. The constellation of Ursa Minor, or the Little Dipper, which revolves around the North Star.
2. A marsh bird. "Hern": heron.

As year by year the labourer tills
    His wonted glebe,[3] or lops the glades;
    And year by year our memory fades
From all the circle of the hills.

CII

We leave the well-beloved place
    Where first we gazed upon the sky;
    The roofs, that heard our earliest cry,
Will shelter one of stranger race.

5   We go, but ere we go from home,
    As down the garden-walks I move,
    Two spirits of a diverse love[1]
Contend for loving masterdom.

One whispers, 'Here thy boyhood sung
10   Long since its matin song,[2] and heard
    The low love-language of the bird
In native hazels tassel-hung.'

The other answers, 'Yea but here
    Thy feet have stray'd in after hours
15   With thy lost friend among the bowers,
And this hath made them trebly dear.'

These two have striven half the day,
    And each prefers his separate claim,
    Poor rivals in a losing game,
20   That will not yield each other way.

I turn to go: my feet are set
    To leave the pleasant fields and farms;
    They mix in one another's arms
To one pure image of regret.

CIII

On that last night before we went
    From out the doors where I was bred,

3. His usual plot of land.
1. "First, the love of native place; second, this enhanced by the memory of A.H.H." [T.].
2. I.e., Tennyson's youthful poetry; compare section LXXVI, line 9.

I dream'd a vision of the dead,
Which left my after-morn content.

5   Methought I dwelt within a hall,
      And maidens with me: distant hills
      From hidden summits fed with rills
   A river sliding by the wall.[1]

The hall with harp and carol rang.
10   They sang of what is wise and good
      And graceful. In the centre stood
   A statue veil'd, to which they sang;

And which, tho' veil'd, was known to me,
      The shape of him I loved, and love
15   For ever: then flew in a dove
   And brought a summons from the sea:[2]

And when they learnt that I must go
      They wept and wail'd, but led the way
      To where a little shallop[3] lay
20   At anchor in the flood below;

And on by many a level mead,
      And shadowing bluff that made the banks,
      We glided winding under ranks
   Of iris, and the golden reed;

25   And still as vaster grew the shore
      And roll'd the floods in grander space,
      The maidens gather'd strength and grace
   And presence, lordlier than before;[4]

And I myself, who sat apart
30   And watch'd them, wax'd in every limb;
      I felt the thews of Anakim,
   The pulses of a Titan's heart;[5]

1. According to Tennyson, the maidens "are the Muses, poetry, arts—all that made life beautiful here, which we hope will pass with us beyond the grave." The hidden summits represent "the divine," and the river, "life" [T.].
2. "Eternity" [T.].
3. A small open boat.
4. This stanza suggests "the progress of the Age" [T.].
5. The Titans were the giants of Greek mythology. "The thews of Anakim": the strength of "the children of Anak," a biblical race of giants (Numbers 13, Deuteronomy 9).

As one would sing the death of war,
   And one would chant the history
35   Of that great race, which is to be,
And one the shaping of a star;[6]

Until the forward-creeping tides
   Began to foam, and we to draw
   From deep to deep, to where we saw
40   A great ship lift her shining sides.

The man we loved was there on deck,
   But thrice as large as man he bent
   To greet us. Up the side I went,
And fell in silence on his neck:

45   Whereat those maidens with one mind
   Bewail'd their lot; I did them wrong:
   'We served thee here,' they said, 'so long,
And wilt thou leave us now behind?'

So rapt I was, they could not win
50   An answer from my lips, but he
   Replying, 'Enter likewise ye
And go with us:' they enter'd in.[7]

And while the wind began to sweep
   A music out of sheet and shroud,[8]
55   We steer'd her toward a crimson cloud
That landlike slept along the deep.

CIV

The time draws near the birth of Christ;[1]
   The moon is hid, the night is still;
   A single church below the hill
Is pealing, folded in the mist.

5   A single peal of bells below,
   That wakens at this hour of rest
   A single murmur in the breast,
That these are not the bells I know.

6. The songs describe "the great hopes of humanity and science" [T.].
7. Tennyson commented that the speaker "was wrong to drop his earthly hopes and powers—
they will still be of use to him" in the afterlife.
8. Types of rope on a ship.
1. Compare the opening of section XXVIII, the first Christmas lyric in the poem, with which
this section is paired.

Like strangers' voices here they sound,
10   In lands where not a memory strays,
        Nor landmark breathes of other days,
But all is new unhallow'd ground.[2]

CV[1]

To-night ungather'd let us leave
        This laurel, let this holly stand:
        We live within the stranger's land,
And strangely falls our Christmas-eve.

5   Our father's dust is left alone
        And silent under other snows:
        There in due time the woodbine blows,
The violet comes, but we are gone.

No more shall wayward grief abuse
10   The genial hour with mask and mime;[2]
        For change of place, like growth of time,
Has broke the bond of dying use.

Let cares that petty shadows cast,
        By which our lives are chiefly proved,
15   A little spare the night I loved,
And hold it solemn to the past.

But let no footstep beat the floor,
        Nor bowl of wassail mantle warm;
        For who would keep an ancient form
20 Thro' which the spirit breathes no more?

Be neither song, nor game, nor feast;
        Nor harp be touch'd, nor flute be blown;
        No dance, no motion, save alone
What lightens in the lucid east

25 Of rising worlds by yonder wood.[3]
        Long sleeps the summer in the seed;

2. "High Beech, Epping Forest (where we were then living)" [T.] (see n. 1, p. 74).
1. The third Christmas in the poem (compare sections XXX and LXXVIII) and the first in the new home—away from Somersby where, among other things, the grave of Tennyson's father (lines 5–6) has been left behind.
2. I.e., no more shall grief disguised under merriment wrong ("abuse") the holiday.
3. "The scintillating motion of the stars that rise" [T.]. These stars are addressed in lines 27–28, and told to usher in the golden age to come.

Run out your measured arcs, and lead
The closing cycle rich in good.

CVI

Ring out, wild bells, to the wild sky,
 The flying cloud, the frosty light:
 The year is dying in the night;
Ring out, wild bells, and let him die.

5 Ring out the old, ring in the new,
 Ring, happy bells, across the snow:
 The year is going, let him go;
Ring out the false, ring in the true.

Ring out the grief that saps the mind,
10 For those that here we see no more;
 Ring out the feud of rich and poor,
Ring in redress to all mankind.

Ring out a slowly dying cause,
 And ancient forms of party strife;
15 Ring in the nobler modes of life,
With sweeter manners, purer laws.

Ring out the want, the care, the sin,
 The faithless coldness of the times;
 Ring out, ring out my mournful rhymes,
20 But ring the fuller minstrel in.

Ring out false pride in place and blood,
 The civic slander and the spite;
 Ring in the love of truth and right,
Ring in the common love of good.

25 Ring out old shapes of foul disease;
 Ring out the narrowing lust of gold;
 Ring out the thousand wars of old,
Ring in the thousand years of peace.[1]

Ring in the valiant man and free,
30 The larger heart, the kindlier hand;

1. See Revelation 20.

Ring out the darkness of the land,
Ring in the Christ that is to be.[2]

CVII

It is the day when he was born,[1]
   A bitter day that early sank
   Behind a purple-frosty bank
Of vapour, leaving night forlorn.

5 The time admits not flowers or leaves
   To deck the banquet. Fiercely flies
   The blast of North and East, and ice
Makes daggers at the sharpen'd eaves,

And bristles all the brakes and thorns
10   To yon hard crescent, as she hangs
   Above the wood which grides and clangs
Its leafless ribs and iron horns[2]

Together, in the drifts that pass
   To darken on the rolling brine[3]
15   That breaks the coast. But fetch the wine,
Arrange the board and brim the glass;

Bring in great logs and let them lie,
   To make a solid core of heat;
   Be cheerful-minded, talk and treat
20 Of all things ev'n as he were by;

We keep the day. With festal cheer,
   With books and music, surely we
   Will drink to him, whate'er he be,
And sing the songs he loved to hear.

CVIII[1]

I will not shut me from my kind,
   And, lest I stiffen into stone,

---

2. "The broader Christianity of the future" [T.].
1. Hallam's birthday, "February 1" [T.].
2. The moon ("yon hard crescent") hangs above trees that grate together ("gride") their "leafless" and frozen branches ("iron horns").
3. Snow flurries that blow into the sea and melt.
1. Tennyson paraphrases this section: "Grief shall not make me a hermit, and I will not indulge in vacant yearnings and barren aspirations [lines 1–6]; it is useless trying to find

I will not eat my heart alone,
Nor feed with sighs a passing wind:

5   What profit lies in barren faith,
    And vacant yearning, tho' with might
    To scale the heaven's highest height,
Or dive below the wells of Death?

What find I in the highest place,
10   But mine own phantom chanting hymns?
    And on the depths of death there swims
The reflex[2] of a human face.

I'll rather take what fruit may be
    Of sorrow under human skies:
15   'Tis held that sorrow makes us wise,
Whatever wisdom sleep with thee.

CIX

Heart-affluence in discursive talk
    From household fountains never dry;
    The critic clearness of an eye,
That saw thro' all the Muses' walk;[1]

5   Seraphic intellect and force
    To seize and throw[2] the doubts of man;
    Impassion'd logic, which outran
The hearer in its fiery course;

High nature amorous of the good,
10   But touch'd with no ascetic gloom;
    And passion pure in snowy bloom
Thro' all the years of April blood;[3]

A love of freedom rarely felt,
    Of freedom in her regal seat
15   Of England; not the schoolboy heat,
The blind hysterics of the Celt;[4]

him in the other worlds [lines 6–8]—I find nothing but the reflections of myself [lines 9–12]: I had better learn the lesson that sorrow teaches [lines 13–16]" [T.].
2. Reflection.
1. Hallam had already published several pieces of very mature literary criticism before he died. "Household fountains": i.e., Hallam's ideas sprang from within.
2. Overthrow.
3. Youth.
4. Referring to Irish uprisings.

And manhood fused with female grace
   In such a sort, the child would twine
   A trustful hand, unask'd, in thine,
20 And find his comfort in thy face;

All these have been, and thee mine eyes
   Have look'd on: if they look'd in vain,
   My shame is greater who remain,
Nor let thy wisdom make me wise.[5]

CX

Thy converse drew us with delight,
   The men of rathe and riper years:[1]
   The feeble soul, a haunt of fears,
Forgot his weakness in thy sight.

5 On thee the loyal-hearted hung,
   The proud was half disarm'd of pride,
   Nor cared the serpent at thy side
To flicker with his double tongue.

The stern were mild when thou wert by,
10 The flippant put himself to school
   And heard thee, and the brazen fool
Was soften'd, and he knew not why;

While I, thy nearest, sat apart,
   And felt thy triumph was as mine;
15 And loved them more, that they were thine,
The graceful tact, the Christian art;

Nor mine the sweetness or the skill,
   But mine the love that will not tire,
   And, born of love, the vague desire
20 That spurs an imitative will.

CXI

The churl in spirit, up or down
   Along the scale of ranks, thro' all,
   To him who grasps a golden ball,
By blood a king, at heart a clown;[1]

5. I.e., "If I do not let thy wisdom make me wise" [T.]; compare Prologue, line 44.
1. I.e., young and old. "Rathe": early.
1. "Churl" and "clown" both mean a rude or low-bred person. "Golden ball": the orb held by
   a king, symbol of power.

5   The churl in spirit, howe'er he veil
        His want in forms for fashion's sake,
        Will let his coltish nature break
    At seasons thro' the gilded pale:[2]

    For who can always act? but he,
10   To whom a thousand memories call,
        Not being less but more than all
    The gentleness he seem'd to be,

    Best seem'd the thing he was, and join'd
        Each office of the social hour
15   To noble manners, as the flower
    And native growth of noble mind;

    Nor ever narrowness or spite,
        Or villain fancy fleeting by,
        Drew in the expression of an eye,
20   Where God and Nature met in light;

    And thus he bore without abuse
        The grand old name of gentleman,
        Defamed by every charlatan,
    And soil'd with all ignoble use.

                    CXII

    His wisdom holds my wisdom less,
        That I, who gaze with temperate eyes
        On glorious insufficiencies,
    Set light by narrower perfectness.[1]

5   But thou, that fillest all the room
        Of all my love, art reason why
        I seem to cast a careless eye
    On souls, the lesser lords of doom.[2]

2. Fence; here, in the sense of "mask."
1. "Glorious insufficiencies": "Unaccomplished greatness such as Arthur Hallam's" [T.].
   Thus "wise" people blame the poet for being more indulgent toward Hallam's promised
   greatness than toward others' actual accomplishments, though less great ("narrower per-
   fectness"). "Set light by": "make light of" [T.].
2. But love for Hallam obscures my perception of those who can act as they wish (are "lords
   of doom," i.e., fate) but who remain "lesser." The poet admits that his estimation of Hallam's extraordinary talents, expressed in sections CIX–CXIII, is biased. But Tennyson was
   not alone in thinking that Hallam would have been one of the leading figures of his age
   (see Introduction, p. xi).

For what wert thou? some novel power
10   Sprang up for ever at a touch,
        And hope could never hope too much,
In watching thee from hour to hour,

Large elements in order brought,
        And tracts of calm from tempest made,
15   And world-wide fluctuation sway'd
In vassal tides that follow'd thought.[3]

CXIII

'Tis held that sorrow makes us wise;
        Yet how much wisdom sleeps with thee[1]
        Which not alone had[2] guided me,
But served the seasons that may rise;

5   For can I doubt, who knew thee keen
        In intellect, with force and skill
        To strive, to fashion, to fulfil—
I doubt not what thou wouldst have been:

A life in civic action warm,
10   A soul on highest mission sent,
        A potent voice of Parliament,
A pillar steadfast in the storm,

Should licensed boldness gather force,[3]
        Becoming, when the time has birth,
15   A lever to uplift the earth
And roll it in another course,

With thousand shocks that come and go,
        With agonies, with energies,
        With overthrowings, and with cries,
20   And undulations to and fro.

CXIV

Who loves not Knowledge? Who shall rail
        Against her beauty? May she mix

3. I.e., great political issues were marshaled into logical order.
1. Compare section CVIII, lines 15–16 (the original reading of which was identical to this).
2. I.e., would have.
3. If a justified social revolution should occur (with the consequent "storm" of complications described in the two final stanzas).

With men and prosper! Who shall fix
    Her pillars?[1] Let her work prevail.

5   But on her forehead sits a fire:
        She sets her forward countenance
        And leaps into the future chance,
    Submitting all things to desire.[2]

    Half-grown as yet, a child, and vain—
10   She cannot fight the fear of death.
        What is she, cut from love and faith,
    But some wild Pallas from the brain[3]

    Of Demons? fiery-hot to burst
        All barriers in her onward race
15   For power. Let her know her place;
    She is the second, not the first.

    A higher hand must make her mild,
        If all be not in vain; and guide
        Her footsteps, moving side by side
20 With wisdom, like the younger child:

    For she is earthly of the mind,
        But Wisdom heavenly of the soul.
        O, friend, who camest to thy goal
    So early, leaving me behind,

25 I would the great world grew like thee,
        Who grewest not alone in power
        And knowledge, but by year and hour
    In reverence and in charity.

                        CXV

        Now fades the last long streak of snow,
            Now burgeons every maze of quick[1]

1. Limits. The Pillars of Hercules (the Strait of Gibraltar) represented the limits of the known
   world in classical geography.
2. In her forward sweep, "Knowledge" subordinates everything to desire (for more knowledge).
3. In Greek mythology Pallas Athena (goddess of Wisdom) was born full-grown from the
   brain of Zeus. "Cut": cut off.
1. Hedgerow (as in section LXXXVIII, line 2). "Burgeons": "buds" [T.]. This is the third spring
   since Hallam's death.

About the flowering squares, and thick
By ashen roots the violets blow.

5   Now rings the woodland loud and long,
        The distance takes a lovelier hue,
        And drown'd in yonder living blue
The lark becomes a sightless song.

Now dance the lights on lawn and lea,
10   The flocks are whiter down the vale,
        And milkier every milky sail
On winding stream or distant sea;

Where now the seamew pipes, or dives
        In yonder greening gleam, and fly
15   The happy birds, that change their sky
To build and brood; that live their lives

From land to land; and in my breast
        Spring wakens too; and my regret
        Becomes an April violet,
20 And buds and blossoms like the rest.

CXVI

Is it, then, regret for buried time
        That keenlier in sweet April wakes,
        And meets the year, and gives and takes
The colours of the crescent prime?[1]

5   Not all: the songs, the stirring air,
        The life re-orient[2] out of dust,
        Cry thro' the sense to hearten trust
In that which made the world so fair.

Not all regret: the face will shine
10   Upon me, while I muse alone;
        And that dear voice, I once have known,
Still speak to me of me and mine:

Yet less of sorrow lives in me
        For days of happy commune dead;

1. "Growing spring" [T.].
2. Rising again.

15 Less yearning for the friendship fled,
   Than some strong bond which is to be.

CXVII

 O days and hours, your work is this
   To hold me from my proper place,
   A little while from his embrace,
 For fuller gain of after bliss:

5 That out of distance might ensue
   Desire of nearness doubly sweet;
   And unto meeting when we meet,
 Delight a hundredfold accrue,

 For every grain of sand that runs,
10   And every span of shade that steals,
   And every kiss of toothed wheels,[1]
 And all the courses of the suns.

CXVIII

 Contemplate all this work of Time,
   The giant labouring in his youth;
   Nor dream of human love and truth,
 As dying Nature's earth and lime,[1]

5 But trust that those we call the dead
   Are breathers of an ampler day
   For ever nobler ends. They say,
 The solid earth whereon we tread

 In tracts of fluent heat began,
10   And grew to seeming-random forms,
   The seeming prey of cyclic storms,
 Till at the last arose the man;[2]

 Who throve and branch'd from clime to clime,
   The herald of a higher race,

---

1. Referring to the hourglass, sun dial, and clock, respectively.
1. Consider the vast stretches of geological time but without letting it cause you to think that the soul is as mortal as the body ("Nature's earth and lime"). The speaker thus counters his own doubts in sections LV and LVI, which sprang from his observations of nature and particularly of extinction. The "giant" is Time, "labouring" to shape the earth.
2. "They" (line 7) include Cuvier, Laplace, Lyell, and Chambers, scientists who introduced such theories as the nebular hypothesis (lines 8–9) and catastrophism (line 11). These theories are revisited in section CXXIII.

15   And of himself in higher place,[3]
       If so he type this work of time

       Within himself, from more to more;
         Or, crown'd with attributes of woe
         Like glories,[4] move his course, and show
20   That life is not as idle ore,

       But iron dug from central gloom,
         And heated hot with burning fears,
         And dipt in baths of hissing tears,
       And batter'd with the shocks of doom

25   To shape and use. Arise and fly
         The reeling Faun, the sensual feast;
         Move upward, working out the beast,
       And let the ape and tiger die.[5]

CXIX

       Doors, where my heart was used to beat[1]
         So quickly, not as one that weeps
         I come once more; the city sleeps;
       I smell the meadow in the street;

5   I hear a chirp of birds; I see
         Betwixt the black fronts long-withdrawn
         A light-blue lane of early dawn,
       And think of early days and thee,

       And bless thee, for thy lips are bland,[2]
10   And bright the friendship of thine eye;
         And in my thoughts with scarce a sigh
       I take the pressure of thine hand.

CXX

       I trust I have not wasted breath:
         I think we are not wholly brain,

3. Human development not only presages more highly evolved generations here on earth but also hints at what we shall ourselves be in heaven ("higher place").
4. But the human race evolves only if individuals reproduce ("type") its development in their own lives, either gradually ("from more to more") or in large steps achieved through suffering ("woe"), as described in the lines that follow.
5. The faun (a mythical creature, half-goat and half-human), ape, and tiger all represent sensual, bestial qualities. Since evolution is partly a matter of individual will (lines 16–25), the speaker urges us to progress ("Move upward") to a higher nature.
1. Hallam's old house, as in section VII.
2. Gentle; soothing.

Magnetic mockeries;[1] not in vain,
Like Paul with beasts, I fought with Death;[2]

5   Not only cunning casts in clay:
          Let Science prove we are, and then
          What matters Science unto men,
      At least to me? I would not stay.[3]

      Let him, the wiser man who springs
10   Hereafter, up from childhood shape
          His action like the greater ape,[4]
      But I was *born* to other things.

                    CXXI[1]

Sad Hesper o'er the buried sun
      And ready, thou, to die with him,
      Thou watchest all things ever dim
And dimmer, and a glory done:

5   The team is loosen'd from the wain,[2]
          The boat is drawn upon the shore;
          Thou listenest to the closing door,
      And life is darken'd in the brain.

      Bright Phosphor, fresher for the night,
10   By thee the world's great work is heard
          Beginning, and the wakeful bird;
      Behind thee comes the greater light:

      The market boat is on the stream,
          And voices hail it from the brink;
15   Thou hear'st the village hammer clink,
      And see'st the moving of the team.

1. I trust that there is more to the soul than electrical impulses in the brain. Tennyson apparently understood "magnetic" and electrical as roughly equivalent; he refers to nerve impulses as "electric" in section CXXV, line 15.
2. Tennyson cites 1 Corinthians 15:32: "If after the manner of men I have fought with beasts at Ephesus, what advantageth it me, if the dead rise not?"
3. If science can prove that we are no more than bodies (and hence that there is no immortality), then life is of no use to me.
4. "Spoken ironically against mere materialism, not against evolution" [T.]. The poet does not abandon the evolutionary model of section CXVIII but reminds the "wiser man" (used ironically of the scientist) that the theory is debasing unless it applies to the soul as well as to the body.
1. "The evening star is also the morning star" [T.]. At certain times of the year, the planet Venus is the first "star" visible after sunset; it was then called "Hesper" in ancient astronomy. At other times Venus is the last "star" still shining just before sunrise and was called "Phosphor."
2. The oxen ("the team") are unyoked.

Sweet Hesper-Phosphor, double name
  For what is one, the first, the last,
  Thou, like my present and my past,
20 Thy place is changed; thou art the same.

CXXII

Oh, wast thou with me, dearest, then,
  While I rose up against my doom,[1]
  And yearn'd to burst the folded gloom,
To bare the eternal Heavens again,

5 To feel once more, in placid awe,
  The strong imagination roll
  A sphere of stars about my soul,
In all her motion one with law;

If thou wert with me, and the grave
10 Divide us not, be with me now,
  And enter in at breast and brow,
Till all my blood, a fuller wave,

Be quicken'd with a livelier breath,
  And like an inconsiderate boy,
15 As in the former flash of joy,
I slip the thoughts of life and death;

And all the breeze of Fancy blows,
  And every dew-drop paints a bow,[2]
  The wizard[3] lightnings deeply glow,
20 And every thought breaks out a rose.

CXXIII

There rolls the deep where grew the tree.
  O earth, what changes hast thou seen![1]
  There where the long street roars, hath been
The stillness of the central sea.[2]

1. "That of grief" [T.]. "Then" does not necessarily refer to any known occasion, but to the
time when the speaker first wished to feel joy again. For "dearest," see n. 1, p. 51.
2. "Every dew-drop turns into a miniature rainbow" [T.].
3. Magical, as in section LXX, line 14.
1. Here, as in section XXXV, Tennyson draws his images of changes in the earth's surface from
Charles Lyell, *Principles of Geology* (1830–33).
2. "Balloonists say that even in a storm the middle sea is noiseless" [T.].

5   The hills are shadows, and they flow
     From form to form, and nothing stands;
     They melt like mist, the solid lands,
  Like clouds they shape themselves and go.

  But in my spirit will I dwell,
10   And dream my dream, and hold it true;
     For tho' my lips may breathe adieu,
  I cannot think the thing farewell.[3]

CXXIV

  That which we dare invoke to bless;
     Our dearest faith; our ghastliest doubt;
     He, They, One, All; within, without;
  The Power in darkness whom we guess;

5   I found Him not in world or sun,
     Or eagle's wing, or insect's eye;
     Nor thro' the questions men may try,
  The petty cobwebs we have spun:[1]

  If e'er when faith had fall'n asleep,
10   I heard a voice 'believe no more'
     And heard an ever-breaking shore
  That tumbled in the Godless deep;

  A warmth within the breast would melt
     The freezing reason's colder part,
15   And like a man in wrath the heart
  Stood up and answer'd 'I have felt.'

  No, like a child in doubt and fear:
     But that blind clamour made me wise;[2]
     Then was I as a child that cries,
20   But, crying, knows his father near;

  And what I am beheld again
     What is, and no man understands;

3. I.e., in spite of all evidence of change, I cannot believe we will never meet again. Compare section LVII, lines 15–16 and note.
1. Faith comes neither from "natural theology" (which deduced God from evidence in nature) nor from philosophical arguments.
2. His reaction to his doubts was not that of "a man" (line 15), but of a child: the "blind clamour" (described in lines 10–12) inspired fear, but also prompted the recognition that a comforting presence was near. Compare the image in section LIV, lines 17–20.

And out of darkness came the hands
That reach thro' nature, moulding men.

CXXV

Whatever I have said or sung,
    Some bitter notes my harp would give,
    Yea, tho' there often seem'd to live
A contradiction on the tongue,

5   Yet Hope had never lost her youth;
    She did but look through dimmer eyes;
    Or Love but play'd with gracious lies,
Because he felt so fix'd in truth:[1]

And if the song were full of care,
10   He breathed the spirit of the song;
    And if the words were sweet and strong
He set his royal signet there;

Abiding with me till I sail
    To seek thee on the mystic deeps,
15   And this electric force, that keeps
A thousand pulses dancing, fail.

CXXVI

Love is and was my Lord and King,
    And in his presence I attend
    To hear the tidings of my friend,
Which every hour his couriers bring.

5   Love is and was my King and Lord,
    And will be, tho' as yet I keep
    Within his court on earth, and sleep
Encompass'd by his faithful guard,

And hear at times a sentinel
10   Who moves about from place to place,
    And whispers to the worlds of space,
In the deep night, that all is well.

1. Love was so confident that he could afford to entertain hypothetical doubts. "He" in the following lines refers to Love.

CXXVII

And all is well, tho' faith and form
    Be sunder'd in the night of fear;[1]
    Well roars the storm to those that hear
A deeper voice across the storm,

5   Proclaiming social truth shall spread,
    And justice, ev'n tho' thrice again
    The red fool-fury of the Seine
Should pile her barricades with dead.[2]

But ill for him that wears a crown,
10   And him, the lazar,[3] in his rags:
    They tremble, the sustaining crags;
The spires of ice are toppled down,

And molten up, and roar in flood;
    The fortress crashes from on high,
15   The brute earth lightens to the sky,
And the great Aeon sinks in blood,

And compass'd by the fires of Hell;
    While thou, dear spirit, happy star,
    O'erlook'st the tumult from afar,
20   And smilest, knowing all is well.

CXXVIII

The love that rose on stronger wings,
    Unpalsied when he met with Death,
    Is comrade of the lesser faith
That sees the course of human things.[1]

5   No doubt vast eddies in the flood
    Of onward time shall yet be made,
    And throned races may degrade;[2]
Yet O ye mysteries of good,

1. Faith can no longer depend on established religious doctrine ("form") that has been called into doubt; compare sections XXXIII and XCVI.
2. A reference to the French revolutions of 1789, 1830, and 1848. The Seine runs through Paris, and the revolutionaries of 1789 wore red caps (and were also bloody, hence "red"). This section may have been composed before the revolution of 1848; the word "thrice" was added only in 1850.
3. A poor and diseased person. The images in the following stanzas symbolize political upheaval.
1. Faith in the immortality of love "is comrade" to the faith expressed in the previous section, that upheaval in human affairs eventually leads to good.
2. I.e., races now in power may degenerate.

Wild Hours that fly with Hope and Fear,
10   If all your office had to do
        With old results that look like new;[3]
If this were all your mission here,

To draw, to sheathe a useless sword,
        To fool the crowd with glorious lies,
15   To cleave a creed in sects and cries,
To change the bearing of a word,

To shift an arbitrary power,
        To cramp the student at his desk,
        To make old bareness picturesque
20 And tuft with grass a feudal tower;

Why then my scorn might well descend
        On you and yours.[4] I see in part
        That all, as in some piece of art,
Is toil coöperant to an end.

CXXIX

Dear friend, far off, my lost desire,
        So far, so near in woe and weal;
        O loved the most, when most I feel
There is a lower and a higher;

5   Known and unknown; human, divine;
        Sweet human hand and lips and eye;
        Dear heavenly friend that canst not die,
Mine, mine, for ever, ever mine;

Strange friend, past, present, and to be;
10   Loved deeplier, darklier understood;
        Behold, I dream a dream of good,
And mingle all the world with thee.

CXXX

Thy voice is on the rolling air;
        I hear thee where the waters run;
        Thou standest in the rising sun,
And in the setting thou art fair.

3. If time brought about only superficial change, but no real progress (examples of which are given in the following stanzas).
4. The "Wild Hours" and the accompanying "Hope and Fear" (line 9).

5   What art thou then? I cannot guess;
        But tho' I seem in star and flower
        To feel thee some diffusive power,
    I do not therefore love thee less:

    My love involves the love before;
10   My love is vaster passion now;
        Tho' mix'd with God and Nature thou,
    I seem to love thee more and more.

    Far off thou art, but ever nigh;
        I have thee still, and I rejoice;
15   I prosper, circled with thy voice;
    I shall not lose thee tho' I die.

CXXXI

O living will that shalt endure[1]
    When all that seems shall suffer shock,
    Rise in the spiritual rock,[2]
Flow thro' our deeds and make them pure,

5   That we may lift from out of dust
    A voice as unto him that hears,
    A cry above the conquer'd years
To one that with us works, and trust,

With faith that comes of self-control,
10   The truths that never can be proved
    Until we close with all we loved,
And all we flow from, soul in soul.

[EPILOGUE][1]

O true and tried, so well and long,
    Demand not thou a marriage lay;
    In that it is thy marriage day
Is music more than any song.

1. "That which we know as Free-will in man" [T.].
2. See 1 Corinthians 10:4: "They drank of that spiritual Rock that followed them: and that Rock was Christ."
1. This concluding section (which, like the "Prologue," Tennyson left untitled) is an *epithalamium* or "marriage lay" (line 2), celebrating the wedding of Tennyson's sister Cecilia to his friend Edmund Lushington. The wedding took place in October 1842, nine years after Hallam's death (lines 9–10). Lushington is the person addressed, as he was also in section LXXXV.

5 Nor have I felt so much of bliss
  Since first he told me that he loved
  A daughter of our house; nor proved
Since that dark day a day like this;[2]

 Tho' I since then have number'd o'er
10 Some thrice three years: they went and came,
  Remade the blood and changed the frame,
And yet is love not less, but more;

No longer caring to embalm
  In dying songs a dead regret,
15 But like a statue solid-set,
And moulded in colossal calm.

Regret is dead, but love is more
  Than in the summers that are flown,
  For I myself with these have grown
20 To something greater than before;

Which makes appear the songs I made
  As echoes out of weaker times,
  As half but idle brawling rhymes,
The sport of random sun and shade.

25 But where is she, the bridal flower,
  That must be made a wife ere noon?
  She enters, glowing like the moon
Of Eden on its bridal bower:

On me she bends her blissful eyes
30 And then on thee; they meet thy look
  And brighten like the star that shook
Betwixt the palms of paradise.

O when her life was yet in bud,
  He too foretold the perfect rose.[3]
35 For thee she grew, for thee she grows
For ever, and as fair as good.

2. Lines 6–7 refer to Hallam's engagement to Tennyson's sister Emily; "that dark day" (line 8) refers to the day of Hallam's death. "Proved": experienced.
3. I.e., Hallam foretold that she would grow up to be beautiful. Cecilia was eight years younger than her brother. Since their father died in 1831, Tennyson gave away the bride at the wedding (line 42).

And thou art worthy; full of power;
    As gentle; liberal-minded, great,
    Consistent; wearing all that weight
40 Of learning lightly like a flower.

But now set out: the noon is near,
    And I must give away the bride;
    She fears not, or with thee beside
And me behind her, will not fear.

45 For I that danced her on my knee,
    That watch'd her on her nurse's arm,
    That shielded all her life from harm
At last must part with her to thee;

Now waiting to be made a wife,
50   Her feet, my darling, on the dead;
    Their pensive tablets round her head,[4]
And the most living words of life

Breathed in her ear. The ring is on,
    The 'wilt thou' answer'd, and again
55   The 'wilt thou' ask'd, till out of twain
Her sweet 'I will' has made you one.

Now sign your names,[5] which shall be read,
    Mute symbols of a joyful morn,
    By village eyes as yet unborn;
60 The names are sign'd, and overhead

Begins the clash and clang that tells
    The joy to every wandering breeze;
    The blind wall rocks, and on the trees
The dead leaf trembles to the bells.

65 O happy hour, and happier hours
    Await them. Many a merry face
    Salutes them—maidens of the place,
That pelt us in the porch with flowers.

O happy hour, behold the bride
70   With him to whom her hand I gave.

4. She stands on the grave of those buried in the church and with their memorial "tablets"
   on the wall above her.
5. In the parish register.

They leave the porch, they pass the grave
That has to-day its sunny side.

To-day the grave is bright for me,
    For them the light of life increased,
75   Who stay to share the morning feast,
Who rest to-night beside the sea.

Let all my genial spirits advance
    To meet and greet a whiter sun;
    My drooping memory will not shun
80 The foaming grape of eastern France.[6]

It circles round, and fancy plays,
    And hearts are warm'd and faces bloom,
    As drinking health to bride and groom
We wish them store of happy days.

85 Nor count me all to blame if I
    Conjecture of a stiller guest,
    Perchance, perchance, among the rest,
And, tho' in silence, wishing joy.

But they must go, the time draws on,
90   And those white-favour'd horses wait;
    They rise, but linger; it is late;
Farewell, we kiss, and they are gone.

A shade falls on us like the dark
    From little cloudlets on the grass,
95   But sweeps away as out we pass
To range the woods, to roam the park,

Discussing how their courtship grew,
    And talk of others that are wed,
    And how she look'd, and what he said,
100 And back we come at fall of dew.

Again the feast, the speech, the glee,
    The shade of passing thought, the wealth
    Of words and wit, the double health,
The crowning cup, the three-times-three,[7]

6. Champagne.
7. I.e., cheers.

105   And last the dance;—till I retire:
         Dumb is that tower which spake so loud,
         And high in heaven the streaming cloud,
      And on the downs a rising fire:

      And rise, O moon, from yonder down,
110   Till over down and over dale
         All night the shining vapour sail
      And pass the silent-lighted town,

      The white-faced halls, the glancing rills,
         And catch at every mountain head,
115   And o'er the friths[8] that branch and spread
      Their sleeping silver thro' the hills;

      And touch with shade the bridal doors,
         With tender gloom the roof, the wall;
         And breaking let the splendour fall
120   To spangle all the happy shores

      By which they rest, and ocean sounds,
         And, star and system rolling past,
         A soul shall draw from out the vast
      And strike his being into bounds,

125   And, moved thro' life of lower phase,[9]
         Result in man, be born and think,
         And act and love, a closer link
      Betwixt us and the crowning race[1]

      Of those that, eye to eye, shall look
130   On knowledge; under whose command
         Is Earth and Earth's, and in their hand
      Is Nature like an open book;

      No longer half-akin to brute,
         For all we thought and loved and did,
135   And hoped, and suffer'd, is but seed
      Of what in them is flower and fruit;

8. Waterways.
9. The soul of the child that will be conceived on this wedding night (lines 123–24) will
   progress through stages in which it resembles lower forms of life. Tennyson was familiar
   with the theory that the human embryo's development recapitulates the evolution of the
   species.
1. The new child will be one step closer to the perfect humanity of the future ("the crowning
   race"), described in the following stanzas.

Whereof the man, that with me trod
   This planet, was a noble type[2]
   Appearing ere the times were ripe,
140 That friend of mine who lives in God,

That God, which ever lives and loves,
   One God, one law, one element,
   And one far-off divine event,
To which the whole creation moves.

2. Archetype; model.

CRITICISM

HALLAM, LORD TENNYSON

In Memoriam†

* * *

At first the reviews of the volume were not on the whole sympathetic. One critic in a leading journal, for instance, considered that "a great deal of poetic feeling had been wasted," and "much shallow art spent on the tenderness shown to an Amaryllis of the Chancery Bar." Another referred to the poem as follows: "These touching lines evidently come from the full heart of the widow of a military man." However, men like Maurice and Robertson thought that the author had made a definite step towards the unification of the highest religion and philosophy with the progressive science of the day; and that he was the one poet who "through almost the agonies of a death-struggle" had made an effective stand against his own doubts and difficulties and those of the time, "on behalf of those first principles which underlie all creeds, which belong to our earliest childhood, and on which the wisest and best have rested through all ages; that all is right; that darkness shall be clear; that God and Time are the only interpreters; that Love is King; that the Immortal is in us; that, which is the keynote of the whole, 'All is well, tho' Faith and Form be sundered in the night of Fear.' " Scientific leaders like Herschel, Owen, Sedgwick and Tyndall regarded him as a champion of Science, and cheered him with words of genuine admiration for his love of Nature, for the eagerness with which he welcomed all the latest scientific discoveries, and for his trust in truth. Science indeed in his opinion was one of the main forces tending to disperse the superstition that still darkens the world.

* * *

"It must be remembered," writes my father,[1] "that this is a poem, *not* an actual biography. It is founded on our friendship, on the engagement of Arthur Hallam to my sister, on his sudden death at Vienna, just before the time fixed for their marriage, and on his burial at Clevedon Church. The poem concludes with the marriage of my youngest sister Cecilia. It was meant to be a kind of *Divina Commedia*,[2] ending with happiness. The sections were written at many different places, and as the phases of our intercourse came to my

† From *Alfred Lord Tennyson, A Memoir* vol. I, (New York: Macmillan, 1897), pp. 298–99, 304–6, 308–9, 311–14, 321–23, 327. The author's footnotes have been omitted; all notes are the editor's.
1. Hallam Tennyson was the poet's son; throughout the selection, therefore, "my father" refers to the poet.
2. Dante's *Divine Comedy*, which moves from hell to heaven.

memory and suggested them. I did not write them with any view of weaving them into a whole, or for publication, until I found that I had written so many. The different moods of sorrow as in a drama are dramatically given, and my conviction that fear, doubts, and suffering will find answer and relief only through Faith in a God of Love. 'I' is not always the author speaking of himself, but the voice of the human race speaking thro' him. After the Death of A.H.H., the divisions of the poem are made by First Xmas Eve (Section XXVIII.), Second Xmas (LXXVIII.), Third Xmas Eve (CIV. and CV. etc.). I myself did not see Clevedon till years after the burial of A.H.H. Jan. 3rd, 1834, and then in later editions of 'In Memoriam' I altered the word 'chancel,' which was the word used by Mr Hallam in his Memoir, to 'dark church.' As to the localities in which the poems were written, some were written in Lincolnshire, some in London, Essex, Gloucestershire, Wales, anywhere where I happened to be."

"And as for the metre of 'In Memoriam' I had no notion till 1880 that Lord Herbert of Cherbury had written his occasional verses in the same metre. I believed myself the originator of the metre, until after 'In Memoriam' came out, when some one told me that Ben Jonson and Sir Philip Sidney had used it.

* * *

That my father was a student of the Bible, those who have read "In Memoriam" know. He also eagerly read all notable works within his reach relating to the Bible, and traced with deep interest such fundamental truths as underlie the great religions of the world. He hoped that the Bible would be more and more studied by all ranks of people, and expounded simply by their teachers; for he maintained that the religion of a people could never be founded on mere moral philosophy: and that it could only come home to them in the simple, noble thoughts and facts of a Scripture like ours.

* * *

His creed, he always said, he would not formulate, for people would not understand him if he did; but he considered that his poems expressed the principles at the foundation of his faith.

He thought, with Arthur Hallam, "that the essential feelings of religion subsist in the utmost diversity of forms," that "different language does not always imply different opinions, nor different opinions any difference in *real* faith." "It is impossible," he said, "to imagine that the Almighty will ask you, when you come before Him in the next life what your particular form of creed was: but the question will rather be, 'Have you been true to yourself, and given in My Name a cup of cold water to one of these little ones?' "

"This is a terrible age of unfaith," he would say. "I hate utter unfaith, I cannot endure that men should sacrifice everything at the cold altar of what with their imperfect knowledge they choose to call truth and reason. One can easily lose all belief, through giving up the continual thought and care for spiritual things."

And again, "In this vale of Time the hills of Time often shut out the mountains of Eternity."

* * *

Assuredly Religion was no nebulous abstraction for him. He consistently emphasized his own belief in what he called the Eternal Truths; in an Omnipotent, Omnipresent and All-loving God, Who has revealed Himself through the human attribute of the highest self-sacrificing love; in the freedom of the human will; and in the immortality of the soul. But he asserted that "Nothing worthy proving can be proven," and that even as to the great laws which are the basis of Science, "We have but faith, we cannot know." He dreaded the dogmatism of sects and rash definitions of God. "I dare hardly name His Name" he would say, and accordingly he named Him in "The Ancient Sage" the "Nameless." "But take away belief in the self-conscious personality of God," he said, "and you take away the backbone of the world." "On God and God-like men we build our trust." A week before his death I was sitting by him, and he talked long of the Personality and of the Love of God, "That God, Whose eyes consider the poor," "Who catereth even for the sparrow." "I should," he said, "infinitely rather feel myself the most miserable wretch on the face of the earth with a God above, than the highest type of man standing alone." He would allow that God is unknowable in "his whole world-self, and all-in-all," and that therefore there was some force in the objection made by some people to the word "Personality," as being "anthropomorphic," and that perhaps "Self-consciousness" or "Mind" might be clearer to them: but at the same time he insisted that, although "man is like a thing of nought" in "the boundless plan," our highest view of God must be more or less anthropomorphic: and that "Personality," as far as our intelligence goes, is the widest definition and includes "Mind," "Self-consciousness," "Will," "Love" and other attributes of the Real, the Supreme, "the High and Lofty One that inhabiteth Eternity Whose name is Holy."

* * *

Everywhere throughout the Universe he saw the glory and greatness of God, and the science of Nature was particularly dear to him. Every new fact which came within his range was carefully weighed. As he exulted in the wilder aspects of Nature (see for instance sect. xv.) and revelled in the thunderstorm; so he felt a joy in her orderliness; he felt a rest in her steadfastness, patient progress and hope-

fulness; the same seasons ever returned; the same stars wheeled in
their courses; the flowers and trees blossomed and the birds sang
yearly in their appointed months; and he had a triumphant appreciation of her ever-new revelations of beauty. One of the "In Memoriam" poems, written at Barmouth, gives preeminently his sense of
the joyous peace in Nature, and he would quote it in this context
along with his Spring and Bird songs:

> Sweet after showers, ambrosial air,
>   That rollest from the gorgeous gloom
>   Of evening over brake and bloom
> And meadow, slowly breathing bare
>
> The round of space, and rapt below
>   Thro' all the dewy-tassell'd wood,
>   And shadowing down the horned flood
> In ripples, fan my brows and blow
>
> The fever from my cheek, and sigh
>   The full new life that feeds thy breath
>   Throughout my frame, till Doubt and Death,
> Ill brethren, let the fancy fly
>
> From belt to belt of crimson seas
>   On leagues of odour streaming far,
>   To where in yonder orient star
> A hundred spirits whisper "Peace."
>
>   [LXXXVI]

But he was occasionally much troubled with the intellectual problem of the apparent profusion and waste of life and by the vast
amount of sin and suffering throughout the world, for these seemed
to militate against the idea of the Omnipotent and All-loving Father.[3]

No doubt in such moments he might possibly have been heard to
say what I myself have heard him say: "An Omnipotent Creator Who
could make such a painful world is to me *sometimes* as hard to believe
in as to believe in blind matter behind everything. The lavish profusion too in the natural world appals me, from the growths of the
tropical forest to the capacity of man to multiply, the torrent of
babies."

                            *   *   *

I need not enlarge upon his faith in the Immortality of the Soul
as he has dwelt upon that so fully in his poems. "I can hardly understand," he said, "how any great, imaginative man, who has deeply
lived, suffered, thought and wrought, can doubt of the Soul's con-

3. See section LV.

tinuous progress in the after-life." His poem of "Wages" he liked to quote on this subject.

He more than once said what he has expressed in "Vastness": "Hast Thou made all this for naught! Is all this trouble of life worth undergoing if we only end in our own corpse-coffins at last? If you allow a God, and God allows this strong instinct and universal yearning for another life, surely that is in a measure a presumption of its truth. We cannot give up the mighty hopes that make us men."

> My own dim life should teach me this,
>   That life shall live for evermore,
>   Else earth is darkness at the core,
> And dust and ashes all that is.
>
> *   *   *
>
> What then were God to such as I?
>   [XXXIV, 1–4, 9]

I have heard him even say that he "would rather know that he was to be lost eternally than not know that the whole human race was to live eternally"; and when he speaks of "faintly trusting the larger hope" he means by "the larger hope" that the whole human race would through, perhaps, ages of suffering, be at length purified and saved, even those who now "better not with time"; so that at the end of "The Vision of Sin" we read

> God made Himself an awful rose of dawn.

One day towards the end of his life he bade me look into the Revised Version and see how the Revisers had translated the passage "Depart from me, ye cursed, into everlasting fire." His disappointment was keen when he found that the translators had not altered "everlasting" into "æonian" or some such word: for he never would believe that Christ could preach "everlasting punishment."

> "Fecemi la divina potestate
> La somma sapienza, e 'l primo amore,"[4]

were words which he was fond of quoting in this relation, as if they were a kind of unconscious confession by Dante that Love must conquer at the last.

Letters were not unfrequently addressed to him asking what his opinions were about Evolution, about Prayer, and about Christ.

Of Evolution he said: "That makes no difference to me, even if the Darwinians did not, as they do, exaggerate Darwinism. To God all is present. He sees present, past, and future as one."

*   *   *

4. "Divine power created me [i.e., hell], highest wisdom, and primal love" (*Inferno* III, 5–6); this is inscribed over the gates of hell.

In the poem "By an Evolutionist," written in 1888 when he was dangerously ill, he defined his position; he conceived that the further science progressed, the more the Unity of Nature, and the purpose hidden behind the cosmic process of matter in motion and changing forms of life, would be apparent. Someone asked him whether it was not hard to account for genius by Evolution. He put aside the question, for he believed that genius was the greatest mystery to itself.

To Tyndall he once said, "No evolutionist is able to explain the mind of Man or how any possible physiological change of tissue can produce conscious thought." Yet he was inclined to think that the theory of Evolution caused the world to regard more clearly the "Life of Nature as a lower stage in the manifestation of a principle which is more fully manifested in the spiritual life of man, with the idea that in this process of Evolution the lower is to be regarded as a means to the higher."

*   *   *

I cannot end this chapter on "In Memoriam" more fitly than by quoting Henry Hallam's[5] letter on receiving in 1850 what he calls "the precious book."

> I know not how to express what I have felt. My first sentiment was surprise, for, though I now find that you had mentioned the intention to my daughter, Julia, she had never told me of the poems. I do not speak as another would to praise and admire: few of them indeed I have as yet been capable of reading, the grief they express is too much akin to that they revive. It is better than any monument which could be raised to the memory of my beloved son, it is a more lively and enduring testimony to his great virtues and talents that the world should know the friendship which existed between you, that posterity should associate his name with that of Alfred Tennyson.

EDGAR FINLEY SHANNON, JR.

The Pinnacle of Success: *In Memoriam*†

The Reception of In Memoriam

In Memoriam, that monument to the religious questioning of the nineteenth century as well as to the memory of Arthur Henry Hallam, was published by Moxon on June 1, 1850. The product of seven-

5. Arthur Hallam's father.
† From *Tennyson and the Reviewers*, (Cambridge: Harvard University Press, 1952), pp. 141–54. Copyright © 1952 by the President and Fellows of Harvard College. The author's footnotes have been omitted; all footnotes are the editor's.

teen years of rumination engendered by the sudden death of Tennyson's college friend in Vienna on September 15, 1833, the elegy came before the reading public unheralded by publisher's advertisements and without its author's name on the title page.

There was little doubt, however, as to the identity of the pen from which the unusual work emanated. On Wednesday, May 29, Mudie's Select Library advertised in the London daily papers that fifty copies of Tennyson's new poem would be available on Saturday, the day of publication. And on that day the fifty copies were announced as in circulation. The *Sun* in August complained that the opportunity of revealing the author's name from internal evidence had been cut off by the rumors linking the poem with Tennyson "even prior to the day of its publication." The first periodicals to notice the book, the *Spectator* and the *Examiner*, unhesitatingly informed their readers on June 8 that Tennyson was the writer and Hallam the person to whom the poem was addressed. A week later the *Atlas* pretended to be vexed that speculations and learned disquisitions had thus been anticipated by the "outspokenness of our periodical critics, who blurt out the secret before the volume is a week old. . . . the whole truth even now stands revealed to the world. There is no mystery about it." Only the *Literary Gazette* distinguished itself by welcoming on June 15 "a female hand" to "the Muses' banquet," after it had already listed *In Memoriam* as by Tennyson in its column of new books on June 1.

The reception of *In Memoriam* by the periodicals during the year of its publication was in general extremely laudatory. The weekly journals printed in London, as usual the first to notice a new work, responded with no fewer than nine reviews during the month of June. The *Leader*, the newly established republican paper captained by George Henry Lewes and Thornton Hunt, and the faithful *Examiner* were fervid in their commendation. Lewes, who wrote the encomium in the *Leader*, called Tennyson the "greatest living poet" and judged *In Memoriam* superior to "Lycidas." "The comparison," he said, "is not here of genius, but of feeling. Tennyson sings a deeper sorrow, utters a more truthful passion, and singing truly, gains the predominance of passion over mere sentiment." He concluded with a prophetic opinion of the poem, "We shall be surprised if it does not become the solace and delight of every house where poetry is loved. A true and hopeful spirit breathes from its pages. . . . All who have sorrowed will listen with delight to the chastened strains here poured forth *In Memoriam*." The *Examiner*, in an article presumably by Forster, was no less eulogistic. *In Memoriam* was not unworthy of comparison to Milton's "Lycidas," Petrarch's and Shakespeare's sonnets, and Dante's "Purgatorio" and "Paradiso." Tennyson's poem, the writer said, is a pathetic tale of real human sorrow, suggested rather than told. It exhibits the influence of a sudden and appalling shock, and lasting bereavement, in the formation of character and opinion. It is the record of a healthy and vigorous mind working its way, through suffering, up to settled equipoise and hopeful resignation. The effect of the poem, as a whole, is to soften yet to strengthen the heart; while every separate part is instinct with intense beauty, and with varied and profound reflections on individual man, on society, and on their mutual relations. It is perhaps the author's greatest achievement. A passion, deep-felt throughout it, has informed his ever subtle thoughts and delicate imagery with a massive grandeur and a substantial interest.

The *Guardian*, which had approved of *The Princess*,[1] was as appreciative of *In Memoriam*. Although it was not so enthusiastic as the *Leader* and the *Examiner*, it declared, "Judged even by the standard of Shakespeare and Spenser, Mr. Tennyson will not be found wanting."

Even the weeklies that had handled *The Princess* severely had overcome their aversion for Tennyson to a remarkable degree. The *Spectator* quoted approvingly sections LXXXIX ("Witch-elms that counterchange the floor") and CVI ("Ring out, wild bells") and said, "The volume is pervaded by a religious feeling, and an ardent aspiration for the advancement of society. . . . These two sentiments impart elevation, faith, and resignation; so that memory, thought, and a chastened tenderness, generally predominate over deep grief." The *Spectator* found fewer of the eccentricities of style against which it had been protesting for twenty years and felt that the scheme of the poem was "favourable to those pictures of common landscape and daily life, redeemed from triviality by genial feeling and a perception of the lurking beautiful, which are the author's distinguishing characteristic." If the reviewer in the *Literary Gazette*, possibly Jerdan, whose long editorship was just coming to an end, mistook the identity of the author, he had only the warmest praise for the poem. The *Atlas* had been completely won over, though the critic doubted that the poem would "find as large a circle of readers as other emanations of Tennyson's muse." The series of poems which make up the whole work "are entirely worthy of the poet," he said. "They overflow with plaintive beauty. They are the touching heart-utterances of a genuine and noble sorrow. There is a homeliness and simplicity about them which bear ample testimony to their truth. There is nothing ornate or elaborate in them; they are thoughtful, chastened, and subdued." The *Britannia*, which had looked upon *The Princess* as despicable, conceded that in the new poem, amidst some repetition of the poet's

1. Tennyson's last major poem (1847) before *In Memoriam*.

old faults, there were beauties "which take their place at once and for ever in the poetry of England." The *Athenaeum*, in another review by J. Westland Marston, firmly endorsed the volume:

> It belongs to those deepest forms of poetic expression which grow out of the heart and stand distinguished from those which have their origin in the imagination. . . . In its moral scope the book will endear itself to all who suffer, both by its vivid appreciation of their grief and by its transmutation of that grief into patience and hope. No worthier or more affecting tribute could be rendered to the dead than one which like this, converts the influence of their memory into solace for the living.

Reviewing Tennyson for the first time, the Unitarian *Inquirer* alone found more to blame than to praise; but its attitude cannot be called hostile. It was "grateful for the purity and elegance that breathe throughout the volume" and desisted from quoting examples of the "mellow fruit" shining out amid the "weeds" in order not to overthrow "our critical objections to the poem as a whole." The objections of this sectarian journal, whose reviews were devoted almost entirely to religious works, could not have had much effect upon the literary world in the face of the approval of the *Athenaeum*, the *Examiner*, the *Spectator*, and the *Atlas*, not to mention the other weeklies.

It was somewhat curious that Forster in the *Examiner*, sharing the view of the critic for the *Atlas*, should think that *In Memoriam* would not "become immediately popular." Henry Taylor privately expressed the same opinion. On July 1, 1850, he wrote to Miss Isabella Fenwick, "Have you read Tennyson's 'In Memoriam'? It is a wonderful little volume. Few—very few—words of such power have come out of the depths of this country's poetic heart. They might do much, one would think, to lay the dust in its highways and silence its market towns. But it will not be felt for a while, I suppose; and just now people are talking of the division of last Friday."

But Lewes' forecast was the correct one, and the prophets of gloom had reckoned without the people and without the praise of the press. Besides the notices in the London weeklies, favorable reviews and excerpts from *In Memoriam* were printed by various newspapers throughout the United Kingdom during the month of June. In July additional complimentary articles appeared. Encomiums of the poem flowered in the periodicals for August. The *North British Review*, in the first elaborate critique of *In Memoriam*, sounded the note that succeeding critics echoed: "There are certain great epochs in the history of poetry. The publication of 'Paradise Lost'[2] was one of these. The next, which was at all similar in impor-

2. By John Milton (1667).

tance, was the appearance of the 'Excursion.'[3]. . . . Our immediate impression upon the perusal of 'In Memoriam' was that it claimed a place in the very highest rank, and that it was the first poem of historical importance which has appeared since the 'Excursion.' " Franklin Lushington, one of the family to whom Tennyson was so closely bound by ties of affection and marriage, proclaimed in *Tait's Edinburgh Magazine* that *In Memoriam* was "the finest poem the world has seen for very many years." "Its title," he said, "has already become a household word among us. Its deep feeling, its wide sympathies, its exquisite pictures, its true religion, will soon be not less so. The sooner the better." Patmore, writing in the *Palladium*, a newly established Edinburgh magazine, was practically breathless with adulation. Tennyson's new work contained "the best religious poetry that has ever been written in our language—if we except a very few of the lovely and too seldom appreciated effusions of George Herbert." After quoting section CIII ("On that last night"), Patmore remarked, "In our opinion, there is nothing nearly equal to the above, in splendour of language and imagination, depth and classicality of thought and feeling, perfection of form, and completeness in every way, in the whole scope of modern English poetry." *Sharpe's London Journal* exclaimed,

> All the qualifications which have rendered him [Tennyson] so acceptable to the critical readers and discreet lovers of poetry, are here displayed in their matured excellence:—the graceful diction and exquisite harmony of versification; the subtle flights of thought and fancy; the delicate sense of beauty and keen appreciation of the beautiful; the power of condensation, and of presenting the commonest objects in a new and unexpected light;—these and many more characteristics of his genius are observable in the pages of *"In Memoriam."*

Hogg's Instructor found "high merit" in the poem's "general tone of lofty spiritualism. . . .The thoughts awakened by reflections on life and death—on the reality life and the reality death—give to this work that vitality which outlives mere beauty of description and mere pathos of sentiment." The *Court Journal* cried, "Never yet did fairer wreath deck the tomb where lies the loved and lost; chisel never yet fashioned monumental marble more graceful, more expressive of the homage paid by the living to the dead, than in this tribute of a sorrowing heart to the memory of one so beloved."

At the end of August, two of the London daily newspapers added their voices to these paeans. The *Sun* called *In Memoriam* a "masterpiece of poetic composition" and asserted, "Of the exquisite simplicity of the whole effusion we cannot speak in terms of too earnest

3. By William Wordsworth (1814).

admiration." The ever-loyal *Morning Post* maintained, "Only a poet would have conceived the idea; and Wordsworth himself, in his happiest moments, would not have produced a more touching or beautiful composition." Concerning the sections which make up the poem, the *Post* remarked, "It is not merely the intensity of feeling which they manifest nor the musical power and simplicity of the language which gives so great a charm and so absorbing an interest to these stanzas; it is the harmony and depth of thought, illustrated and adorned with the riches of a fertile fancy and a well-stored intellect, which form their chief excellence and repay with the disclosure of new beauties every fresh perusal."

By the beginning of September *In Memoriam* had reached a second edition and probably a third. Sir Charles Tennyson says that there were 5,000 copies in the first edition; and it is likely that a larger number was printed for the second and third editions. The book was selling at a phenomenal rate, setting at naught all predictions to the contrary.

Three articles in the magazines and reviews for September, which appeared about the first of the month, continued the flood of panegyric. For the *Eclectic Review* the chief importance of the poem lay in "the revealment of greatness in the spirit of the artist." And "the second great value of the book" was said to be its "expression of a cycle of experience common to thoughtful humanity." Charles Kingsley in *Fraser's Magazine* thought *In Memoriam* "the noblest English Christian poem which several centuries have seen." The *English Review*, while mercilessly exposing Tennyson's lack of faith (to which I shall return presently), described the poem as "an heirloom bequeathed to our nation, and to be treasured by it, as long as the English tongue endures."

The October number of the *Westminster Review* devoted nineteen pages to an article which was in no sense critical and can only be described as a fulsome eulogy of both author and work.

In the criticism of *In Memoriam* during the first four months after its publication, the reviewers had a good deal to say concerning the poem's technical or literary qualities—its unity, diction, meter, and monotony. They generally agreed that the sometimes almost unconnected sections of the work did not destroy its total effect. *Hogg's Instructor* felt that though the poem was "thus made up of a series of detached parts, yet is the unity of the whole unbroken, because there is ever a recurrence to one and the same melancholy event." The *Morning Post* said, "Not only is the unity of design and of subject apparent throughout, but the thoughts follow each other in a natural sequence, the continuity of which renders it necessary to contemplate the work as a whole in order fully to appreciate its beauties." The *Eclectic* declared, "An organic unity informs the whole; unity of feeling and of interest." And Lushington in *Tait's* asserted that the poem was "perfect and unique as a whole, to a degree and in a style very rarely reached."

The diction, always one of the focal points of attack on Tennyson, met with more approval than censure. Some critics, such as those in the *Inquirer*, the *Britannia*, and the *Court Journal*, repeated the old charges of quaint and obscure phraseology. Marston and Lushington, in the *Athenaeum* and *Tait's*, respectively, were more directly concerned with the poet's problem of expressing succinctly metaphysical conceptions and objected that the language did not always represent with sufficient clarity abstract ideas. More representative of the prevailing opinion was that of the *Eclectic*: "As regards words merely, Tennyson is undeniably one of the greatest of *Expressers*. His is the master's facility. His are the 'aptest words to things.' In expert 'fitting' of the one to the other, his present practice far exceeds even his original gift. Unerring is his speech, as opulent. It is ever *adequate* to the thought. The balance of the two brings about lucidness, unexampled, in thought so large, feeling so deep, poetry so subtle."

The stanza in which the poem was written provoked extensive comment, but the weight of critical opinion was strongly in its favor. The *Leader* remarked, "How exquisitely adapted the music of the poem is to its burden; the stanza chosen, with its mingling rhymes, and its slow, yet not imposing march, seems to us the very perfection of stanza for the purpose." The *Eclectic* called the stanza a "happy one"; *Sharpe's London Journal* said that it was "most happily selected"; and Kingsley in *Fraser's* pronounced it "exquisitely chosen." The *North British Review* went so far as to say, "This seems to us to be one of the most perfect rhymed measures for continuous verse ever invented."

There were, however, a few dissenting voices. The *Inquirer*, for instance, complained, "The measure is of too obvious facility, and, in a less masterly hand, might break into the very false gallop of verses. Even in spite of the division into short canzonets or sonnets, which breaks the continuity of the air, there is a poverty and sameness in it which produces weariness and fatigue, so that there is danger of losing the full appreciation of the burden for want of greater variety and strength in the verse." The *Christian Reformer*, also wishing for more variety, regretted that Tennyson had confined himself to one meter. The *Sun* thought the stanza "at the first somewhat unpalatable from its monotony," yet confessed in the end to being overcome by its "irresistible fascination." The *Westminster*, charmed by the rhyme scheme of the stanzas, maintained that "the sweetness of the notes, the earnest truth of the thought, the comprehensiveness of the love, relieve them of all monotony."

The question of the monotony of the poem was also raised by other reviewers. The *Spectator* felt that there was "inevitably something of sameness in the work" and that the subject was "unequal to its long expansion." The *Atlas* believed that the sections were "too mournfully monotonous," and even Forster in the *Examiner* conceded an "unavoidable monotony." But this point of view did not go unchallenged. *Hogg's Instructor* said that, although the poem might appear to be monotonous, "to many this very monotony will be its chief beauty." And the *English Review* asserted, "It might be presumed, that such a work, extending to pages 210, upon the same simple theme, would be monotonous: but this is scarcely the case. At least, if there be any monotony here, the monotony of sorrow, it is so eminently beautiful, that we could not wish it other than it is."

Among the general features of the poem, the portrayal of English landscape and of domestic scenes and affections elicited unanimous approbation. But probably the most interesting aspect of the criticism of *In Memoriam* is the attitude of the reviewers toward its religious doctrine. A vast majority commended this element of the work and, with a somewhat human tendency to read more into the meaning than the poet had actually expressed, found the theology sound and the faith inspiring. Kingsley rejoiced as follows: "Blessed it is to find the most cunning poet of our day able to combine the complicated rhythm and melody of modern times with the old truths which gave heart to the martyrs at the stake, to see in the science and history of the nineteenth century new and living fulfilments of the words which we learnt at our mothers' knee!" Patmore maintained that the reader was exalted by the strains in which "sorrow is gradually shown to be the teacher of a pure, or rather the only pure philosophy" and "secular knowledge is humbled before loving faith." The *Guardian* and the *Spectator* said that the volume was "full of religious feeling." The *Morning Post*, in a notice of *Fraser's Magazine* for September, spoke of "the pure Christianity" of *In Memoriam*. The *North British Review* asserted that the poem uttered primary Christian truths, which the age, having lost, was in the process of recovering; and *Tait's* mentioned the volume's "true religion." For the *Sun* the "philosophy" of the poem was "ever pure and lofty." The *Westminster* thought the poem was thoroughly devout, and the *Prospective Review* cherished the poet's declaration for faith over knowledge.

In this overwhelming tide of laudation, only three instances of protest have come to light. The *Britannia* noticed "an almost total absence of those higher consolations which religion should suggest." "We miss," the reviewer said, "those hues of cheerfulness and manly resignation with which Christianity invests the outpourings of her stricken children." Yet he was moved to comment on section CVI ("Ring out, wild bells"), "It is suggestive, healthy, full of generous aspirations, poetical, sympathetic, Christian." The *Court Journal* feared that Tennyson did "not always seek his consolation at the one sufficing source," but hoped that the passages which compelled such a remark had been misconstrued. The critic for the High Church *English Review* alone examined in detail Tennyson's theological position. Although some of his views were extreme, he anticipated by some eighty-six years Mr. T. S. Eliot's dictum that *In Memoriam* is more conspicuous for the doubt than for the faith which it expresses.[4] In the first place, he took the poet to task for not capitalizing in the proem the pronouns referring to the Divinity. Concerning the lines,

> O thou that after toil and storm
>   Mayst seem to have reach'd a purer air,
>   Whose faith has centre everywhere,
> Nor cares to fix itself to form,
>
> Leave thou thy sister when she prays,
>   Her early Heaven, her happy views;
>   Nor thou with shadow'd hint confuse
> A life that leads melodious days,
>
> (XXXIII, 1–8)

he charged, "It is most falsely, and, we may add, offensively assumed, that the unbeliever in Christianity can possess a faith of his own, quite as real and as stable as that of the believer!" He suspected Tennyson of being "*an exclusive worshipper of the beautiful.*" The lines,

> There lives more faith in honest doubt,
> Believe me, than in half the creeds,
>
> (XCVI, 11–12)

he pronounced "infinitely mischievous." The stanza,

> Tho' truths in manhood darkly join,
>   Deep seated in our mystic frame,
>   We yield all blessing to the name
> Of Him that made them current coin,
>
> (XXXVI, 1–4)

he declared to be "simply and purely blasphemy." He viewed with distrust Tennyson's apparent acceptance of the principles of evolution and concluded, "We remain undecided as to Mr. Tennyson's faith, though we opine, that, strictly speaking, *he has none*, whether negative or affirmative, and advise him, for his soul's good, to try to get one!"

---

4. See Eliot's essay on p. 138 herein.

But in spite of this attack upon the poet's theology, the critic preserved an adulatory respect for his work. For the first time in the contemporary criticism of Tennyson, aesthetic qualities outweighed moral values. Tennyson, he said, "*teaches* us nothing; he needs teaching himself; he is rather an exponent of this age's wants, than one who can in any measure undertake to satisfy them. And yet, with all this, we repeat, he is a great poet; and great he for ever will remain."

It was now generally agreed that Tennyson was not only the leading poet of the day but a poet of commanding genius. The *Leader* had already proclaimed him the "greatest living poet." The *Eclectic* had found his "greatness" revealed by *In Memoriam*. The *Standard of Freedom*, noticing *Fraser's* for September, called him "that great poet." As one reviewer put it, he had become "the rage," and the *Globe* said on September 4, 1850, "For one genuine reader of Wordsworth there are thousands who relish Tennyson."

At last Tennyson was thought to have fulfilled his promise and to have accepted the mission that had been envisaged for him. *Sharpe's London Journal* had felt it necessary to lament "the apparent absence of any direct or intelligible aim" in his previous poetry and had been unable to "discover in it that genuine sympathy . . . with . . . human progress generally found in the highest order of poetry." "But the present volume," the critic said, "abounds with noble aspirations and generous sentiments which reflect equal glory on the philanthropist and the poet, and which prove to us that we have not been wrong in classing Alfred Tennyson among the great and moving spirits of the age." The *Eclectic* also testified to the poet's achievement. *Poems*, 1842, and *The Princess* had shown that Tennyson's nature was "eminently elevated, pure . . . sympathizing, genuine, refined," but also that it was "a reserved and fastidious one." His skill and artistry had made him seem "removed and distant. Rarely was a direct sentiment or sympathy, the central influence of a poem." With *In Memoriam*, however, "All wants are now amply compensated by one continuous revealment of our poet in his spiritual individuality; one exclusive outlet of personal feeling and sympathies. Their expression is enlarged into relevance with universal humanity." The poem contains "the poetic solution of every-day problems of thought." In addition, "More than once, a penetrating poet's glance is turned on this age itself. A calmly attuned voice is raised in testimony to 'The mighty hopes that make us men:' a voice of large trust, of deep-seated faith, of long prophecy; singing of that 'crowning race,' the 'flower and fruit' of that, in us the seed."

Thus *In Memoriam* was believed to embody all the qualities which the age expected of poetry. The poem awakened chords of universal human sympathy. It played upon and ministered to emotions expe-

rienced by all men at one time or another. It was eminently of the
day and concerned itself with the solution of current problems; it
was complete with prophecy and the doctrine of progress; it incul-
cated the moral of faith and hope derived from the catharsis of suffering. Tennyson had finally produced an elevated, sustained, and
unified poem of a philosophical nature and had convinced most of
his contemporaries that he was a vigorous and profound thinker.

It was the consensus of the reviewers that *In Memoriam* was the
great work which had been awaited from Tennyson's pen. The poem
was neither an epic nor a drama, as had been prescribed, but it was
a work to stand beside *Paradise Lost* and *The Excursion*, beside the
"Purgatorio" and "Paradiso" of Dante, and the sonnets of Petrarch
and Shakespeare. Of the periodicals that made the comparison, only
the *Inquirer*, admittedly reactionary in matters of literary taste,
thought *In Memoriam* inferior to "Lycidas."[5]

A work of such eminence was naturally thought to be of timeless
significance. Through his mastery of poetic technique, Tennyson was
said to have embalmed his "great thoughts" and "elevated feeling"
"for the ages." *In Memoriam* contained "joys, in which our children
and our children's children will participate as largely as ourselves."
The thoughts of the poet "who revolves the problems of free-will and
fate, and gives utterance to his feelings of awe and hope . . . [are]
not 'such perishable stuff as dreams are made of,' but they 'wander
through eternity.' " And to the memory of Arthur Hallam, the poem
was "a monument 'more lasting than brass,' " "a memorial more lasting than bronze."

The Laureateship

Wordsworth had died on April 23, 1850; and, while the praise of
In Memoriam was steadily mounting, the office of poet laureate, left
vacant by his death, remained unfilled. The discussion prevalent in
literary circles about an appropriate successor was echoed in the
press. Although Chorley assiduously advanced Mrs. Browning's
claims in the *Athenaeum*, the most likely candidates were conceded
to be Tennyson and Leigh Hunt. The Queen had acted promptly in
offering the post on May 8 to Samuel Rogers, the literary veteran,
famous as a host and connoisseur as well as a poet. But Rogers, then
eighty-seven, declined the honor because of his age, and the
laureateship went unoccupied until the autumn.

On September 7, 1850, the Prime Minister wrote to the Queen:
"Lord John Russell has had the honour of receiving at Taymouth a
letter from the Prince. He agrees that the office of Poet Laureate
ought to be filled up. There are three or four authors of nearly equal

5. Major elegy by Milton (1638).

merit, such as Henry Taylor, Sheridan Knowles, Professor Wilson, and Mr Tennyson, who are qualified for the office." On October 3 Russell wrote to Rogers, "H. M. is inclined to bestow it on Mr Tennyson, but I should wish, before the offer is made, to know something of his character, as well as of his literary merits." The old poet having vouched for Tennyson's respectability, Russell informed Prince Albert on October 21, "Mr Tennyson is a fit person to be Poet Laureate"; and on November 5 Sir Charles Phipps, Keeper of the Privy Purse, wrote to Tennyson for the Queen, offering him the post "as a mark of Her Majesty's appreciation of your literary distinction." Tennyson, after a day's hesitation, accepted; and the appointment was officially made on November 19, 1850. It seems to have been received with general satisfaction by the public, though Chorley, who admitted there was no question of Tennyson's merit, grumbled about the "multiplication of . . . benefices to a single subject." The *Leader* reported the appointment with pleasure, saying that "the name of ALFRED TENNYSON is so beloved that any good fortune befalling him will delight the public." Hunt like a good loser, wrote in his new periodical, *Leigh Hunt's Journal*,

> If the Office in future is really to be bestowed on the highest degree of poetical merit, and on that only (as being a solitary office, it unquestionably ought to be, though such has not hitherto been the case), then Mr. Alfred Tennyson is entitled to it above any other man in the kingdom; since of all living poets he is the most gifted with the sovereign poetical faculty, Imagination. May he live to wear his laurel to a green old age; singing congratulations to good Queen Victoria and human advancement, long after the writer of these words shall have ceased to hear him with mortal ears.

Wordsworth had raised the dignity of the laureateship to a new level in public esteem; and if the Queen's intention was to preserve this high standing, Tennyson was the obvious, and actually the only, choice. *In Memoriam* had elevated him to an unassailable pinnacle. His appointment as poet laureate was the accolade for twenty years of poetic endeavor.

* * *

122

A. C. BRADLEY

[The Structure and Effect of *In Memoriam*]†

The Structure of In Memoriam

I. The most obvious sign of definite structure in *In Memoriam* consists in the internal chronology, and it will be well to begin by making this clear.

Tennyson[1] himself tells us (*Memoir*, I. 305) that the divisions of the poem are made by the Christmas-tide sections (XXVIII., LXXVIII., CIV.). That the first of these refers to the first Christmas after the death of the friend in autumn is evident from XXX., 14–16:

> We sung, tho' every eye was dim,
> A merry song we sang with him
> *Last year:*[2]

and we certainly receive the impression from the other Christmas poems that the second refers to the Christmas of the next year, and the third to that of the next again. Thus, when we have reached section CIV., we are distant from the death of the friend about two years and a quarter; and there is nothing in the sections after CIV. to make us think that they are supposed to cover any length of time. Accordingly, the time imagined to elapse in the poem may be set down as rather less than three years.

These results are confirmed by other facts. Between the Christmas poems there come occasional sections indicating the progress of time by reference to the seasons and to the anniversaries of the death of the friend; and between two Christmas poems we never find a hint that more than one spring or one summer has passed, or that more than one anniversary has come round. After the third Christmas we have a spring poem (CXV.), but after this no sign of summer or of the return of the anniversary of the friend's death.

The unmistakable indications of the internal chronology are shown in the following table:

---

† From *A Commentary on Tennyson's In Memoriam* (London: Macmillan, 1901), pp. 20–48.
1. It will be understood that generally, both in this Introduction and in the Notes, when I speak of 'the poet' I mean the poet who speaks *in* the poem. I refer to the author who composed the poem as 'Tennyson' or 'the author.'
2. These lines are decisive, and their evidence is not weakened by the fact that some poems referring to the burial precede this first Christmas section, whereas the burial of Arthur Hallam did not really take place until after Christmas, 1833. The author did not choose to make the internal chronology coincide with the actual order of events.

Section XI.	Early Autumn.
XV.	Later.
XXVIII.–XXX.	Christmastide.
XXXVIII.–IX.	Spring.
LXXII.	Anniversary.
LXXVIII.	Christmastide.
LXXXIII.	Delaying spring.
LXXXVI., LXXXVIII.	Spring.
LXXXIX., XCV., XCVIII.	Summer.
XCIX.	Anniversary.
CIV.–CV.	Christmastide.
CVI.	New Year's Day.
CVII.	Winter.
CXV., CXVI.	Spring.

Against all these indications there seems nothing to be set except the few passages, already noted, where a phrase or the tone of a section appears to be not quite in harmony with this internal chronology. That these passages are so few is a proof of the care taken by the author to preserve the clearness and consistency of the scheme. And it is undoubtedly of use in giving the outlines of a structure to the poem, and of still greater use in providing beautiful contrasts between the sections which deal with the recurring seasons and anniversaries; though it is somewhat unfortunate that the contents of some of the final sections imply a greater distance of time from the opening of the series than is suggested by the chronological scheme.

II. If we describe in the most general terms the movement of thought and feeling in *In Memoriam*, the description will be found to apply also to *Lycidas* or *Adonais*.[3] In each case the grief of the opening has passed at the close into triumph: at first the singer thinks only of loss and death, and at last his eyes are fixed upon the vision of a new and greater life. But in *Lycidas* and *Adonais* this change is expressed in one continuous strain and is therefore felt by the reader to occupy but a few hours of concentrated experience; and in *Adonais* especially the impression of passionate rapidity in the transition from gloom to glory is essential to the effect. In *In Memoriam* a similar change is supposed to fill a period of some years, and the impression of a very gradual and difficult advance is no less essential. It is conveyed, of course, not only by the indications of time which have just been considered, but by the mere fact that each of the 131 sections is, in a sense, a

3. Elegies by Milton (1638) and Percy Shelley (1821), respectively [Editor].

poem complete in itself and accordingly felt to be the expression of
the thought of one particular time.

In many cases, however, we soon observe that a single section is
not really thus independent of its predecessor and successor. On the
contrary, some are scarcely intelligible if taken in isolation; and again
and again we discover groups which have one subject, and in which
the single sections are devoted to various aspects of this one subject.
The poet in his progress has come upon a certain thought, which
occupies him for a time and is developed through a series of stages
or contrasted with a number of other thoughts. And even in cases
where we cannot trace such a close connection in thought we often
find that several consecutive sections are bound together, and separated from the poems that surround them, by a common tone of
feeling. These groups or clusters correspond with single paragraphs
of *Lycidas*, or with single stanzas or groups of stanzas in *Adonais*;
and their presence forms a second means by which a certain amount
of structure is given to the poem.

There are many readers of *In Memoriam* who have never read the
poem through, but probably everyone who has done so has recog-
nised to some extent the existence of groups. Everyone remarks, for
instance, that near the beginning there are a number of sections
referring to the coming of the ship, and that there are other consecutive poems which deal with Christmastide. But perhaps few readers
are aware of the large part played by these groups. The fact is that,
taken together, they account for considerably more than one-half of
the poem; and in this estimate no notice has been taken of mere
pairs of connected sections, such as XIX., XX.; XLVIII., XLIX.; LVII., LVIII.;
CXV., CXVI.; or of parts of the poem where the sections, though not
so closely connected as to form a distinct group, are yet manifestly
united in a looser way. If these additions are made to our estimate,
it will be found to include nearly 100 poems out of the total of 131.

Of the remaining sections (*a*) a small number may properly be
called occasional poems, though the positions which they occupy in
the whole are always more or less significant. Such are LXXXVII.,
which describes the visit to Cambridge; XCVIII., on the brother's tour
to Vienna; the long retrospective poem, LXXXV.; or the poem on Hallam's birthday, CVII. (*b*) Others at once remind us of preceding sections suggested by a like occasion, and in this way bring home to us
the change which has taken place in the poet's mind during the
interval. The Christmas poems are the most prominent instance; the
later spring poems recall the earlier; the second 'Risest thou thus'
brings back the first; the two sections beginning, 'Dark house,' and
the two poems on the Yew-tree, form similar pairs. (*c*) Lastly, we find
that the sections which immediately follow connected groups are

often of one and the same kind. The subject which has occupied the poet's thoughts being dismissed, there follows a kind of reaction. He looks inward, and becomes more keenly conscious of the feeling from which his attention had been for the time diverted (*e.g.* XXXVIII.), or of the feeling in which his thoughts have culminated (*e.g.* LVII.). Not seldom this feeling suggests to him some reflection on his own songs: his singing comforts him on his dreary way, or he feels that it is of no avail, or that it expresses nothing of his deepest grief. And not only thus at the close of groups, but at various other points throughout *In Memoriam* there occur sections in which the poet's songs form the subject, pointing backwards and forwards to one another, and showing the change which passes over his mind as time goes on (*e.g.* V., XXI., LVIII., CXXV.). In these various ways, as well as by the presence of definite groups, some kind of connection is established between section and section almost throughout the whole of the poem.

III. We are now in a position to observe the structure of this whole, reserving for the Commentary the fuller characterisation of particular parts.

The 'Way of the Soul' we find to be a journey from the first stupor and confusion of grief, through a growing acquiescence often disturbed by the recurrence of pain, to an almost unclouded peace and joy. The anguish of wounded love passes into the triumph of love over sorrow, time and death. The soul, at first almost sunk in the feeling of loss, finds itself at last freed from regret and yet strengthened in affection. It pines no longer for the vanished hand and silent voice; it is filled with the consciousness of union with the spirit. The world which once seemed to it a mere echo of its sorrow, has become the abode of that immortal Love, at once divine and human, which includes the living and the dead.

Is it possible to find in this 'Way' any turning-point where grief begins to yield to joy,—such a turning-point as occurs in *Adonais* when indignation rouses the poet from his sorrow and the strain suddenly rises into the solemn affirmation,

'Peace, peace! he is not dead, he doth not sleep'?

If so, *In Memoriam* may be considered to fall into two fairly distinct parts, though the dividing-line would not necessarily come, any more than in *Adonais*, at the centre of the poem.

It might seem natural to take the long section LXXXV. as marking such a line of division, for here the poet himself looks back over the way he has traversed, and when he renews his journey the bitterness of grief seems to have left him. But the passing away of this bitterness has been already clearly observable before section LXXXV. is reached, and the change of tone after that section does not seem sufficiently decided to justify us in regarding it as a central point in the whole.

More tempting would be a proposal to consider section LVII. as marking the centre of *In Memoriam*. In these verses the most troubled and passionate part of the poem reaches the acme of a climax, while after them there is, on the whole, a steady advance towards acquiescence. But in reality the distress which culminates in section LVII. is characteristic only of the group which closes with that section; it is not a distress which has deepened from the outset of the poem; indeed, many tokens of advance have been visible before that group is reached, and the main direction of the movement towards it is definitely upward.[4]

If a turning-point in the general feeling of *In Memoriam* is to be sought at all, it must certainly be found not in section LVII., nor in section LXXXV., but in the second Christmas poem, LXXVIII. It seems true that, in spite of gradual change, the tone of the poem so far is, on the whole, melancholy, while after LXXVIII. the predominant tone can scarcely be called even sad; it is rather the feeling of spring emerging slowly and with difficulty from the gloom of winter. And it is probable that Tennyson himself intended this change to be associated with the second coming of Christmas, since the first and the third coming also announce a definite change, and since he says that the divisions of *In Memoriam* are made by the Christmas sections. At the same time it is questionable whether the transition at section LXXVIII. is so marked as to strike a reader who was not looking for signs of transition; and, this being so, it would seem to be a mistake to regard *In Memoriam* as a poem which, like *Adonais*, shows a dividing line clearly separating one part of the whole from the other. Its main movement is really one of advance almost from the first, though the advance is for a long time very slow.

Falling back, then, on the divisions pointed out by the author, we may attempt to characterise the four parts into which the poem will fall, to show the groups contained in each, and to indicate the principal changes in the course of ideas through which the mind of the poet moves.

4. I am not converted, therefore, by Mr. Beeching's words, which have appeared since the above was written: 'Here the poem, as at first designed, seems to have ended. The 57th elegy [58th in the copyright text] represents the Muse as urging the poet to a new beginning; and the 58th [59th] was added in the fourth edition, as though to account for the difference in tone between the earlier and later elegies' (Introduction, p. x). Apart from the objection urged above, the first sentence here seems to be scarcely consistent with Tennyson's own account of the composition of *In Memoriam*, nor can I believe that he ever thought of ending his poem in tones of despair. But it is certainly true that there is a more marked *break* at Section LVII. than at LXXVIII. or LXXXV.

Part I. To the First Christmas.

The general tone of this part, which is supposed to cover a space of about three months, is that of absorption in grief; but the poet gradually rises from mere suffering to a clearer conviction that

> 'Tis better to have loved and lost
> Than never to have loved at all,

and that love may, and ought to, survive the loss of the beloved. There is throughout scarcely any reference to the continued existence of the lost friend.

This part contains two distinct groups:

(1) Sections IX.–XVII. (or XX.),[5] referring to the coming of the ship (or to this and to the burial).
(2) Sections XXII.–XXV., a retrospect of the years of friendship.

Part II. To the Second Christmas.

This part of the poem has some marked characteristics. (*a*) From beginning to end the idea of the continued life of the dead is prominent, far more prominent than in any of the other three parts. (*b*) It is through reflection on this idea and on the problems suggested by it that the poet wins his way forward; so that this is the part of *In Memoriam* which contains most semi-philosophic speculation. (*c*) Hence this part consists almost wholly of distinct groups with intervening sections, and there are but few 'occasional' poems.

The following brief analysis of the groups will indicate the course of the poet's thoughts:

(1) Sections XXVIII.–XXX. Christmastide. The thought of the continued life of the dead emerges in an hour of exaltation.
(2) Sections XXXI.–XXXVI. This continued life is at once a truth revealed, and a fact implied in the constitution of human nature. The group accordingly is concerned in part with the difference between two forms of faith in immortality.
(3) Sections XL.–XLVII. Immortality being assumed, the question of future reunion is raised. This involves the question (which is the main subject of the group) whether the earthly

5. Here, as in a few other cases, it is a matter of doubt, and even of indifference, at which of two sections the group is best taken to close.

life is remembered beyond death. Only an affirmative answer would satisfy the demand of love.

(4) Sections L.–LVI. The poet's desire that the dead friend should remember him and be near him *now* (as well as in a future life) is followed by fears and doubts raised by the thought, first, of his own unworthiness, and then of all the pain, waste, and evil in the world. These doubts cannot be silenced by reason; and the poet's hope that good is the end of evil, and love the law of creation, is sustained only by blind trust.

(5) Sections LX.–LXV. The poet returns to his desire that his friend should think of him *now*. His hopes and fears on this subject are free from the distress of the preceding group, and issue in the acceptance of ignorance, and in faith that love cannot be lost. Here, and in the remainder of Part II., there is a gradual advance towards quiet regret, sympathy with others, and a peaceful recognition of the beauty of the past and the influence of the lost friend.

(6) Sections LXVII.–LXXI. On Night, Sleep, and Dreams.

(7) Sections LXXIII.–LXXVII. On Fame. The poet writes of his friend's loss of fame on earth and gain of fame in another world, and of the brevity of any fame which his own songs could win for his friend.

Part III. To the Third Christmas.

SECTIONS LXXVIII.–CIII.

Of the four parts this contains the greatest number of sections which may be called 'occasional.' The idea of the future life retires again into the background.

(1) The prevailing tone of sections LXXIX.–LXXXIX. (not to be considered a group) is that of quiet and not unhappy retrospection, and a sense of new and joyful life begins to appear.

(2) Sections XC.–XCV. form a closely connected group on the possible contact of the living and the dead. The idea is considered from various sides, and appears to be realised in the trance recorded in XCV.

(3) Sections C.–CIII. form a group which has for its subject the poet's farewell to the home of childhood. He begins to turn his eyes from the past.

Part IV. From the Third Christmas.

SECTIONS CIV.–CXXXI.

Throughout this part, even when the poet is thinking of the past, he is looking forward into the future. Regret is passing away, but love is growing and widening. The dead friend is regarded not only as a friend, but as a type of the nobler humanity to come, and as mingled with that Love which is the soul of the universe.

(1) Sections CIV.–CVI. form a group dealing with Christmas and New Year in the new home.

(2) Sections CVII.–CVIII. express the poet's resolve to turn from the grief of the past.

(3) Sections CIX.–CXIV. describe the character of the dead friend, and incidentally the dangers of the progress of mankind.

(4) Sections CXVII.–CXXXI. are not so closely connected as to form a group, but they are united by their expression of faith in the future both of the individual and of humanity. In form many of them are retrospective, the poet looking back to the struggles through which he has won his way to entire faith in the omnipotence of love.[6]

The 'Way of the Soul.'

It is a fashion at present to ascribe the great popularity of *In Memoriam* entirely to the 'teaching' contained in it, and to declare that its peculiar position among English elegies has nothing to do with its poetic qualities. This is equivalent to an assertion that, if the so-called substance of the poem had been presented in common prose,[7] the work would have gained the same hold upon the mass of educated readers that is now possessed by the poem itself. Such an assertion no one would make or consciously imply. The ordinary reader does not indeed attempt to separate the poetic qualities of a work from some other quality that appeals to him; much less does he read the work in terror of being affected by the latter; but imagination and diction and even versification can influence him much as they influence the people who talk about them, and he would never have taken *In Memoriam* to his heart if its consoling or uplifting

---

6. In conversation with Mr. James Knowles, Tennyson gave a division of *In Memoriam* into nine parts, as follows: (I) I.–VIII.; (2) IX.–XX.; (3) XXI.–XXVII.; (4) XXVIII.–XLIX.; (5) L.–LVIII.; (6) LIX.–LXXI.; (7) LXXII.–XCVIII.; (8) XCIX.–CIII.; (9) CIV.–CXXXI. As nothing is said of this arrangement in his notes on *In Memoriam* printed in the *Memoir*, it is to be supposed that he was not satisfied with it. It ignores the Second Christmas poem.

7. This, in strictness, is an impossible supposition. Anything that could be so presented would not be really the substance of the poem.

thoughts had not also touched his fancy and sung in his ears. It is true, however, that he dwells upon these thoughts, and that the poem is often valued by him for its bearing upon his own life; and true again that this is why he cares for it far more than for elegies certainly not inferior to it as poems. And perhaps here also many devotees of poetry may resemble him more than they suppose.

This peculiar position of *In Memoriam* seems to be connected with two facts. In the first place, it alone among the most famous English elegies is a poem inspired by deep personal feelings. Arthur Hallam was a youth of extraordinary promise, but he was also 'dear as the mother to the son.' The elegy on his death, therefore, unlike those on Edward King or Keats or Clough, bears the marks of a passionate grief and affection; and the poet's victory over sorrow, like his faith in immortality, is felt to be won in a struggle which has shaken the centre of his being. And then, as has been observed already, this struggle is portrayed in all its stages and phases throughout months and years; and each is represented, not as it may have appeared when the victory was won, but as it was experienced then and there. Hence much of *In Memoriam* is nearer to ordinary life than most elegies can be, and many a reader has found in it an expression of his own feelings, or has looked to the experience which it embodies as a guide to a possible conquest over his own loss. 'This,' he says to himself as he reads this section or that, 'is what I dumbly feel. This man, so much greater than I, has suffered like me and has told me how he won his way to peace. Like me, he has been forced by his own disaster to meditate on "the riddle of the painful earth," and to ask whether the world can really be governed by a law of love, and is not rather the work of blind forces, indifferent to the value of all that they produce and destroy.'

A brief review, first of the experience recorded in *In Memoriam*, and then of the leading ideas employed in it, may be of interest to such readers, and even to others, as it may further the understanding of the poem from one point of view, although it has to break up for the time that unity of substance and form which is the essence of poetry.

The early sections portray a soul in the first anguish of loss. Its whole interest is fixed on one thing in the world; and, as this thing is taken away, the whole world is darkened. In the main, the description is one of a common experience, and the poem shows the issue of this experience in a particular case.

Such sorrow is often healed by forgetfulness. The soul, flinching from the pain of loss, or apprehensive of its danger, turns away, at first with difficulty, and afterwards with increasing ease, from the thought of the beloved dead. 'Time,' or the incessant stream of new impressions, helps it to forget. Its sorrow gradually perishes, and with its sorrow its love; and at last 'all it was is overworn,' and it stands whole and sound. It is not cynical to say that this is a frequent history, and that the ideas repelled in section XC are not seldom true.

Sometimes, again, the wound remains unhealed, although its pain is dulled. Here love neither dies nor changes its form; it remains a painful longing for something gone, nor would anything really satisfy it but the entire restoration of that which is gone. All the deeper life of the soul is absorbed in this love, which from its exclusively personal character is unable to coalesce with other interests and prevents their growth.

In neither of these extreme cases is there that victory of which the poet thinks even in the first shock of loss, when he remembers how it has been said.

> That men may rise on stepping-stones
> Of their dead selves to higher things.
> [I, 3–4]

In the first case there is victory of a kind, but it is a victory which in the poet's eyes is defeat: the soul may be said to conquer its sorrow, but it does so by losing its love; it is a slave in the triumph of Time. In the second case, the 'self' refuses to die and conquers time, but for that very reason it is bound to the past and unable to rise to higher things. The experience portrayed in *In Memoriam* corresponds with neither case, but it resembles each in one particular. Sorrow is healed, but it is not healed by the loss of love: for the beloved dead is the object of continual thought, and when regret has passed away love is found to be not less but greater than before. On the other hand regret does pass away, and love does not merely look forward to reunion with its object but unites freely with other interests. It is evident that the possibility of this victory depends upon the fact that, while love does not die, there is something in the soul which does die. The self 'rises' only on the basis of a 'dead self.' In other words, love changes though it does not perish or fade; and with the change in it there is a corresponding change in the idea of its object. The poem exhibits this process of two-fold change.

At the beginning love desires simply that which was, the presence and companionship of the lost friend; and this it desires unchanged and in its entirety. It longs for the sight of the face, the sound of the voice, the pressure of the hand. These doubtless are desired as tokens of the soul; but as yet they are tokens essential to love, and that for which it pines is the soul as known and loved through them. If the mourner attempts to think of the dead apart from them, his heart remains cold, or he recoils: he finds that he is thinking of a phantom; 'an awful thought' instead of 'the human-hearted man he loved'; 'a spirit, not a breathing voice.' This he does not and cannot love. It is an object of awe, not of affection; the mere dead body is a thousand-fold dearer than this,—naturally, for this is not really a spirit, a thinking and loving soul, but a ghost. As then he is unable to think of the object of his love except as 'the hand, the lips, the eyes,' and 'the meeting of the morrow,' he feels that what he loves is simply gone and lost, and he finds his one relief in allowing fancy to play about the thought of the tokens that remain (see the poems to the ship).

The process of change consists largely in the conquest of the soul over its bondage to sense. So long as this bondage remains, its desire is fixed on that which really is dead, and it cannot advance. But gradually it resigns this longing, and turns more and more to that which is not dead. The first step in its advance is the perception that love itself is of infinite value and may survive the removal of the sensible presence of its object. But no sooner has this conviction been reached and embraced (xxix.) than suddenly the mourner is found to have transferred his interest from the sensible presence to the soul itself, while, on the other hand, the soul is no longer thought of as a mere awful phantom, but has become what the living friend had been, something both beloved and loving (xxx.). This conquest is, indeed, achieved first in a moment of exaltation which cannot be maintained; but its result is never lost, and gradually strengthens. The feeling that the soul of the dead is something shadowy and awful departs for ever, and step by step the haunting desire for the bodily presence retires. Thought is concentrated on that which lives, the beauty of the beloved soul, seen in its remembered life on earth, and doubtless shown more fully elsewhere in a life that can be dimly imagined. At last the pining for what is gone dies completely away, but love is found to be but stronger for its death, and to be no longer a source of pain. It has grown to the dimensions of its object, and this object is not only distant and desired, but also present and possessed. And more—the past (which is not wholly past, since it lives and acts in the soul of the mourner) has lost its pang and retained its loveliness and power: 'the days that are no more' become a life in death instead of a 'death in life'; and even the light of the face, the sound of the voice, and the pressure of the hand, now that the absorbing desire for them is still, return in the quiet inward world.

Another aspect of this change is to be noticed. So long as the mourner's sorrow and desire are fixed on that which dies they withdraw his interest from all other things. His world seems to depend for its light on that which has passed away, and he cries 'All is dark where thou art not.' But as his love and its object change and grow, this exclusiveness lessens and its shadow shrinks. His heart opens itself to other friendships; the sweetness of the spring returns; and the 'mighty hopes' for man's future which the friend had shared, live again as the dead friend ceases to be a silent voice and becomes a living soul. Nor do the reviving activities simply flourish side by side with love for this soul, and still less do they compete with it. Rather they are one with it. The dead man lives in the living, and 'moves him on to nobler ends.' It is at the bidding of the dead that he seeks a friendship for the years to come. His vision of the ideal man that is to be is a memory of the man that trod this planet with him in his youth. He had cried, 'All is dark where thou art not,' and now he cries,

> Thy voice is on the rolling air;
>   I hear thee where the waters run;
>   Thou standest in the rising sun,
> And in the setting thou art fair.
>
> [CXXX, 1–4]

For the sake of clearness little has been so far said of the thoughts of the mourner regarding the life beyond death. These thoughts touch two main subjects, the hope of reunion, and the desire that the dead friend should think of the living and should even communicate with him. The recurrent speculations on the state of the dead spring from this hope and this desire. They recur less frequently as the soul advances in its victory. This does not mean that the hope of reunion diminishes or ceases to be essential to the mourner's peace and faith; but speculation on the nature both of this reunion and of the present life of the dead is renounced, and at last even abruptly dismissed (CVII., CVIII.). The singer is content to be ignorant and to wait in faith.

It is not quite so with the desire that the dead friend should now remember the living, and should even communicate with him. True, this desire is at one moment put aside without unhappiness (LXV.), and it ceases to be an urgent and disturbing force. But long after the pining for the bodily presence has been overcome, it remains and brings with it pain and even resentment. It seems to change from a hope of 'speech' or 'converse' to a wish that the dead should in some way be 'near' to or 'touch' the living; and thus it suggests the important group of sections XC.-XCV. Here the poet even wishes at first for a vision; and although he at once reflects that neither this nor any other appeal to sense could convince him that the dead was really with him,[8] he does not surrender either here or later (CXXII.) the idea of some more immediate contact of souls.[9] On the other hand, he is not sure that the idea is realised, nor does his uncertainty disturb his peace. What he desires while he remains on earth is contact with

---

8. His reflections on the difficulty or impossibility of any such proof are expressed in XCII. with a conciseness which is characteristic of Tennyson and conceals from many readers the full force and bearing of his thoughts.

9. This idea is not confined to *In Memoriam*. Tennyson, we are told, thought 'that there might be a more intimate communion than we could dream of between the living and the dead, at all events for a time' (*Memoir*, i. 320).

'that which is,' the reality which is half revealed and half concealed
by nature and man's earthly life, and which, by its contact, convinces
him of the reason and love that rule the world; and, as now he thinks
of his friend as 'living in God,' he neither knows nor seeks to know
whether that which touches him is to be called the soul of his friend
or by some higher name.

It appears then that the victory over sorrow portrayed in the poem
is dependent upon a change in the love felt by the living for the dead,
and upon a corresponding change in the idea of the dead. And some
readers may even be inclined to think that the change is so great
that at last the dead friend has really ceased to be to the living an
individual person. He is, they will say, in some dim fashion 'mixed
with God and Nature,' and as completely lost in 'the general soul' as
is Adonais in Shelley's pantheistic poem: and so the poet's love for
him has not merely changed, it has perished, and its place has been
taken by a feeling as vaguely general and as little personal as the
object to which it is directed. As my purpose is neither to criticise
nor to defend the poet's ideas, but simply to represent them, I will
confine myself to pointing out that the poem itself flatly denies the
charge thus brought against it, and by implication denies the validity
of the antitheses on which the charge rests. It is quite true that, as
the poet advances, he abandons all attempts to define the life beyond
death, and to form an image of his friend, 'whate'er he be.' It is quite
true also that he is conscious that his friend, at once human and
divine, known and unknown, far and near, has become something
'strange,' and is 'darklier understood' than in the old days of earthly
life. But it is equally clear that to the poet his friend is not a whit
less himself because he is 'mixed with God and Nature,' and that he
is only 'deeplier loved' as he becomes 'darklier understood.' And if
the hope of reunion is less frequently expressed as the sense of present possession gains in strength, there is nothing in the poem to
imply that it becomes less firm as the image of reunion becomes less
definite. The reader may declare that it ought to do so. He may apply
to the experience here portrayed his customary notions of human
and divine, personal and impersonal, individual and general, and he
may argue that whatever falls under one of these heads cannot fall
under the other. But whether his ideas and his argument are true or
false, the fact is certain that for the experience portrayed in *In Memoriam* (and, it may be added, in *Adonais* also) they do not hold. For
the poets the soul of the dead in being mingled with nature does not
lose its personality; in living in God it remains human and itself; it
is still the object of a love as 'personal' as that which was given to

> the touch of a vanished hand,
> And the sound of a voice that is still.

135

T. S. ELIOT

In Memoriam†

Tennyson is a great poet, for reasons that are perfectly clear. He has three qualities which are seldom found together except in the greatest poets: abundance, variety, and complete competence. We therefore cannot appreciate his work unless we read a good deal of it. We may not admire his aims: but whatever he sets out to do, he succeeds in doing, with a mastery which gives us the sense of confidence that is one of the major pleasures of poetry.

* * *

It is, in my opinion, in *In Memoriam*, that Tennyson finds full expression. Its technical merit alone is enough to ensure its perpetuity. While Tennyson's technical competence is everywhere masterly and satisfying, *In Memoriam* is the most unapproachable of all his poems. Here are one hundred and thirty-two passages, each of several quatrains in the same form, and never monotony or repetition. And the poem has to be comprehended as a whole. We may not memorize a few passages, we cannot find a 'fair sample'; we have to comprehend the whole of a poem which is essentially the length that it is. We may choose to remember:

> Dark house, by which once more I stand
>   Here in the long unlovely street,
>   Doors, where my heart was used to beat
> So quickly, waiting for a hand,
>
> A hand that can be clasp'd no more—
>   Behold me, for I cannot sleep,
>   And like a guilty thing I creep
> At earliest morning to the door.
>
> He is not here; but far away
>   The noise of life begins again,
>   And ghastly thro' the drizzling rain
> On the bald street breaks the blank day.
>   [VII]

This is great poetry, economical of words, a universal emotion in what could only be an English town: and it gives me the shudder

† From *Essays Ancient and Modern* (London: Faber & Faber, 1936), pp. 175–90. Copyright © 1936 Faber & Faber, Ltd. Reprinted by permission of Faber & Faber, Ltd. The author's footnotes have been omitted; all footnotes are the editor's.

that I fail to get from anything in *Maud*.[1] But such a passage, by itself, is not *In Memoriam*: *In Memoriam* is the whole poem. It is unique: it is a long poem made by putting together lyrics, which have only the unity and continuity of a diary, the concentrated diary of a man confessing himself. It is a diary of which we have to read every word.

Apparently Tennyson's contemporaries, once they had accepted *In Memoriam*, regarded it as a message of hope and reassurance to their rather fading Christian faith. It happens now and then that a poet by some strange accident expresses the mood of his generation, at the same time that he is expressing a mood of his own which is quite remote from that of his generation. This is not a question of insincerity: there is an amalgam of yielding and opposition below the level of consciousness. Tennyson himself, on the conscious level of the man who talks to reporters and poses for photographers, to judge from remarks made in conversation and recorded in his son's Memoir, consistently asserted a convinced, if somewhat sketchy, Christian belief. And he was a friend of Frederick Denison Maurice[2]—nothing seems odder about that age than the respect which its eminent people felt for each other. Nevertheless, I get a very different impression from *In Memoriam* from that which Tennyson's contemporaries seem to have got. It is of a very much more interesting and tragic Tennyson. His biographers have not failed to remark that he had a good deal of the temperament of the mystic—certainly not at all the mind of the theologian. He was desperately anxious to hold the faith of the believer, without being very clear about what he wanted to believe: he was capable of illumination which he was incapable of understanding. The 'Strong Son of God, immortal Love', with an invocation of whom the poem opens, has only a hazy connexion with the Logos, or the Incarnate God. Tennyson is distressed by the idea of a mechanical universe; he is naturally, in lamenting his friend, teased by the hope of immortality and reunion beyond death. Yet the renewal craved for seems at best but a continuance, or a substitute for the joys of friendship upon earth. His desire for immortality never is quite the desire for Eternal Life; his concern is for the loss of man rather than for the gain of God.

> shall he,
> Man, her last work, who seem'd so fair,
> Such splendid purpose in his eyes,
> Who roll'd the psalm to wintry skies,
> Who built him fanes of fruitless prayer,

1. Tennyson's next major poem (1855).
2. The Reverend F. D. Maurice was a prominent writer on theology, whose unorthodox views led to his dismissal from his position at King's College, London, in 1853; he was godfather to Tennyson's son Hallam.

> Who trusted God was love indeed,
>   And love Creation's final law—
>   Though Nature, red in tooth and claw
> With ravine shriek'd against his creed—
>
> Who loved, who suffer'd countless ills.
>   Who battled for the True, the Just,
>   Be blown about the desert dust,
> Or seal'd within the iron hills?
>
>   [LVI, 8–20]

That strange abstraction, 'Nature', becomes a real god or goddess, perhaps more real, at moments, to Tennyson than God ('Are God and Nature then at strife?'). The hope of immortality is confused (typically of the period) with the hope of the gradual and steady improvement of this world. Much has been said of Tennyson's interest in contemporary science, and of the impression of Darwin. *In Memoriam*, in any case, antedates *The Origin of Species* by several years,[3] and the belief in social progress by democracy antedates it by many more; and I suspect that the faith of Tennyson's age in human progress would have been quite as strong even had the discoveries of Darwin been postponed by fifty years. And after all, there is no logical connexion: the belief in progress being current already, the discoveries of Darwin were harnessed to it:

> No longer half-akin to brute,
>   For all we thought, and loved and did
>   And hoped, and suffer'd, is but seed
> Of what in them is flower and fruit;
>
> Whereof the man, that with me trod
>   This planet, was a noble type
>   Appearing ere the times were ripe,
> That friend of mine who lives in God,
>
> That God, which ever lives and loves,
>   One God, one law, one element,
>   And one far-off divine event,
> To which the whole creation moves.
>
>   [Epilogue, 133–144]

These lines show an interesting compromise between the religious attitude and, what is quite a different thing, the belief in human perfectibility; but the contrast was not so apparent to Tennyson's contemporaries. They may have been taken in by it, but I don't think

---

3. Charles Darwin's *On the Origin of Species by Means of Natural Selection* was published in 1859.

that Tennyson himself was, quite: his feelings were more honest than his mind. There is evidence elsewhere—even in an early poem, *Locksley Hall*, for example—that Tennyson by no means regarded with complacency all the changes that were going on about him in the progress of industrialism and the rise of the mercantile and manufacturing and banking classes; and he may have contemplated the future of England, as his years drew out, with increasing gloom. Temperamentally, he was opposed to the doctrine that he was moved to accept and to praise.

Tennyson's feelings, I have said, were honest; but they were usually a good way below the surface. *In Memoriam* can, I think, justly be called a religious poem, but for another reason than that which made it seem religious to his contemporaries. It is not religious because of the quality of its faith, but because of the quality of its doubt. Its faith is a poor thing, but its doubt is a very intense experience. *In Memoriam* is a poem of despair, but of despair of a religious kind. And to qualify its despair with the adjective 'religious' is to elevate it above most of its derivatives. For *The City of Dreadful Night*, and the *Shropshire Lad*,[4] and the poems of Thomas Hardy, are small work in comparison with *In Memoriam*: it is greater than they and comprehends them.

In ending we must go back to the beginning and remember that *In Memoriam* would not be a great poem, or Tennyson a great poet, without the technical accomplishment. Tennyson is the great master of metric as well as of melancholia; I do not think any poet in English has ever had a finer ear for vowel sound, as well as a subtler feeling for some moods of anguish:

> Dear as remember'd kisses after death,
> And sweet as those by hopeless fancy feign'd
> On lips that are for others; deep as love,
> Deep as first love, and wild with all regret.[5]

And this technical gift of Tennyson's is no slight thing. Tennyson lived in a time which was already acutely time-conscious: a great many things seemed to be happening, railways were being built, discoveries were being made, the face of the world was changing. That was a time busy in keeping up to date. It had, for the most part, no hold on permanent things, on permanent truths about man and god and life and death. The surface of Tennyson stirred about with his time; and he had nothing to which to hold fast except his unique and unerring feeling for the sounds of words. But in this he had something that no one else had. Tennyson's surface, his technical accomplishment, is intimate with his depths: what we most quickly

---

4. Poems by James Thomson (1874) and A.E. Housman (1896), respectively.
5. From "Tears, Idle Tears," one of the lyrics in Tennyson's long poem *The Princess* (1847).

see about Tennyson is that which moves between the surface and the depths, that which is of slight importance. By looking innocently at the surface we are most likely to come to the depths, to the abyss of sorrow. Tennyson is not only a minor Virgil, he is also with Virgil as Dante saw him, a Virgil among the Shades, the saddest of all English poets, among the Great in Limbo, the most instinctive rebel against the society in which he was the most perfect conformist.

Tennyson seems to have reached the end of his spiritual development with *In Memoriam*; there followed no reconciliation, no resolution.

> And now no sacred staff shall break in blossom,
> No choral salutation lure to light
> A spirit sick with perfume and sweet night,[6]

or rather with twilight, for Tennyson faced neither the darkness nor the light, in his later years. The genius, the technical power, persisted to the end, but the spirit had surrendered. A gloomier end than that of Baudelaire: Tennyson had no *singulier avertissement*.[7] And having turned aside from the journey through the dark night, to become the surface flatterer of his own time, he has been rewarded with the despite of an age that succeeds his own in shallowness.

ELEANOR BUSTIN MATTES

The Challenge of Geology to Belief in Immortality and a God of Love†

i

As far as "the way of the soul" was concerned, the year 1837 brought Tennyson an experience more crucial to the further development of *In Memoriam* than either the moment of mystical union with Hallam or the departure from Somersby; for "during some months" of that year he was "deeply immersed in . . . Lyell's *Geology*."[1]

Charles Lyell's *Principles of Geology*, which appeared in three volumes from 1830–1833, proved revolutionary not only to the geologic theories of the period but to religious thought as well. On the basis

---

6. From Algernon Charles Swinburne's "Ave Atque Vale: In Memory of Charles Baudelaire" (1867), lines 166–68.
7. In 1862 the French poet Charles Baudelaire (1821–1867) had a *singulier avertissement* or "sudden warning" that his poetic ability was passing from him.
† From *In Memoriam: The Way of a Soul* (New York: Exposition Press, 1951), p. 55–63. The author's footnotes have been abridged. Reprinted by permission of the author.
1. *Memoir*, I, 162.

of studies made by his predecessors and his own geologic observations over a number of years, Lyell sought to demonstrate that the present state of the earth is wholly the result of natural forces like wind and water erosion, rock faulting, and sedimentation, operating over long periods of time. This hypothesis challenged Cuvier's theory that various catastrophic disturbances were responsible for the present configurations of the earth. In his second volume Lyell then proceeded to explain that the continual physical changes which geology revealed pointed to the certain extinction of species after species throughout the earth's history, as they found themselves unable to cope with the new conditions they encountered.

None of Lyell's conclusions were actually new. James Hutton, in his *Theory of the Earth*, published in 1795, had asserted that one can account for all the past changes of the earth's surface by reference to natural forces still in operation. And the French naturalist Buffon had insisted upon the inevitable extinction of man and all his works.

But Hutton's *Theory of the Earth* had no popular sale like that of Lyell's *Geology*, and Buffon had few English readers. The whole situation in England was, moreover, markedly different from that in France, where the astronomer Laplace is said to have brushed aside Napoleon's question as to where the Creator figured in his nebular theory, with the reply, "Sire, I have no need of that hypothesis." In England, in the early 1830's, the official Church of England theology was predominantly rationalist, and the outstanding scientists were also religious men, so that there had been no serious questioning of the eighteenth-century assumption that science is the handmaid of religion, since it leads men to appreciate "the Power, Wisdom, and Goodness of God as manifested in the Creation." And as late as 1837, when the distinguished geologist Adam Sedgwick was Chairman of the British Association (for the advancement of scientific research), he concluded its annual meeting by declaring that if he found his science "interfere in any of its tenets with the representations of doctrines of Scripture, he would dash it to the ground."[2]

Lyell, although he by no means shared Sedgwick's sentiments, was no iconoclast, and he therefore did everything possible to conceal the disturbing religious implications of his theories. He found that most churchmen were willing to accept almost any description of the *manner* of God's activity in the universe, so long as the *fact* of such divine activity was affirmed. He accordingly cloaked and minimized the revolutionary nature of his conclusions, as he disclosed in a confidential statement of his strategy:

2. Caroline Fox, *Memories of Old Friends, Being Extracts from the Journals and Letters of Caroline Fox from 1835 to 1871* (Philadelphia, J. B. Lippincott and Co., 1882), p. 25.

If you don't triumph over them, but compliment the liberality and candour of the present age, the bishops and enlightened saints will join us in despising both the ancient and modern physico-theologians . . . I give you my word that full *half* of my history and comments was cut out, and even many facts, because . . . I . . . felt that it was anticipating twenty or thirty years of the march of honest feeling to declare it undisguisedly.[3]

And those who read to the end of the *Principles of Geology* might well have any uncomfortable doubts allayed by its eloquent, pious conclusion:

In vain do we aspire to assign limits to the works of creation in *space*, whether we examine the starry heavens, or that world of minute animalcules which is revealed to us by the microscope. We are prepared, therefore, to find that in *time* also, the confines of the universe lie beyond the reach of mortal ken. But in whatever direction we pursue our researches, whether in time or space, we discover everywhere the clear proofs of a Creative Intelligence, and of His foresight, wisdom, and power.[4]

For Tennyson, however, such a conclusion—if he read it—did not gloss over the shocking implications that he sensed in Lyell's descriptions of geologic process. He had never been interested in the deist's Master Mind, nor convinced that His existence and wisdom could be demonstrated from the wonders of nature. When the Apostles at Cambridge had asked: "Is an intelligible First Cause deducible from the phenomena of the Universe?" he had voted "no."[5] And when he looked through a microscope at the minute life it revealed he said: "Strange that these wonders should draw some men to God and repel others. No more reason in one than in the other."[6] But in the early sections of *In Memoriam* he had assumed, with Wordsworth, that nature does testify to immortality, and had repeatedly affirmed the eternal quality of love. Lyell's conclusions challenged both these premises, the first directly, the second implicitly; and the next phase of *In Memoriam* was the recording of Tennyson's reaction to this shock.

ii

Writing a hundred years earlier than Lyell, Joseph Butler had challenged the supposed "reasonableness" of natural religion by pointing

3. Mrs. (Katherine) Lyell, ed., *Life, Letters and Journals of Sir Charles Lyell* (London, J. Murray, 1881), I, 271.
4. Charles Lyell, *Principles of Geology, Being an Attempt to Explain the Former Changes of the Earth's Surface, by Reference to Causes Now in Operation* (1st ed.; London, 1830–33), III, 384.
5. *Memoir*, I, 44, n. 1.
6. *Ibid.*, I, 102.

out that nature by no means shares the solicitous concern for every creature which the New Testament ascribes to God, since "of the numerous Seeds of Vegetables and Bodies of Animals, which are adapted and put in the Way, to improve to such a Point or State of natural Maturity and Perfection, we do not see perhaps that one in a million actually does."[7] And Tennyson, who must have read Butler's *Analogy of Religion* at Cambridge if not before, may have been indebted to this thought in section 55 of *In Memoriam*:

> Are God and Nature then at strife,
>   That Nature lends such evil dreams?
>   So careful of the type she seems,
> So careless of the single life;
>
> That I, considering everywhere
>   Her secret meaning in her deeds,
>   And finding that of fifty seeds
> She often brings but one to bear,
>
> I falter where I firmly trod.
>   (55:5–13)

But it was almost certainly his reading in the *Principles of Geology* that led Tennyson to write section 56.

Lyell's second volume has this disconcerting quotation[8] on its title page: "The inhabitants of the globe, like all the other parts of it, are subject to change. It is not only the individual that perishes, but whole species."[9] The volume then presents an accumulation of evidence which leads relentlessly to the conclusion that

> . . . the reader has only to reflect on what we have said of the habitations and the stations of organic beings in general, and to consider them in relation to those effects . . . resulting from the igneous and aqueous causes now in action, and he will immediately perceive that, amidst the vicissitudes of the earth's surface, species cannot be immortal, but must perish one after the other, like the individuals which compose them.[1]

Section 56 of *In Memoriam* takes up the assumption of section 55 and gives it the drastic revision required by Lyell's findings:

> "So careful of the type?" but no.
>   From scarped cliff and quarried stone

7. Joseph Butler, *The Analogy of Religion, Natural and Revealed, to the Constitution and Course of Nature* (London, 1881), p. 146.
8. From John Playfair's *Illustrations of the Huttonian Theory.*
9. Charles Lyell, *op. cit.*, II, title page.
1. *Ibid.*, II, 168–69.

> She cries, "A thousand types are gone;
>   I care for nothing, all shall go.
>
> "Thou makest thine appeal to me:
>   I bring to life, I bring to death:
>   The spirit does but mean the breath:
>   I know no more."
>
> (56 :1–8)

It states in specific and personal terms what these findings imply for man's hope of immortality:

> And he, shall he,
>
> Man, her last work, who seem'd so fair,
> Such splendid purpose in his eyes,
>
> (56:8–10)
>
> . . . .
> Be blown about the desert dust,
> Or seal'd within the iron hills?
>
> No more? . . .
>
> (56:19–21)

and the lines echo Lyell's conclusion " 'that none of the works of a mortal being can be eternal.' . . . And even when they have been included in rocky strata, . . . they must nevertheless eventually perish, for every year some portion of the earth's crust is shattered by earthquakes or melted by volcanic fire, or ground to dust by the moving waters on the surface."[2] It recognizes that Lyell's theory of natural laws operating ruthlessly throughout the earth's history is incompatible with belief that God is love and love is the law of creation (56:13–14). And it suggests that a horrible mockery and self-delusion permeates the entire structure of Western civilization, in which men build churches to worship a God of love whom nature disproves, and fight for supposedly eternal values like truth and justice, which die with the species that cherishes them.

It is easy to see how the whole fabric of assurance that Tennyson had woven in the earlier-written sections seemed destroyed by his reading of Lyell. The arguments for immortality he found in Wordsworth, and Isaac Taylor's confident assertions that the departed retain their affections for their earthly friends in their new spheres of life, took for granted a benevolent Nature and a loving God, which all Lyell's evidence seemed to deny. And, although Tennyson could long for his dead friend's "voice to soothe and bless" (56:26), as it had always done while Hallam lived, he could find no actual rebuttal

2. *Ibid.*, II, 271.

to Lyell in what he remembered of Hallam's religious views or in the *Remains*.

Tennyson could not, however, accept such a dismal conception of man as a transient phenomenon on the earth's surface, who vainly believes in an immortality and a God of love that ruthless nature belies. So he closed this disturbed section 56 by asserting that the questions raised by Lyell's findings must remain unanswered until he could penetrate "behind the veil" (56:28). One cannot state the exact meaning or certain source of this allusive phrase. But Tennyson was seeking refuge in the position that the so-called realities of the physical world hide as much as they reveal of the truth, which man can have full access to only at death, when the "veil" of finite, mortal limitations is withdrawn.

iii

When Tennyson came to write section 123, Lyell's findings were still vivid in his mind, and the first stanza,

> There rolls the deep where grew the tree.
>   O earth, what changes hast thou seen!
>   There where the long street roars hath been
> The stillness of the central sea.
>
> (123:1–4)

is a poetic summary of descriptions like the following:

> . . . seas and lakes have since been filled up, the lands whereon the forests grew have disappeared or changed their form, the rivers and currents which floated the vegetable masses can no longer be traced . . . [3]

> . . . how constant an interchange of sea and land is taking place on the face of our globe. In the Mediterranean alone, many flourishing inland towns, and a still greater number of ports, now stand where the sea rolled its waves since the era when civilized nations first grew up in Europe. If we could compare with equal accuracy the ancient and actual state of all the islands and continents, we should probably discover that millions of our race are now supported by lands situated where deep seas prevailed in earlier ages. [4]

At this time, however, Tennyson could borrow word pictures from Lyell without being distressed by his theories, and he concluded 123 on a note very different from that of 56.—But this is anticipating a later phase of his spiritual journey.

3. *Ibid.*, I, 2.
4. *Ibid.*, I, 255.

BASIL WILLEY

[Tennyson's Honest Doubts]†

If 1833 had been Tennyson's black year, 1850 was his *annus mira-bilis*. That year, *In Memoriam* was published, and a fortnight later he was married to Emily Sellwood, after a broken engagement which had dragged on for twelve years. And as if this were not enough to atone for all that Tennyson had endured of neglect, disparagement, bereavement and loneliness, Wordsworth died, leaving vacant the Laureateship at the very moment when Tennyson, with the immense success of *In Memoriam*, had become a national institution.

The success and influence of *In Memoriam* illustrate its truly representative quality. The Victorians loved it, and were moved by it, because it dealt seriously and beautifully with the very problems that most concerned them: problems arising from the gradual fading-out of the older spiritual lights in the harsh dawn of a new and more positive age. For *In Memoriam* (it need hardly be said) is far from being a continuous lament over Arthur Hallam. It begins, of course, with the bereavement, with personal grief and lamentation, and with the inevitable questionings about the soul's survival in a future life. Gradually the immediate sorrow recedes, giving place to poignant recollection, and then to more general meditations on man's place in Nature and the impact of science upon religious faith. As in *The Two Voices*, a mood of reconciliation, even hope, is at last reached and the reasons of the heart are vindicated against the reasonings of the intellect. It is needless and beside the mark to look for any greater unity or closer pattern in the poem than this. Tennyson gave a semblance of design to it by rearranging many of the sections and by introducing recurrent Christmases. But it remains a series of elegiac poems strung upon the thread of the poet's own life and following the curve of his development. It is in fact Tennyson's intimate spiritual journal of those years, and it succeeds largely *because* it lacks, a more formal structure. Its desultory, informal character ensures its freedom from bardic posturings or routine gestures; the various sections come straight from Tennyson's heart, and were—as he calls them—'brief lays, of sorrow born', or

> Short swallow-flights of song, that dip
> Their wings in tears, and skim away.
> [XLVIII, 15–16]

† From *More Nineteenth Century Studies* (London: Chatto & Windus, 1956), pp. 79–92; 98–101; 103–5.

This meant that Tennyson's lyric power, the greatest of his gifts, was allowed full play, and we get therefore something very unusual: a long poem free from epic pomp, and built up, like a coral-reef, entirely from living organisms. Moreover, in this poem we find all Tennyson's distinctive graces in fragrant blow together. His artistry is at its height, every verse and line being wrought as near perfection as he could make it; yet such is the pressure of emotion, so compelling the need for utterance, that artificiality is avoided. Similarly, *In Memoriam* is the richest of all repositories of the five-word jewels, exquisite landscapes, renderings of the shifting panorama of the seasons; but these are here employed as vehicles and symbols of the poet's changing moods and share in his imaginative life: they never strike us, as often elsewhere (especially in the *Idylls of the King*),[1] as decoration mechanically and coldly applied from without.

The problems confronted in *In Memoriam*, though forced upon Tennyson by personal experience and by the spirit of his age, are neither local nor ephemeral; they are universal, in that they are those which are apt to beset a sensitive and meditative mind in any age. Has man an immortal soul? Is there any meaning in life? any purpose or design in the world-process? any evidence in Nature, in philosophy or in the human heart, for a beneficent Providence? These issues are dealt with by Tennyson, not in the manner of a thinker—whether philosopher, theologian or scientist—but in the manner of a well-informed modern poet: that is, in the manner of one who, though not ignorant of what the specialists are saying, cares for their results only insofar as they are felt in the blood, and felt along the heart, affecting there the inmost quality of living.

There is another significant point about the way in which Tennyson faces experience in this poem: he faces it, virtually, as a soul unprovided with Christian supports. In spite of the Prologue, 'Strong Son of God, immortal Love' (which was in fact composed at the end), *In Memoriam* is not a distinctively Christian poem. The doubts, misgivings, discouragements, probings and conjectures which make it humanly moving could not have existed in a mind equipped with the Christian solutions. It is well to remember, sometimes, how much in literature as a whole presupposes a suspension, not of disbelief, but of belief. Most of literature lives on the level of Nature, not of grace. And thus *In Memoriam* is not concerned with the impact of the Zeitgeist upon Christian doctrine or apologetic, nor does it proffer Christian consolation. It goes behind Christianity, or passes it by, confronting the preliminary question which besets the natural man, the question whether there can be any religious interpretation of life at all. What made the poem acceptable even to the Christian

1. Tennyson's epic poem on King Arthur, published in parts between 1859 and 1885 [Editor].

reader in the Victorian age was that having, though with diffidence and humility, vindicated the believing temper, accepted the reasons of the heart, Tennyson had opened a door which gave access to the Christian territory.

Those who mistake Tennyson for an 'escapist' might ponder the following remark of A. C. Bradley:

> . . . with the partial exception of Shelley, Tennyson is the only one of our great poets whose attitude towards the sciences of Nature was what a modern poet's ought to be; . . . the only one to whose habitual way of seeing, imagining, or thinking, it makes any real difference that Laplace, or for that matter Copernicus, ever lived.[2]

From his earliest manhood Tennyson breathed the atmosphere of scientific theory and discovery, and throughout his life his meditations were governed by the conceptions of law, process, development and evolution—the characteristic and ruling ideas of his century. Of course, the challenge of science to religious orthodoxy was no new manifestation peculiar to the century. Copernicus had challenged it by destroying the geocentric world-picture; the mechanico-materialism of the seventeenth and eighteenth centuries had undermined the miraculous elements of Christianity. Nevertheless the middle decades of the nineteenth century are rightly felt to be the *locus classicus* of the science-and-religion conflict; and that, perhaps, for two main reasons. First because, to the older idea of immutable law operating throughout the physical universe in the inorganic sphere, there was now added the idea of inexorable development proceeding within the organic world, moulding and modifying living species. Secondly, because this great idea, arriving upon the scene in a century of cheap printing and a vastly augmented reading public, soon advanced outside the studies of philosophers and noblemen— to which 'advanced' thought had hitherto been largely confined— and reached the average man, the sort of man who had generally been in possession of a simple conventional faith.

The first aspects of science that interested the young Tennyson seem to have been astronomy (in particular the nebular theory, propounded by Laplace in 1796) and embryology. Wordsworth, in an oft-quoted passage of the Preface to Lyrical Ballads, had predicted that poetry would eventually be able to absorb the results of science and carry them alive into the heart; Tennyson fulfilled that prophecy in Wordsworth's lifetime. Here is his poetic version of the nebular theory (it is the exordium of Professor Psyche's lecture in *The Princess*):

2. *A Miscellany* (1929), pp. 30–1.

> This world was once a fluid haze of light,
> Till toward the centre set the starry tides,
> And eddied into suns, that wheeling cast
> The planets: then the monster, then the man.[3]

It will be noticed that he does not stop at the planets, but carries the development on to man, conceiving the whole process as one. But years before *The Princess* he had written, and deleted from the published version, the following stanzas for *The Palace of Art* (1832):

> Hither, when all the deep unsounded skies
>   Shudder'd with silent stars, she clomb,
> And as with optic glasses her keen eyes
>   Pierced thro' the mystic dome,
>
> Regions of lucid matter taking forms,
>   Brushes of fire, hazy gleams,
> Clusters and beds of worlds, and bee-like swarms
>   Of suns, and starry streams.

Two more of the excised stanzas run thus:

> "From shape to shape at first within the womb
>   The brain is moulded", she began.
> "And thro' all phases of all thought I come
>   Unto the perfect man.
>
> All nature widens upward. Evermore
>   The simple essence lower lies,
> More complex is more perfect, owning more
>   Discourse, more widely wise."[4]

Here we see not only the conception of biological evolution but supporting evidence for it taken from the new science of embryology, which taught that the brain of the foetus passed through all the previous phases of evolution, recapitulating in brief the whole history of the species. It is recorded of Tennyson that, right back in his undergraduate days, he once propounded, at a Trinity discussion, the theory that 'the development of the human body might possibly be traced from the radiated, vermicular, molluscous and vertebrate organisms.'[5]

But it was from geology that Tennyson received the most decisive shock. We know that for some months in 1837 he was 'deeply immersed' in Charles Lyell's celebrated *Principles of Geology* (1830–33). What was there in this book to disturb him or any other reader?

---

3. *The Princess* II, 101–4 [Editor].
4. Quoted in *Memoir*, p. 101.
5. Quoted by Sir C. Tennyson, *Alfred Tennyson* (1949), p. 83.

Its main thesis was that the present state of the earth's crust is to be accounted for, not, as in Cuvier's theory, by a series of catastrophic changes, but by the continuous operation, through immense tracts of time, of the natural forces still at work (erosion, gradual earth-movement, sedimentation, etc.). This sounds innocent enough, but the sting of it was that it presupposed for the earth a vastly greater age than was allowed for in the accepted biblical chronology, and thrust far back, if not out of the picture altogether, the notion of divine creation and superintendence. First cooling gases, then aeons of erosion: what, then, of the Seven Days creation, Adam and Eve, and the Flood? Secondly, Lyell went on to show that in the course of these gradual changes species after species of living creatures had become extinct through inability to adapt themselves to changed environments. 'The inhabitants of the globe', says he,

> like all the other parts of it, are subject to change. It is not only the individual that perishes but whole species.
>   None of the works of a mortal being can be eternal. . . . And even when they have been included in rocky strata, . . . they must nevertheless eventually perish, for every year some portion of the earth's crust is shattered by earthquakes or melted by volcanic fires, or ground to dust by the moving waters on the surface.[6]

This teaching, though it might have no direct bearing upon the doctrine of immortality, seemed to weaken its probability, and certainly weakened any alleged support derivable by analogy from Nature. Worse still, it seemed hard to reconcile with the belief that 'God is love indeed, and love Creation's final law'. What, according to Lyell, has become of the Heavenly Father without whose care and compassion not one sparrow falls to the ground?

Before quitting Lyell's *Geology*, it is worth noting that Lyell himself was quite willing to profess belief in the *fact* of divine activity, provided that science were left free to investigate and demonstrate the mode of it. This was the formula adopted (quite rightly) by the nineteenth century reconcilers of science and religion in general. Lyell was astute enough, moreover, to have thought out a suitably insinuating manner of approaching the orthodox:

> If you don't triumph over them, but compliment the liberality and candour of the present age, the bishops and enlightened saints will join us in despising both the ancient and modern physico-theologians. . . . I give you my word that full *half* of my history and comments was cut out, and even many facts;

6. Quoted by E. B. Mattes, *In Memoriam* (New York: Exposition Press, 1951), pp. 58 ff. This dissertation is an excellent guide to the sources and structure of the poem, and I owe much to it in this section of the present chapter. [See above, pp. 142–43.]

because . . . I . . . felt that it was anticipating twenty or thirty years of the march of honest feeling to declare it undisguisedly.[7]

It was, of course, all very well to take this line, and to say: "Science the enemy of religion? Not a bit of it, my dear sir! We're not denying that God does all this, we're merely showing you how he does it." I say, 'all very well', because there were many who felt that a God who moved in such a very mysterious way was not the God of their fathers. Some found it more comforting to ascribe to him the attribute of non-existence. Others, of whom Tennyson was one, felt (or came to feel) that the whole spectacle of Nature was somehow irrelevant to faith. Even in the early days, at one of the Apostles' debates at Cambridge, he had voted 'No' on the question 'Is an Intelligible First Cause deducible from the Phenomena of the Universe?' And later, he is reported to have said, of the wonders disclosed by the microscope, 'Strange that these wonders should draw some men to God and repel others. No more reason in one than in the other.' This attitude distinguishes Tennyson, and others of this period, not only from Wordsworth but from that line of thinkers who, from the seventeenth century onwards, had been demonstrating the Wisdom of God from the Creation. I suspect that it was also at variance with his own subconscious feeling.

However, Tennyson read other books in which a scientific attitude was combined with more explicit reassurances. Mrs Mattes has shown that in October 1843 he possessed a copy of Herschel's *Preliminary Discourse on the Study of Natural Philosophy* (first published 1830). She quotes these typical extracts, illustrating the optimistic gloss which Herschel put upon the grim story of geology.

> Is it wonderful that a being so constituted [i.e. man] should first encourage a hope, and by degrees acknowledge an assurance, that his intellectual existence will not terminate with the dissolution of his corporeal frame but rather that, in a future state of being . . . endowed with acute senses, and higher faculties, he shall drink deep at that fountain of beneficent wisdom for which the slight taste obtained on earth has given him so keen a relish?
> . . . we cannot fail to be struck with the rapid rate of dilatation which every degree upward of the scale, so to speak, exhibits, and which, in an estimation of averages, gives an immense preponderance to the present over every former condition of mankind, and, for aught we can see to the contrary, will place succeeding generations in the same degree of superior relation to the present that this holds to those passed away.[8]

7. Quoted *ibid.*, p. 57. [See p. 141, above.]
8. *Ibid.*, p. 77.

In short (if we can pick out way through the verbiage), man is rapidly getting bigger and better, and after all a future life seems quite probable—anyway, let's believe it!

About a year later (November 1844) Tennyson wrote to his publisher Edward Moxon:

> I want you to get me a book which I see advertised in the *Examiner*: it seems to contain many speculations with which I have been familiar for years, and on which I have written more than one poem. The book is called *Vestiges of the Natural History of Creation*. . . .

This book (as was pointed out by Mr W. R. Rutland in a very instructive essay called "Tennyson and the Theory of Evolution", over fifteen years ago[9]) contains so many passages which seem to be paraphrased in *In Memoriam* that we cannot doubt its consonance with Tennyson's own thought, and in some particulars its direct influence. Hallam Tennyson has a footnote in his *Memoir*: 'The sections of "In Memoriam" about Evolution had been read by his friends [i.e. in MS.] some years before the publication of *The Vestiges of Creation* in 1844.'[1] But as Mrs Mattes points out, this note does not say which sections, and her evidence indicates that the Epilogue, at least, was not written before 1844. However, only those (if there are still any) who think that Darwin invented Evolution in 1859 will be surprised to find that it is anticipated by Robert Chambers in *Vestiges*, or that Tennyson had anticipated them both. Romanes said that 'In "In Memoriam" Tennyson noted the fact [of Natural Selection], and a few years later Darwin supplied the explanation'.[2] The truth is that the idea of continuous unfolding, development or 'evolution' had been in the air since the latter part of the eighteenth century, being foreshadowed for example by Kant, Goethe and Lamarck. What Darwin did was to collect evidence, not for the fact of evolution, but for the mode of its operation.

Many readers found *Vestiges* disturbing; not so Tennyson. Its harsher implications were already familiar to him, and its consolations were to him truly reassuring. We can form an idea of both these aspects from the following passages (both quoted by Mr Rutland in the above-mentioned essay):

> We have seen powerful evidence that the construction of this globe and its associates, and inferentially of all the other globes of space, was the result, not of any immediate or personal exertion on the part of the Deity, but of natural laws which are the expressions of His will. What is to hinder our supposing that

9. *Essays and Studies by Members of the English Association*, 1940.
1. *Op. cit.*, p. 186.
2. *Ibid.*, p. 186.

the organic creation is also a result of natural laws, which are in like manner an expression of His will?

The Great Ruler of Nature has established laws for the operation of inanimate matter, which are quite unswerving, so that when we know them we have only to act in a certain way with respect to them in order to obtain all the benefits and avoid all the evils connected with them. He has likewise established moral laws in our nature; which are equally unswerving, and from obedience to which unfailing good is to be derived. But the two sets of laws are independent of each other. . . . It is clear, moreover, from the whole scope of the natural laws, that the individual, as far as the present sphere of being is concerned, is to the Author of Nature a consideration of inferior moment. Everywhere we see the arrangements for the species perfect; the individual is left, as it were, to take his chance amidst the mêlée of the various laws affecting him.

Man is thus part of the animal or organic creation, and subject to its laws. Yet Chambers has this reflection to add:

It may be, that, while we are committed to take our chance in a natural system of undeviating operation, and are left with apparent ruthlessness to endure the consequences of every collision into which we knowingly or unknowingly come with each law of the system, there is a system of Mercy and Grace behind the screen of nature, which is to make up for all the casualties endured there, and the very largeness of which is what makes these casualties a matter of indifference to God. For the existence of such a system, the actual constitution of nature is itself an argument. . . . Thinking of all the contingencies of this world as to be in time melted into or lost in the greater system, to which the present is only subsidiary, let us wait the end with patience, and be of good cheer.[3]

And lastly, this, which parallels the conclusion of *In Memoriam*:

It is startling to find an appearance of imperfection in the circle to which man belongs, and the ideas which rise in consequence are no less startling. Is our race but the initial of the grand crowning type? Are there yet to be species superior to us in organization, purer in feeling, more powerful in device and act, and who shall take a rule over us? . . . There may be then occasion for a nobler type of humanity, which shall complete the zoological circle on this planet, and realize some of the dreams of the purest spirits of the present race.[4]

3. Rutland, *loc. cit.*, p. 19; Mattes, *op. cit.*, p. 80.
4. Rutland, *loc. cit.*, p. 23; Mattes, *op. cit.*, p. 80.

It was, then, in the context of such ideas as these that *In Memoriam* was composed. But, needless to say (I hope it is needless), we have not 'accounted for' the poem by mentioning some of the books that Tennyson was reading at the time. If *In Memoriam* were merely a versification of such trite reflexions as I have been quoting, it would be of little more account than they. This consideration applies in general to all philosophical poetry, poetry with a 'message'. Readers (and Victorian readers were especially prone to this) often discuss such poetry as if its doctrine were something detachable, something which could be expressed in prose and presented as its essence or inmost meaning. True, it *can* be so presented, but in that case the 'message' of *In Memoriam* (for instance) could as well be learnt direct from Lyell, Herschel or Chambers. It is not that the 'thought' is unimportant in this or other reflective poetry; the point is that it is important in a different way. If its importance were equivalent to that of its prose counterpart, I should not be devoting this attention to Tennyson now. Instead, I should only be entitled to say something like this: 'Lyell, Herschel, Chambers and Tennyson all considered that, while there was no direct evidence for a life after death, the evidence against its probability was not sufficient to preclude any reasonable man from believing in it if he found it comforting.' But, in fact, Tennyson's statement of this great thought has generally been felt to be worth more than that of the other three authors. Why? not because he 'means' anything different, but because he means it from a far greater depth and in a far richer context. Meaning in poetry, as we all know, is far more complex than meaning in logical statement; it operates through image, symbol, rhythm, suggestion and association, and therefore calls forth from us a far more complete response—'complete' in that the emotions, imagination and sensibility are involved as well as the intelligence. A poem, like a piece of ritual, *enacts* what a credal statement merely *propounds*; "this", says the poem in effect, "is a tract of experience lived through in the light of such-and-such a thought or belief; this is what it feels like to accept it". As Professor I. A. Richards has said, a poet is usually more valuable to us when he is feeling something than when he is 'feeling that' something. I think it likely that what, for Tennyson, chiefly kept alive the heart in the head was the influence of Carlyle, working upon a soul prepared by a Christian upbringing and not unacquainted with flashes of mystical insight.

Perhaps the reader may find it convenient to have before him here a few of the stanzas (familiar though they be) which show most clearly how Messrs Lyell, Herschel and Chambers appear when felt along the heart:

LV

. . . .
Are God and Nature then at strife,
   That Nature lends such evil dreams?
   So careful of the type she seems,
So careless of the single life;

That I, considering everywhere
   Her secret meaning in her deeds,
   And finding that of fifty seeds
She often brings but one to bear,

I falter where I firmly trod,
   And falling with my weight of cares
   Upon the great world's altar-stairs
That slope thro' darkness up to God,

I stretch lame hands of faith, and grope,
   And gather dust and chaff, and call
   To what I feel is Lord of all,
And faintly trust the larger hope.

LVI

"So careful of the type?" but no.
   From scarped cliff and quarried stone
   She cries, "A thousand types are gone:
I care for nothing, all shall go.

"Thou makest thine appeal to me:
   I bring to life, I bring to death:
   The spirit does but mean the breath:
I know no more." And he, shall he,

Man, her last work, who seem'd so fair,
   Such splendid purpose in his eyes,
   Who roll'd the psalm to wintry skies,
Who built him fanes of fruitless prayer,

Who trusted God was love indeed
   And love Creation's final law—
   Tho' Nature, red in tooth and claw
With ravine, shriek'd against his creed—

Who loved, who suffer'd countless ills,
   Who battled for the True, the Just,

Be blown about the desert dust,
Or seal'd within the iron hills?

No more? A monster, then, a dream,
    A discord. Dragons of the prime,
    That tare each other in their slime,
Were mellow music match'd with him.

O life as futile, then, as frail!
    O for thy voice to soothe and bless!
    What hope of answer, or redress?
Behind the veil, behind the veil.

In these two Sections (LV and LVI) we have Tennyson feeling the
first shock of Lyell and Chambers (or of the interpretations they
stand for). Nature seems to deny the law of love, and man is (in Mrs
Mattes's phrase) 'a prospective fossil'. After faintly trusting the larger
hope, Tennyson sinks to even dimmer depths of perplexity; hope
seems to vanish, truth is for ever hidden behind the veil, and he
vainly longs for Hallam's reassuring voice. However, in a later Section (CXVIII) he makes a new synthesis of his former thoughts; above
all, he unites in one comprehensive view what Chambers separates:
physical and moral law:

CXVIII

Contemplate all this work of Time,
    The giant labouring in his youth;
    Nor dream of human love and truth,
As dying Nature's earth and lime;

But trust that those we call the dead
    Are breathers of an ampler day
    For ever nobler ends: They say,
The solid earth whereon we tread

In tracts of fluent heat began,
    And grew to seeming-random forms,
    The seeming prey of cyclic storms,
Till at the last arose the man;

Who throve and branch'd from clime to clime
    The herald of a higher race,
    And of himself in higher place,
If so he type this work of time

Within himself, from more to more;
    Or, crown'd with attributes of woe

Like glories, move his course, and show
That life is not as idle ore,

But iron dug from central gloom,
 And heated hot with burning fears,
 And dipt in baths of hissing tears,
And batter'd with the shocks of doom

To shape and use. Arise and fly
 The reeling Faun, the sensual feast;
 Move upward, working out the beast,
And let the ape and tiger die.

Man is the product of the natural law, but he must now take conscious part in the evolutionary process, transferring it from the physical to the moral level. Moreover, this very obligation strengthens the probability that the process does not end with physical death, but that the dead are breathers of an ampler day.

   * * *

We come at length to Section CXXIV, where, at the climax of the poem, Tennyson states the faith he has attained. For a man of his upbringing, a man so awake to spiritual reality and so mystically inclined, a believing attitude was inevitable and necessary. But, as we have seen, it was not achieved without conflict, or by putting out the eyes of the mind. What especially gives Tennyson his representative quality, and also earns him our respect, is that to the best of his ability he kept pace with all new truths, and, much as he longed for religious assurance, would accept none unless it was compatible with them. It was thus that he came to base his faith on what seemed the only invulnerable foundation: the needs and affirmatives of the heart.

That which we dare invoke to bless;
 Our dearest faith; our ghastliest doubt;
 He, They, One, All; within, without;
The Power in darkness whom we guess;

I found Him not in world or sun,
 Or eagle's wing, or insect's eye;
 Nor thro' the questions men may try,
The petty cobwebs we have spun:

If e'er when faith had fall'n asleep,
 I heard a voice "believe no more"
 And heard an ever-breaking shore
That tumbled in the Godless deep;

A warmth within the breast would melt
The freezing reason's colder part,
And like a man in wrath the heart
Stood up and answer'd "I have felt".
[cxxiv, 1–16]

'I found Him not in world or sun': in spite of his impassioned and lifelong attention to Nature, and his incomparable success in rendering her, it was not there, not in the classic evidences of wisdom and design in the universe, that he found God. I mentioned his remark about the microscopic world—how strange it seemed to him that its wonders should either strengthen or weaken faith: he found Him not in 'insect's eye'. We recall that even at Cambridge he had voted 'No' at a College discussion on the question 'Is an Intelligible First Cause deducible from the Phenomena of the Universe?' And if not in Nature, certainly not in metaphysical cobweb-spinning. Because, rejecting these former props of orthodoxy, Tennyson fell back upon the inward evidence, the reasons of the heart, he has been accused, like other believers of his and other times, of wishful thinking. This is perhaps not the place to discuss such a question; I would only remark that in taking up this position Tennyson was in accord with some of the profoundest insights of the ages, and of his own age in particular. From the time of David, through St Anselm with his *'crede ut intelligas'*,[5] Pascal with his 'this then is faith, God known in the heart, not proved by the reason', down to Coleridge and Carlyle and Kierkegaard, there had been a recognition that faith is not a matter of rational demonstration; that were it so, it would cease to be faith—i.e. a matter of religious duty, a vital commitment—and become compulsory knowledge; and that its acceptance means an act of the will: a plunge, a venture, or what is now sometimes called 'an existential choice'. If we remember all this, we may be less ready to despise Tennyson—as some of his critics have done—for coming to rest in a similar affirmation. If a man persisted in believing that the earth was flat, or that it rested in space upon the horns of a bull, and the bull upon the shell of a tortoise—if he obstinately clung to these views simply because he felt them in his heart to be true, we should rightly consider him eccentric, and possibly mad. But the shape and position of the earth are matters of empirical observation and mathematical calculation, whereas religious belief is not. In this sphere, the writ of the rational understanding does not run, and we are permitted—no, enjoined—by our experience as responsible moral agents to commit ourselves to those hypotheses without which the good life becomes difficult and, as some find, impossible.

5. "Believe, that you may understand" (Latin), a saying of St. Anselm (1033–1109) [Editor].

Whether or no the reader agrees with this, I hope he will at least
allow that Tennyson's position commands respect.

Very characteristically, he added a qualifying stanza to those above
quoted, feeling, no doubt, that he might seem to have triumphed too
easily over the voice which said "believe no more":

> No, like a child in doubt and fear:
>   But that blind clamour made me wise;
> Then was I as a child that cries,
>   But, crying, knows his father near.

And here let me draw attention to what seems to me the most
remarkable of Victorian comments on Tennyson. It is by Henry Sidgwick, who, having resigned his Trinity Fellowship on account of
'honest doubt', and spent the rest of his life fluctuating between faith
and agnosticism, was peculiarly well qualified to offer an opinion.
There are two comments recorded in the *Memoir of Henry Sidgwick*
(1906); the first, written in his Journal for February 10, 1887, is this:

> Perhaps a certain balancedness is the most distinctive char-
> acteristic of Tennyson among poets . . . Perhaps this specially
> makes him the representative poet of an age whose most char-
> acteristic merit is to see both sides of a question. Thus in *In
> Memoriam* the points where I am most affected are where a
> certain *retour sur soi-même*[6] occurs. Almost any poet might have
> written,

> And like a man in wrath the heart
>   Stood up and answered, I have felt.

> But only Tennyson would have immediately added:

> *No*, like a child in doubt and fear.[7]

*   *   *

No better illustration could be found, I think, of that poised uncertainty of the devoutly inclined agnostic mind, to which *In Memoriam*
made so strong an appeal. At the same time Tennyson's deeply religious nature, and the intensity of his longing for assurance, could
not but reach the hearts of his Christian readers also, even though
with them a touch of pity would mix itself with their sympathetic
response. For when all was said, Tennyson had *not* found that degree
and kind of certainty which revealed religion, through dogma and
Church, claimed to give. The Churchman R. H. Hutton (editor of
The Spectator) wrote in 1892:

6. Return upon itself (French) [Editor].
7. *Henry Sidgwick, A Memoir*, by A. S. and E. M. S. (1906), pp. 468–9.

There was an agnostic element in Tennyson, as perhaps in all the greatest minds, though in him it may have been in excess, which kept re-iterating: "We have but faith, we cannot know", and which, I should say, was never completely satisfied even of the adequacy of dogmatic definitions which his Church recognized . . . He finds no authoritative last word such as many Christians find in ecclesiastical authority. . . . The generally faltering voice with which Tennyson expresses the ardour of his own hope, touches the heart of this doubting and questioning age, as no more confident expression of belief could have touched it. The lines of his theology were in harmony with the great central lines of Christian thought; but in coming down to detail it soon passed into a region where all was wistful, and dogma disappeared in a haze of radiant twilight.[8]

The Prologue to *In Memoriam* was the last Section to be written (1849). It was written to show the Christian world (and Emily Sellwood in particular) how far Tennyson could, with perfect sincerity, go in the direction of Christianity. Some of its phrases (I have italicized them) show the truth of R. H. Hutton's comment:

> Strong Son of God, immortal Love,
> Whom we, that have not seen thy face,
> By faith, and faith alone, embrace,
> *Believing where we cannot prove*;
> . . . .
> Thou *seemest* human and divine,
> The highest, holiest manhood, thou:
> . . . .
> *Our little systems* have their day;
> They have their day and cease to be:
> They are but broken lights of thee,
> And thou, O Lord, art more than they.

> *We have but faith: we cannot know;*

Yet even this dissatisfied the fastidious Henry Sidgwick: 'I have always felt that . . . the effect of the introduction does not quite represent the effect of the poem. Faith, in the introduction, is too completely triumphant.'

The Two Voices had ended, as we saw, with Sabbath calm and domestic bliss; *In Memoriam* ends with a marriage-song, addressed to Edmund Lushington and Tennyson's sister Cecilia. It was, for more reasons than one, an appropriate conclusion. Hallam had been engaged to another of his sisters, and the approaching wedding of

8. *Aspects of Religious and Scientific Thought* (1901), pp. 406 ff.

Cecilia enabled Tennyson to end on the desired note of hope and
rebirth, all thoughts turned towards the future. By a happy stroke of
synthesis, too, he was able to link the marriage, and its hoped-for offspring, not only with Hallam but also with the main evolutionary drift
of the whole poem—even with that old thought of embryonic development which had interested him long before he had read *Vestiges*;
and, finally, with the Victorian dream of progress and a loftier race:

> 'A soul shall draw from out the vast
>   And strike his being into bounds,
>
> And, *moved thro' life of lower phase* [my italics]
>   Result in man, be born and think,
>   And act and love, a closer link
> Betwixt us and the crowning race
>
> Of those that, eye to eye, shall look
>   On knowledge. . . .
> . . . .
> No longer half-akin to brute,
>   For all we thought and loved and did,
>   And hoped, and suffer'd, is but seed
> Of what in them is flower and fruit;
>
> Whereof the man, that with me trod
>   This planet, was a noble type
>   Appearing ere the times were ripe,
> That friend of mine who lives in God,
>
> That God, which ever lives and loves,
>   One God, one law, one element,
>   And one far-off divine event,
> To which the whole creation moves.'

ALAN SINFIELD

Diction: Simple Words and Complex Meanings†

Diction is concerned with the words selected by the poet. As Mrs.
Nowottny has pointed out, there is some confusion in the use of the
term, resulting from indecision about whether it refers to words in

† From *The Language of Tennyson's* In Memoriam (Oxford: Basil Blackwell, 1971), pp. 41–
   53. Reprinted by permission of Blackwell Publishers.

isolation or as they interact with each other.[1] Sometimes when we talk of diction in literature we say that it is 'ornate' or 'drawn from everyday language' or 'influenced by the terminology of psycho-analysis', and here we seem to be referring in a general and absolute way to the writer's preferences. But when we speak of 'appropriate' diction, of 'every word in place', of 'fruitful ambiguity' or of charac-ters in a novel each having 'a distinctive mode of utterance', we are at least implicitly considering words in relation to their context. Only very limited statements can be made about the diction of a poem without taking into account the context of each word under exami-nation. An alternative way of phrasing this point would be to say that the important issue is the contribution of a word to the density of structure which I described in my first chapter as characteristic of poetic language. Sometimes it will prove possible to generalize about the use of certain types of diction in the poem as a whole, but for the most part I will be concerned with the intricate interrelations between words.

The diction of *In Memoriam* has aroused considerable hostility in unsympathetic critics, and I therefore propose to build this discus-sion round a refutation of Harold Nicolson's all-embracing judgment that 'of all poets, Tennyson should be read very carelessly or not at all'.[2] Studies of Tennyson have often been marked by a crisis of con-fidence which makes the critic assume that if more than one mean-ing is possible at any point then Tennyson was probably confused or, if the complexity seems to fit in, successful despite himself. This is the attitude of Cleanth Brooks, who thinks it 'substantially true' that Tennyson did not build his doubts 'into the structure of the poetry itself as enriching ambiguities'.[3] There is no evidence that, as Brooks claims, Tennyson sought to avoid ambiguity and other kinds of complexity; his quoted remarks suggest the opposite—'Then he spoke of Milton's Latinisms, and delicate play with words, and Shakespeare's play upon words'.[4] I wish to show that the diction of *In Memoriam* is often woven into subtle and complex structures of language and that careless reading is likely to provide the least sat-isfactory approach.

The assumptions underlying this crisis of critical confidence can be illustrated from one of its more extreme exponents, Paull F. Baum in his study, *Tennyson Sixty Years After*. Section i is analysed

1. *The Language Poets Use*, pp. 26ff.; and I. A. Richards, *The Philosophy of Rhetoric* (New York, 1936), pp. 51–7.
2. *Tennyson*, p. 233.
3. Cleanth Brooks. 'The Motivation of Tennyson's Weeper', in John Killham, *Critical Essays on the Poetry of Tennyson* (London, 1960), p. 177.
4. Hallam Tennyson, *Memoir*, I, 277—Mrs. Rundle Charles writing of 1848.

there at some length,[5] and Baum observes that 'dead selves' is ambiguous:

> I held it truth, with him who sings
>   To one clear harp in divers tones,
>   That men may rise on stepping-stones
> Of their dead selves to higher things.

Baum says that 'dead selves' might mean one's past experience during this life or one's improvement from incarnation to incarnation,
but though he finds the ambiguity 'suggestive' he thinks there must
be one 'right' interpretation after all. I would say, on the contrary,
that there are three meanings here, three ways in which men may
rise. The phrase is about a man's development in his life on earth
(the sort of development we see in the poet during *In Memoriam*);
about the individual's progress after death (the poet's desire to
believe that Hallam still exists somewhere becomes an important
theme); and about the perfectibility of mankind as a whole (the possibility, which the poet eventually affirms, that man may be 'The
herald of a higher race'). Hallam's death has opened up three principal areas of deep anxiety, and they are all comprised in this one
phrase; the poet's optimism has been destroyed in one blow. The
lines express in embryo the main themes of the whole poem.

Baum is even less happy about the rest of the section, for he persists in finding confusion where I see complexity. The poet wants to
cling to his grief for fear that love should vanish with it: 'Let Love
clasp Grief lest both be drown'd,/Let darkness keep her raven gloss'.
Baum objects to the latter line because Milton's parallel usage in
Comus (line 251) is in a very different context.[6] Comus is speaking
of the enchanting power of the Lady's song: 'At every fall smoothing
the Raven downe/Of darkness till it smil'd'. There is no contradiction
here. The effect of the virtuous Lady's song is so great that it even
smooths the raven down of darkness—that is, it softens the deathly
evil of Comus. Tennyson's poet, however, is more extreme, and
would not have his darkness of grief and death charmed away even
for a moment. The allusion boldly links the poet with Comus, and
his determination to resist consolation with opposition to Christian
virtue. The poet's desire to preserve his love whatever the cost is most
forcibly expressed.

The parallel with *Comus* runs right through the section. The first
lines we considered ('men may rise on stepping-stones') reflect the
opening lines of Milton's poem:

5. Pp. 303–6. On section i see also L. Metzer, 'The Eternal Process: Some Parallels between
   Goethe's *Faust* and Tennyson's *In Memoriam*', *Victorian Poetry*, I (1963), 189–96.
6. In John Milton's *A Masque Presented at Ludlow Castle*, also known as *Comus* (1634),
   Comus is an evil enchanter who tries to tempt the virtuous heroine [Editor].

> Yet som there be that by due steps aspire
> To lay their just hands on that Golden Key
> That opes the Palace of Eternity.[7]

Like those to whom the Attendant Spirit refers here, the poet used to think that men could aspire to eternal life, but he now ranges himself with Comus and darkness and rejects the optimistic Christian creed. The insistence on keeping the raven gloss of darkness develops the loss of faith described in the first lines of the section, for the poet goes further than Comus by refusing to be charmed even temporarily by the virtuous Lady.

The section continues, 'Ah, sweeter to be drunk with loss,/To dance with death, to beat the ground'. Here Baum questions, 'Does "to beat the ground" mean to hurl oneself in despair upon the ground, to beat one's head on the ground; or is it a Latinism merely repeating "To dance"?—a difficult choice'. Once again, we do not have to make a choice. The line partly means 'to despair', with to me the further suggestion of beating on the actual ground where the dead person is buried in a macabre effort to get in. It is also a Latinism, and is in fact the literal meaning of *tripudiare*, 'to dance a religious dance'. The poet's dance is religious, but in a deliberately pagan form. 'To beat the ground' does, at this level, repeat 'To dance with death': all the three phrases in these two lines are ultimately repetitious (they are syntactically similar as well) and may be thought of as simulating the movement of a dance. There is, moreover, a further allusion to *Comus*: 'Come, knit hands, and beat the ground/ In a light fantastic round' (143). These lines end Comus' speech inciting his 'crew' to wantonly abandon themselves to emotion, and the allusion again fits section i exactly. As we have seen, the poet rejects Christian consolation and identifies himself with the pagan Comus, refusing to have darkness smoothed away. Like Comus, he will abandon himself in a ritual dance of emotional indulgence.

This parallel with Milton's poem provides a consistent scheme against which to measure the poet's attitude; the extremity of his position is indicated by the fact that in *Comus* the issue is between good and evil. His resolution to cling to grief is presented as deliberately opposed to an optimistic faith. By means of a delicately sustained allusion Tennyson succeeds in packing his lines with deep religious, moral and mythological implications. There is much more useful complexity here than Baum—or those who think that Tennyson is best read carelessly—will allow. Baum puts his finger on several subtleties of expression, but he begins in each case by assuming mere confusion, so blinding himself to the virtues of the section

---

7. The opening of *Comus* seems relevant also to sections lxiv and xciii, as editors have noted. The epigraph to the early poem 'The Hesperides' is drawn from *Comus*.

—which no one would claim as among the most powerful in *In Memoriam*.

The crisis of confidence in Tennyson's diction seems to break down into two paradoxically related notions. On the one hand it is accepted that the language is simply straightforward and that Tennyson's aim was just to make plain what he meant—this is behind the way Baum takes it for granted that there must be one meaning to 'dead selves'. On the other hand, it is assumed that Tennyson sought, by disguising his meaning in vague or ornate diction, to give his writing a merely artificial elevation which results only in the spuriously 'poetical'. This second idea underlies Baum's criticism of 'Let darkness keep her raven gloss' and 'to beat the ground' and his conclusion that 'Tennyson has chosen to be deliberately cryptic and "poetic" at all costs' (p. 305). The second notion is the subject of the next chapter, the first (that Tennyson is straightforward) I propose to deal with by showing how the juxtaposition of quite unexceptional words produces complex effects if we look closely.

·   ·   ·

One cause of the impression that the diction of *In Memoriam* is straightforward is probably the fact that the words themselves are almost always easy to understand—we do not think of Tennyson as torturing the language into his meaning. The revision of line 9 of section xxxvi suggests that this surface simplicity was Tennyson's aim, for the mention in the Harvard loosepaper and the Trinity manuscript of 'the Logos' is replaced in the published version by 'the Word'. This comprehensible diction certainly seems to have been appreciated by contemporary readers; one wrote, 'A spirit of wonderfully subtle sympathy is displayed in that poem, or series of poems, and in his deepest and tenderest sorrow he is in language most simple'.[8] The concern of the Victorian poet to gain a public for his writing has been much discussed in recent criticism,[9] and the superficial simplicity of the language of *In Memoriam* may have been caused by the desire for a wide public; at any rate, it was no doubt a major factor in the poem's contemporary popularity.

Nevertheless, Tennyson's diction is not always drawn from language in everyday use, or even from the poetic tradition, for he is able to devise new words when he feels the necessity. He is apparently the first user of 'intervital' ('between lives'—xliii), 'orb' as a verb (xxiv) and 'plumelets' ('minute plumes'—xci). Compounding is Tennyson's favourite way of forming new expressions to suit his need, though almost nothing remains in *In Memoriam* of the exces-

8. Archibald C. McMichael, *Reflections By The Way* (Ayr, n.d.—but *Maud* is recently published), p. 114.
9. E.g. E.D.H. Johnson, *The Alien Vision of Victorian Poetry* (Princeton, 1952).

sively delicate usages he is supposed to have spent ten years removing from his first volumes of poetry. The compound is particularly valuable in suggesting the identity or simultaneity of two notions which would otherwise be separated by language as we normally use it. In section xlviii the poet says that Sorrow

> rather loosens from the lip
> Short swallow-flights of song, that dip
> Their wings in tears, and skim away.

'Swallow-flights' catches exactly the idea of a swallow on the wing. The compound has the advantage of making neither element in it seem subordinate. It is not a swallow which is flying, or an act of flying which happens to involve a swallow; it is both at once, a swallow-flight. One thinks also of 'hourly-mellowing' (xci) and 'ever-breaking' (cxxiv). Here is another example:

> O mother, praying God will save
> Thy sailor,—while thy head is bow'd,
> His heavy-shotted hammock-shroud
> Drops in his vast and wandering grave.
>   (vi)

Is it a shroud or a hammock?—a hammock like a shroud or a shroud like a hammock? It is both at once, rather like a metaphor in which tenor and vehicle are completely intertwined. This example links the security of the hammock with the horror of the shroud, whilst playing upon the notion that the dead only sleep. It also looks forward to the process by which the dream, and finally and more satisfyingly the vision, becomes the means of contact with the dead.

The compound is extremely useful for expressing the mystery and paradox of other-worldly experience, as in the 'silent-speaking words' of Hallam's letters in section xcv, or the 'Cloud-towers by ghostly masons wrought' which appear to the poet in the ominous phantasmagoria of section lxx. They are not towers or clouds, but an irreducible amalgam of the two. The rationale of the method is explicit in section cxxi: 'Sweet Hesper-Phosphor, double name / For what is one'. At best, Tennyson's compounds are highly creative. Whereas the device suggests sensuous self-abandonment in the early volumes, in *In Memoriam* it shows a rigorous concern with choosing the right expression for the idea. It can pin down a thought precisely and economically and is particularly useful for preserving intact a notion which ordinary language would falsify by breaking it down into separable elements.

By and large, however, it is true that Tennyson uses simple, straightforward diction. But simple words can achieve complex effects, depending on the context they are placed in. Our use of language is very much involved with the fact that in a given situation there are some expressions which we expect and others which we do not. In the context, say, of a group of people sitting at a meal, we would expect the words 'Please pass the . . . ' to be followed by a word from a rather small range to do with things to eat or drink or which contain food or drink—say 'fruit cake' or 'broccoli'. If, on the other hand, we were behind the counter in a baker's shop, we might still expect 'fruit cake', but 'paper bags' would also be a possibility, whereas this would be as surprising at the dining table as 'broccoli' would be at the baker's. Words which we might expect in a given situation are said to collocate with each other—'by collocation is meant the habitual association of a word in a language with other particular words in sentences'.[1]

The poet, who exploits all the resources of language to the full, can gain great effect from the use of this fact—as Empson puts it, 'a word in a speech which falls outside the expected vocabulary will cause an uneasy stir in all but the soundest sleepers'.[2] In section lxxii the day is commanded to 'sow the sky with flying boughs'. 'Day', the grammatical subject, is so far from 'sow' that we have almost forgotten it, and we assume that the wind is meant. On a literal level, so it is, but in the poet's mind the 'reason' for the storm is that this is the anniversary of Hallam's death, and thus it is right that the day itself should be seen as the originator of the effects in nature. We are thinking of weather and landscape, and therefore sowing, blowing boughs and the sky are not out of place; they are all simple words, but their conjunction is highly meaningful and paradoxical in this section. Sowing the sky is a reversal of the usual practice, and it negates the life-giving natural cycle: it means death. The boughs are torn from their proper, fruitful positions on the trees and flung at random into the air, where they have no place and no useful function—even, perhaps, as Hallam has been frighteningly wrenched from the earth where his potentialities might have been fulfilled, and transplanted to an alien element. Tennyson does not supply a scene of simply arbitrary destruction: it is the active reversal of what is usually a constructive principle which gives the line its strength.

This example shows quite clearly how simple words can be juxtaposed so as to yield complex meanings. It also illustrates the other main reason why the power of Tennyson's diction has been overlooked. The line is one of the most striking in the poem, but it nevertheless relies upon very subtle nuances for its effect; the

1. Robert H. Robins, *General Linguistics, An Introductory Survey* (London, 1964), p. 67. See also J. R. Firth, 'Modes of Meaning', *Essays and Studies*, new series, IV (1951), 118–49, and Spencer and Gregory, *Linguistics and Style*, p. 73.
2. William Empson, *Seven Types of Ambiguity*, 3rd edn. (paperback, London, 1961), p. 4.

collocational gap between the words is at first glance slight and we have to look carefully to see how remarkable the description is. This is almost invariably true of the diction of *In Memoriam*, which is in this respect completely in line with the generalization about Tennyson's language which I made in the previous chapter. He characteristically works in language which is superficially unremarkable: we must expect, not violent shocks, but delicate shades of meaning which gently modify our response. The surface maintains a classical calm, although monsters may be raging in the depths. Tennyson seems to have been very sensitive to slight nuances of language:

> Then he spoke of the great richness of the English language due to its double origin, the Norman and Saxon words. How hard it would be for a foreigner to feel the difference in the line
>
> > An *infant* crying for the light,
>
> had the word *baby* been substituted; which would at once have made it ridiculous.[3]

My argument, then, is that beneath the apparently simple and unremarkable diction of *In Memoriam* are effects of great complexity resulting from the juxtaposing of quite ordinary words. The careless reader may easily miss the point, for Tennyson does not deal in obviously extraordinary collocations. The need is now for further examples to support my claim.

> What hope is here for modern rhyme
> > To him, who turns a musing eye
> > On songs, and deeds, and lives, that lie
> Foreshorten'd in the tract of time?

Section lxxvii is the last of a group concerned with the transience of poetry, and it devalues deeds and lives as well by representing all as deprived of even their actual proportions by the diminishing effect of perspective. The vast, unbounded 'tract of time' is an emotionally charged image, but it is placed alongside a reductive reference to poetry as 'modern rhyme.' We see a similar juxtaposition of great and small in 'a musing eye', where a lurking reminder of the Muses is subordinated to the notion of a casually thoughtful observer. This confrontation of grand and trivial diction continues in the next lines:

> These mortal lullabies of pain
> > May bind a book, may line a box,
> > May serve to curl a maiden's locks,
> Or when a thousand moons shall wane

3. From a conversation of 1892, quoted by Hallam, Lord Tennyson, *Tennyson and His Friends* (London, 1911), p. 218.

> A man upon a stall may find,
>   And, passing, turn the page that tells
>   A grief, then changed to something else,
> Sung by a long-forgotten mind.

'Lullabies' further degrades the poet's art, suggesting that its function is only to soothe the writer; but to link it with 'mortal' is to violate with thoughts of death all its usual connotations of peaceful domesticity providing security and rest for the fretful child. In this packed line 'mortal' has two references—to the poetry itself (it will not live) and to its subject matter (it is about Hallam's death). These are lullabies 'of pain' because they both describe and mitigate the poet's suffering. Such economy is not usually associated with Tennyson. Up to this point the tone of the section has been fairly elevated, but the two central lines of this stanza descend heavily to the mundane with thoughts of binding books, lining boxes and curling hair. We can see Tennyson building up the effect of a random list of trivia in the Trinity manuscript, where the second line of this stanza at first read, 'May be the lining of a box'. The last line requires yet a further shift in our reaction: 'when a thousand moons shall wane' is diction of a quite different kind, and it restores suddenly the wide sweep of time and space which opened the section. The moon also carries connotations of romantic love, but in this context the pair of lovers in the moonlight is overwhelmed by a succession of thousands more such couples. The line therefore suggests not only length of time, but the instability of human aspirations; the moon is also an image of change.

In the third stanza the diction drops again to the mundane man by the bookstall, but he is further juxtaposed with the 'long-forgotten mind', another phrase redolent of dreamy, romantic feelings. The diction puts the fate of modern rhyme before the reader by joining in one sentence the elevated and the inconsequential. The imagination-stretching evocations of the passing of the years correspond to all that is noble in the poet's activity; the trivial events juxtaposed with them figure the insignificance of poetry—or any human action—in the total scheme of things. There is no resolving this disparity; the poet instead decides to disregard it:

> But what of that? My darken'd ways
>   Shall ring with music all the same;
>   To breathe my loss is more than fame,
> To utter love more sweet than praise.

The 'tract of time' of the first stanza is narrowed down to 'my darken'd ways'; though the poet's individual path is gloomy, it forms a more manageable unit than the vast stretch of time with which he began. The strength of the last two lines comes from the fact that their content is almost identical, the great difference being that between the meanings of 'loss' and 'love'. In ordinary language we would not regard these two words as habitually associated, but in *In Memoriam* they have been linked several times already so that by this section they are established as a set collocation—we expect to see them together as we do 'bread and butter'. The affirmation to which they contribute is reinforced by our awareness of their previous occurrences. They carry all the triumph of the poet's victory over time by reminding us of his resolution in the first section of the poem to hold by his love. Their appearance here is therefore at least some kind of answer to the poet's disquiet at the power of time to diminish human achievement, for he has maintained his devotion to his friend. The very fact that he is still pursuing his theme of love and loss asserts human values in the desert of the tract of time. Section lxxvii shows Tennyson precisely controlling his diction so that we must read carefully if we are to appreciate the full connotations of his words and their delicate contributions to the structure.

Section xxi also affords interesting study from this point of view. It is in the pastoral mode with the poet making pipes from the grasses of the grave, but Tennyson's diction does not remain at the conventional level. Travellers pass by and comment unfavourably on his activity; though this happens occasionally in the pastoral tradition, it nevertheless tends to interrupt the mood. But it is quite definitely broken in the fourth and fifth stanzas:

> A third is wroth: 'Is this an hour
>   For private sorrow's barren song,
>   When more and more the people throng
> The chairs and thrones of civil power?
>
> 'A time to sicken and to swoon,
>   When Science reaches forth her arms
>   To feel from world to world, and charms
> Her secret from the latest moon?'

'The chairs and thrones of civil power', and still more 'Science', seem quite out of place in the pastoral world (related considerations appear in 'Lycidas', but even there it is noticeable that Milton is careful to pull the poem together by employing traditional diction whenever he can). The effect is to make the reader conscious, through dramatic presentation, of the differences between the values of the Golden Age and of the modern era. In pastoral poems to sit and pipe love songs is the ideal, but now one is expected to give prime attention to public issues.

If we look more closely at the second stanza quoted, we find that the way in which science is introduced is more subtle yet. The poet

has been rebuked for singing of love, but the language used by the
traveller is in fact that of sexual attraction: science 'reaches forth her
arms/To feel' and 'charms/Her secret from the latest moon'. The
first collocational surprise was the introduction of science into the
pastoral, but then follows a second, for the language of love is used
to describe science so that we come full circle. In the context the
moon must also remind us of love, but '*latest* moon' emphasizes the
irrelevance of such factors to the worldly traveller. He is interested
in novelty and in being up to date, not in the abiding worth of love.
The difference in values between the poet's devotion to his friend
and his critic's pressing of public issues is doubly insisted upon. The
public world breaks in on the pastoral but even as it does so the
pastoral value of love is reasserted through the diction.

My last example is section lxxxii:

> I wage not any feud with Death
>   For changes wrought on form and face;
>   No lower life that earth's embrace
> May breed with him, can fright my faith.
>
> Eternal process moving on,
>   From state to state the spirit walks;
>   And these are but the shatter'd stalks,
> Or ruin'd chrysalis of one.
>
> Nor blame I Death, because he bare
>   The use of virtue out of earth:
>   I know transplanted human worth
> Will bloom to profit, otherwhere.
>
> For this alone on Death I wreak
>   The wrath that garners in my heart;
>   He put our lives so far apart
> We cannot hear each other speak.

Here again we find a highly ironic use of the language of love in the
third and fourth lines. It is the earth which may 'embrace' and 'breed
with' Hallam, whereas the poet is cut off from physical contact. This
gruesome notion is supported by the use of such expressions as 'I
wage not any feud' and 'I wreak the wrath', which have distinctly
Gothic connotations. In such a context the macabre emphasis on
the physical corruption of death seems appropriate.

The references to organic growth continue through the next stanzas. If we compare them, as we are encouraged to do by the repetition, we find a development from the life stimulated by the corpse,
through the suggestion in the second stanza that human life is a
plant which is cut down at death, to the full flowering of the spirit

in an existence after death: 'I know transplanted human worth/Will bloom to profit, otherwise'. This plant diction does not really constitute an extended metaphor—it is largely dead metaphor which might almost occur in conversation—but rather just a recurrence of words from the same area of meaning. We find it at each stage of the thought, taking appropriate connotations from its context but at the same time providing a stable image against which we can measure the development of the argument. We notice also that, despite the poet's claim that he is not disconsolate, the growth in the first two stanzas is linked absolutely to destruction, so that the most obvious and appealing aspect of organic life is denied immediately it is evoked. The third stanza describes a full flowering, but again we find the poet's discontent breaking through in the great prominence given to 'otherwise'. Tennyson uses simple words throughout, but their interactions are complex, for there is a denial underlying the apparent affirmation.

The last stanza gives the cause of the poet's complaint: 'He put our lives so far apart/We cannot hear each other speak' ('far apart' is in clear contrast to 'earth's embrace'). After all the exalted talk of the 'eternal process' the poet's need is revealed as pathetically humble and mundane. The desire for renewed contact with Hallam confirms our suspicion that 'the spirit walks' (line 6) alludes to the possibility of his return as a ghost. Line 6 is primarily about the sublime notion of the soul's progress through its afterlife, but there is an underlying suggestion that a more functional appearance of his friend as a ghost would please the poet much better, for then they might speak. Once again we find that Tennyson's diction is cunningly chosen so as to undermine the apparent equanimity of the early part of the argument. The last stanza also contains the conclusion of the series of words denoting growth. The poet has described various kinds of life, but they provide him with no harvest which could satisfy and fulfil him: he has only 'The wrath that *garners* in my heart'. This is the final, resentful answer to the first three stanzas. Hallam may be blooming somewhere else, but the fruits are hardly available to the poet; he 'garners' only wrath born of frustration. It is that one word which really makes it plain that the section is *not* saying 'I am perfectly happy about all these aspects of death, it is just that one that worries me', but protesting bitterly at the whole process which has deprived the poet of his friend. The structure of the section is more complex and economical than it may appear at first sight, for although Tennyson may seem to employ unremarkable collocations, closer examination shows the words finely interweaving throughout the sixteen lines.

All the examples I have given bring out slightly different aspects of Tennyson's diction and if I gave more this would continue to happen. They have in common the appearance of classical simplicity and unruffled balance which is characteristic of the language of *In Memoriam*, but they also have an underlying complexity. There is no reason to suppose that Tennyson aimed merely to state a plain meaning unambiguously. Only the surface is straightforward and careful reading is essential if we are to probe the subtle interactions of the words in the poetic structure.

CHRISTOPHER RICKS

In Memoriam, 1850†

Tennyson had begun *In Memoriam* during the month when he heard of Arthur Hallam's death, October 1833; and four months later he had indicated to Henry Hallam that he hoped in the future to concentrate his powers on the construction of a tribute to his dead friend. By 1841, 'the number of the memorial poems had rapidly increased', and by 1845 FitzGerald was reporting Spedding's pressure on Tennyson to publish the elegies: 'A.T. has near a volume of poems—elegiac—in memory of Arthur Hallam. Don't you think the world wants other notes than elegiac now? Lycidas is the utmost length an elegiac should reach. But Spedding praises: and I suppose the elegiacs will see daylight—public daylight—one day.'

But Tennyson's uncertainties ran deep. In 1844 he had written to Aunt Russell, 'With respect to the non-publication of those poems which you mention, it is partly occasioned by the considerations you speak of, and partly by my sense of their present imperfectness: perhaps they will not see the light till I have ceased to be. I cannot tell, but I have no wish to send them out yet.' By January 1849, he had promised Aubrey de Vere 'to *print* at least his exquisite Elegies, and let his friends have a few copies'. This private issue, or trial edition, was printed in March 1850, it seems; Tennyson then made some important last-minute revisions, and *In Memoriam A.H.H.* was published anonymously at the end of May 1850. The title *In Memoriam A.H.H.* had been either suggested or preferred by Emily Sellwood, whom Tennyson married in June 1850.

The title *In Memoriam A.H.H.* directs attention firmly to one focus, despite Tennyson's injunction: 'It must be remembered that this is

† From *Tennyson*, 2nd ed. (London and Berkeley: Macmillan and University of California Press, 1989), pp. 201–218. Reprinted by permission of Macmillan Press, Ltd. and the University of California Press. Some of the author's footnotes have been omitted.

a poem, *not* an actual biography.' Another title which Tennyson had
considered would direct attention differently: *The Way of the Soul*.
Yet a third would suggest, with frankness and with some truth, that
the poem as a whole does not possess a firm focus: *Fragments of an
Elegy*. For the critical question about *In Memoriam* remains the first
and most obvious one: in what sense do the 133 separate sections,
ranging in length from 12 lines to 144 lines, constitute a whole, a
poetic unity, a poem?

> The sections were written at many different places, and as
> the phases of our intercourse came to my memory and suggested
> them. I did not write them with any view of weaving them into
> a whole, or for publication, until I found that I had written so
> many. The different moods of sorrow as in a drama are dra-
> matically given, and my conviction that fear, doubts, and suf-
> fering will find answer and relief only through Faith in a God
> of Love. 'I' is not always the author speaking of himself, but the
> voice of the human race speaking through him. After the Death
> of A.H.H., the divisions of the poem are made by First Xmas
> Eve (Section XXVIII), Second Xmas (LXXVIII), Third Xmas Eve (CIV
> and CV etc.).[1]

More informally, Tennyson told his friend James Knowles that 'the
general way of its being written was so queer that if there were a
blank space I would put in a poem'. He also explained to Knowles
that there were nine natural groups or divisions in the poem: I–VIII,
IX–XX, XXI–XXVII, XXVIII–XLIX, L–LVIII, LIX–LXXI, LXXII–XCVIII, XCIX–CIII,
CIV–CXXXI.

Literary criticism since Tennyson's time has become more flexible
in its ideas as to artistic unity, less committed to a narrow or mechanical idea of such unity. But it has also become more skilled at imag-
ining some such unity where it may not exist, and (a natural
consequence of professional academicism) more skilled at exculpat-
ing works of art which deserve the higher compliment of not being
whisked away into the irreproachable. Tennyson himself did not
make large claims for *In Memoriam* as a unity; his sense that the
Christmases provided a serviceable division of the poem should not
be taken as warrant for believing that a poem on the scale of *In
Memoriam*, and with such large concerns, could be adequately unified by such links and cross-connections as modern criticism rightly
delights in and wrongly pretends can be structurally crucial. The
Christmases, or the imagery of dark and light, of water and of the
human hand: these do much in the way of 'weaving them into a
whole', but it remains weaving, not growing or building. Unifying

1. Hallam, Lord Tennyson, *Tennyson: A Memoir* (1897), I, 304–5.

principles which would be adequate to a short poem, and which
might be adequate to a poem on the scale of *Four Quartets*[2] (though
even here there has been special pleading), cannot take the strain
they are asked to bear if we press them to take responsibility for the
unity of a poem as long, various, ranging, and uneven as *In Memoriam*. Admirers of the poem should not protest too much. Charles
Kingsley in 1850 knew that he could afford an important concession:
'Not that there runs throughout the book a conscious or organic
method. The poems seem often merely to be united by the identity
of their metre. . . . ' There is something likewise refreshing about
Humphry House's asseverations, which are uncompromised:

> It is impossible to apprehend it as a unified whole; for it is not
> a whole; and it fluctuates waywardly. . . . The poem then was
> never planned as a whole, and its composition was spread over
> a long period; and also its theme was never properly *appre-
> hended* as a whole. I say its theme; but part of the problem is to
> be sure whether there was a single theme. Is the theme the
> personal sorrow for Arthur Hallam's death? Is the theme the
> whole question of human immortality? Is the theme the inter-
> play of the personal sorrow with the general doubt about sur-
> vival?[3]

House argues persuasively that no convincing case for unity can be
made. Nor does the charting of Tennyson's doubts and hopes within
the poem provide such a unity of apprehended theme; 'The Way of
the Soul' would indeed provide a graph, but a graph is not the same
as an artistic unity. Moreover, such a claim would play into Fitz-
Gerald's unsentimental hands (he was writing in 1845, five years
before Tennyson published the poem):

> We have surely had enough of men reporting their sorrows:
> especially when one is aware all the time that the poet wilfully
> protracts what he complains of, magnifies it in the Imagination,
> puts it into all the shapes of Fancy: and yet we are to condole
> with him, and be taught to ruminate our losses and sorrows in
> the same way. I felt that if Tennyson had got on a horse and
> ridden twenty miles, instead of moaning over his pipe, he would
> have been cured of his sorrows in half the time. As it is, it is
> about three years before the Poetic Soul walks itself out of dark-
> ness and Despair into Common Sense.[4]

Although Tennyson did not ordinarily permit the reprinting of
selected sections from *In Memoriam*, he did let his friend F.T. Pal-

2. Long poem by T. S. Eliot (1943) [Editor].
3. *All in Due Time*, pp. 130–1.
4. *The Letters of Edward FitzGerald*, ed. Terhune, I, 486; 27 February 1845.

grave print such a selection in his volume of *Lyrical Poems* from Tennyson (1885), with the sections moreover in a different order. A remark by Palgrave is acute; he reported that his selections 'from *In Memoriam* (peculiarly difficult to frame, from the reasons which I have noted above in regard to Shakespeare's Sonnets) follow a list which he gave me'. Shakespeare's *Sonnets* are not only an important source for *In Memoriam*; they are its most important analogue. Not that the question of unity simply dissolves if we invoke the authority of the sonnet sequence—no authority attaches as such to the sonnet sequence, which even in Shakespeare's day was less often a creative whole than an inordinately convenient means of gaining some of the advantages of the long poem without having to face its proper responsibilities and difficulties. Nevertheless, the precedent is an illuminating one: separate poems, occasionally and loosely linked into groups, engaging with a multiplicity of matters and achieving the inner interrelationships of a *congeries* rather than of a single poem.[5] From the start, it was seen too that the love of Tennyson for Hallam had a precedent in the *Sonnets*. Charles Kingsley, with some recklessness, exulted in finding a successor to 'the old tales of David and Jonathan, Damon and Pythias, Socrates and Alcibiades, Shakespeare and his nameless friend, of "love passing the love of woman" '; he was drawn twice to this perilous phrase, praising *In Memoriam* for 'a depth and vehemence of affection "passing the love of woman" . . . altogether rivalling the sonnets of Shakespeare.'

It is not only a post-Freudian world which finds some cause for anxiety here. Benjamin Jowett remarked of Tennyson,

> Once again, perhaps in his weaker moments, he had thought of Shakespeare as happier in having the power to draw himself for his fellow men, and used to think Shakespeare greater in his sonnets than in his plays. But he soon returned to the thought which is indeed the thought of all the world. He would have seemed to me to be reverting for a moment to the great sorrow of his own mind. It would not have been manly or natural to have lived in it always. But in that peculiar phase of mind he found the sonnets a deeper expression of the never to be forgotten love which he felt more than any of the many moods of many minds which appear among his dramas. The love of the sonnets which he so strikingly expressed was a sort of sympathy with Hellenism.[6]

5. For the affinities between *In Memoriam* and John Berryman's *Dream Songs* (both are theodicies, are on the death of friends, and are modern equivalents of the sonnet sequence), see an essay by the present writer in the *Massachusetts Review*, Spring 1970. Arthur Hallam had written a theodicy.
6. Hallam Lord Tennyson, *Materials for a Life of A.T.*, IV, 460.

Fearing a homosexual misconstruction, Tennyson's son cut this for the *Memoir*, removing the last sentence and that which begins, 'It would not have been manly'.

Arthur Hallam had worshipped Shakespeare's *Sonnets*. It is likely that Arthur's father, Henry Hallam, was remembering the opinions of Arthur and of Tennyson when he influentially deplored the ardour of the *Sonnets* in 1839, between the death of Arthur and the publication of *In Memoriam*, insisting, 'It is impossible not to wish that Shakespeare had never written them.' Tennyson was to speak bluntly: 'Henry Hallam made a great mistake about them: they are noble.'

But do we too need to speak bluntly? Is Tennyson's love for Hallam a homosexual love? An anthology entitled *Sexual Heretics: Male Homosexuality in English Literature from 1850 to 1900* does not hesitate to quote extensively from ten sections of *In Memoriam*: its editor, anxious to enlist or if necessary pressgang Tennyson, believes that 'the fact that Tennyson evolved an emphatically heterosexual image in later life does nothing to disqualify him as homosexual when he wrote *In Memoriam*'.[7]

The vehemence of Tennyson's love for Hallam is remarkable, but then a powerful and original poem is likely to be remarkable. It is rather some particular turns of speech which disconcert.

> A spectral doubt which makes me cold,
>   That I shall be thy mate no more
>
> (XLI)

Is the metaphor in 'mate' (even allowing for the variety of the word's other uses) an inadvertently revealing one? And what of the manuscript lines which cry to Hallam's spirit?

> Stoop soul and touch me: wed me: hear
>   The wish too strong for words to name;
>
> (XCIII)

But then manuscript readings lend themselves all too easily to a 'heads I win, tails you lose' argument; if the manuscript reading is the same as the final reading, then we can claim that from the start the poet's conception did not waver and is unquestionably such-and-such. And if the manuscript reading differs (as here; what Tennyson published was 'Descend, and touch, and enter', which is in some ways even more disconcerting), we can claim that his original, his truest, conception was subsequently suppressed. Even so, the question about *In Memoriam*, whether moralistic or critical, is a real one. Anybody who believes that Tennyson's feelings for Hallam were not homosexual should try to say why.

7. Brian Reade, *Sexual Heretics* (1970), p. 9.

First, there is the fact that the reiterated metaphor of man and wife in the poem is sufficiently explicable in the simplest terms: that Hallam had been about to marry Tennyson's sister Emily. The frustration by death of such a marriage is an explicit concern of the poem, which speaks often of Emily and of Tennyson's own hopes from the marriage. Moreover, the poem ends with an epilogue in which the happy wedding of another of Tennyson's sisters to another of his dear friends provides both an instance and an augury of joy and aspiration. It is true that the transference of such metaphors so that they include not only Emily but also Tennyson is an extension which could mask other feelings in the poet. But it need not do so, and the family tragedy is sufficiently represented in the poem for it to be clear that there is a strong sense of the word 'too' whenever Tennyson speaks of himself as a widowed heart, or a widower, or no longer Hallam's 'mate'; such moments invoke the community of feeling by saying to Emily, 'I too am widowed.' It may still be strange to cry 'wed me', but at least a critic will need to grant that a point of the cry is that it is addressed to someone who had hoped to wed a Tennyson while alive but could not. Moreover, Tennyson's relationship with his sisters within the poem is presented (this too is faithful to the family situation) as one in which Tennyson had to be father as well as brother.[8] His paternal relationship to his sisters again modifies the metaphors of marriage. Also the metaphors themselves have often been misread, as with xcvii.[9]

Second, there is the fact that Tennyson is both conscious and unselfconscious in ways that work against his being a 'sexual heretic'. His gruff lack of self-consciousness is evident in his comment on cxxii, 'Oh, wast thou with me, dearest, then': 'If anybody thinks I ever called him "dearest" in his life they are much mistaken, for I never even called him "dear" '. Naïve, perhaps, but not tonally suggestive. There is the same directness, altogether unmisgiving, in Tennyson's story of the dream which he had the night before he received the letter offering him the Laureateship: 'That night he had had a dream that the Queen and the Prince had called on him at his Mother's and been very gracious, the Prince kissing him which made him think "very kind but very German".' Yet Tennyson combined this unselfconsciousness with an intelligent consciousness in this vicinity. When he praised Hallam for 'manhood fused with female grace', he was willing to make unembarrassedly explicit the likeness to Christ, 'that union of man and woman'. He saw such a union as

8. Epilogue: 'Nor have I felt so much of bliss / Since first he told me that he loved / A daughter of our house';'For I that danced her on my knee, / That watched her on her nurse's arm, / That shielded all her life from harm / At last must part with her to thee.' As elsewhere in Tennyson, a brother makes a good father.
9. Tennyson: 'The spirit yet in the flesh but united in love with the spirit out of the flesh resembles the wife of a great man of science.'

morally and religiously desirable, not sexually so. But he was careful (and again explicit) in distinguishing this ideal from anything tawdry, as in his epigram 'On One Who Affected an Effeminate Manner', or in his remark that 'Men should be androgynous and women gynandrous, but men should not be gynandrous nor women androgynous.' Moreover, like his friend Aubrey de Vere he was aware of the traditional truth about the poet's sexual empathy; de Vere did not giggle when asked if his devotion was to a lady: 'Certainly, if, as old Coleridge said, every true Poet is inclusively woman, but not the worse man on that account—Alfred Tennyson.' Man must grow more like woman, and vice versa, said Tennyson: 'More as the double-natured Poet each'. He will not have been dismayed at Swinburne's fine praise of the lines about the mother and her son's bones in Tennyson's late poem 'Rizpah': 'But six words of them . . . "they had moved in my side"—give perfect proof once more of the deep truth that great poets are bisexual.'

But, if Tennyson was not self-conscious, his son was—and by the 1890s, when he was writing the *Memoir*, misconstruction and suspicion must have seemed threatening. Hallam Tennyson therefore made the great mistake of censoring exactly those things in Tennyson which are jubilantly straight. A letter from Tennyson to James Spedding in February 1833, for instance, with its jokes about Arthur Hallam; Tennyson mockingly deplored Spedding's remarks about Hallam: 'Ironical sidehits at a person under the same roof with myself and filling more than a first half of the sheet—(i.e. not the person—but the sidehits—it looks as though I meant that the person in question slept with me and I assure you that we have a spare bed and that the bed is not so spare either, but a bed both plump and pulpy and fit for your domeship.' The banter is not strained or anxious.

The one argument in defence (so to speak) of Tennyson which does not effect much is the one that is usually reached for: the general claim that it is somehow unhistorical, naïvely post-Freudian, to imagine any such thing. Thus Gordon Haight said, 'The Victorians' conception of love between those of the same sex cannot be understood fairly by an age steeped in Freud. Where they saw only pure friendship, the modern reader assumes perversion. . . . Even *In Memoriam* for some, now has a troubling overtone.'[1] But, as so often, the position of the historical purist is itself unhistorical. '*Now* has a troubling overtone'? Some Victorians, who found Shakespeare's *Sonnets* troubling, found *In Memoriam* troubling.[2] The reviewer who attributed the poem to 'a female hand' may be dismissed as a joke,

1. *George Eliot: A Biography* (1968), p. 496.
2. Arthur Hallam had discussed Plato's 'frequent commendation of a more lively sentiment than has existed in other times between man and man, the misunderstanding of which has repelled several from the deep tenderness and splendid imaginations of the Phaedrus and the Symposium' ('Essay on Cicero', 1831).

albeit a disconcerting one, but the reviewer in *The Times* was no joke. He deplored 'the tone of . . . amatory tenderness', and after quoting from LXXIV he asked piercingly, 'Very sweet and plaintive these verses are, but who would not give them a feminine application?'

But why does it matter? Because even the least biographical of critics would have to admit that the last two lines of the following poignant section (never published by Tennyson) will have slightly different meanings according to our differing biographical judgments as to Tennyson's love:

> Speak to me from the stormy sky!
>   The wind is loud in holt and hill.
>   It is not kind to be so still.
> Speak to me, dearest, lest I die.
>
> Speak to me: let me hear or see!
>   Alas my life is frail and weak.
>   Seest thou my faults and wilt not speak?
> They are not want of love for thee.

T. S. Eliot said of *In Memoriam*, 'It is a long poem made by putting together lyrics, which have only the unity and continuity of a diary, the concentrated diary of a man confessing himself. It is a diary of which we have to read every word.' The analogy is suggestive, but as with the sonnet sequence the claim for this as an artistic unity should not be pressed; a diary is an ambiguous thing. Moreover, the parallel will have to include all those personal references which both set limits to the kind of success achieved by the poem and are the conditions of that success. Unobtrusively but persistently, Tennyson incorporated details of Hallam's life and writings; the wording of the poem incorporates reminiscences which then modify a reader's response.

> 'Tis well; 'tis something; we may stand
>   Where he in English earth is laid,
>   And from his ashes may be made
> The violet of his native land.
>
>   (XVIII)

With quiet grace and with a deeper timbre (this is no affectionate hyperbole), Tennyson is returning the compliment which Hallam had paid him: in his essay on Tennyson's poems, Hallam had quoted Persius, '*Nunc non e tumulo fortunataque favilla/nascentur violae*', remarking, 'When this Poet dies, will not the Graces and the Loves mourn over him?' Such reminiscences might create a stylistic analogy to the moral fact 'That men may rise on stepping-stones/Of their dead selves to higher things' (1). The phrase 'their dead selves' recalls Tennyson's earlier self, and those of his Cambridge friends, which may yet live as part of a moral evolution: the phrase had formed part of a poem by one of Tennyson's Cambridge friends in 1829 written to another. It is true that such allusions utter their confidences so quietly as to be confidential, and this privacy limits the nature of *In Memoriam*—but it also provides some of its sources of energy. Something of this paradox—*In Memoriam* is anonymous but confessional, private but naked—is caught in a sentence of R. H. Hutton's, which pits 'magnifying' against 'secret' in a delicate discussion of effects of scale within the poem: '*In Memoriam* is full of such magnifying-glasses for secret feelings, and doubts and fears, and hopes, and trusts.'

'Yet art thou oft as God to me': this exclamation (which Tennyson did not permit to emerge from manuscript) lends warrant to George Eliot's remark, 'Whatever was the immediate prompting of *In Memoriam*, whatever the form under which the author represented his aim to himself, the deepest significance of the poem is the sanctification of human love as a religion.' Yet here too there is the paradox in Tennyson which George Gilfillan noticed a few years before *In Memoriam* was published: 'His genius is bold, but is waylaid at almost every step by the timidity and weakness of his temperament.' But we need to distinguish two areas where this does apply from two where it does not. It does not, for example, justify the famous epigram of Verlaine's which Yeats reports: 'M. Verlaine talked . . . of "In Memoriam", which he had tried to translate and could not, because "Tennyson was too noble, too *Anglais*, and when he should have been broken-hearted had many reminiscences." ' Despite the insouciance, it is a torrid sentimentality, too *français*, which takes for granted that a broken heart and reminiscences must necessarily exist on different planes. Hearts may break with different causes and with different effects, and reminiscences may be those memories which are not softened but made even more poignant by being humanised and localised.

Nor does the accusation of timidity properly indict the religious position of *In Memoriam* as a whole. Certain expectations will be false ones; we should heed Tennyson's complaint that 'they are always speaking of me as if I were a writer of philosophical treatises', and we should receive with some scepticism articles on Tennyson and Teilhard de Chardin. The poem is explicit in not claiming to be able to arrive at religious truth by argument. This might be deplored on two quite different grounds: some believers might argue that Tennyson sells Christianity short in underrating the degree to which its beliefs are susceptible of substantiation by argument; or unbelievers might argue that it is bad for people to believe things which are not susceptible of argument. But Tennyson's poem offers almost all that can hereabouts he honestly offered by the Christian, and it is free of the heartlessness which comes from the conviction that the problems of pain, death, and evil can be dealt with by arguments. Dr Johnson rebuked such high-minded heartlessness in Soame Jenyns: 'I do not mean to reproach this author for not knowing what is equally hidden from learning and from ignorance. The shame is to impose words for ideas upon ourselves or others. To imagine that we are going forward when we are only turning round.' *In Memoriam* does not impose words for ideas; it does not claim—in argument, as distinct from mood and feelings—to be going forward but rather is turning round. Indeed, the *In Memoriam* stanza (*abba*) is especially suited to turning round rather than going forward.

Nevertheless, the accusation of timidity does hold in two ways. First, there are Tennyson's disclaimers, which go beyond the prudently modest and become disingenuously disarming.

> If these brief lays, of Sorrow born,
>   Were taken to be such as closed
>   Grave doubts and answers here proposed,
> Then these were such as men might scorn:
>   (XLVIII)

Swinburne was indignant about the 'incompatible incoherences of meditation and profession': 'To say that these effusions of natural sorrow make no pretence, and would be worthy of contempt if they pretended, to solve or satisfy men's doubts—and then to renew the appearance of an incessant or even a fitful endeavour after some such satisfaction or solution—is surely so incongruous as to sound almost insincere.'

Second, there are the local failures of nerve.

> But brooding on the dear one dead,
>   And all he said of things divine,
>   (And dear as sacramental wine
> To dying lips is all he said)
>   (XXXVII)

But *The Times* (28 November 1851) found this shocking: 'Can the writer satisfy his own conscience with respect to these verses? . . . For our part, we should consider no confession of regret too strong for the hardihood that indicated them.' The offending words were changed: '(And dear to me as sacred wine/To dying lips is all he said)'. The words 'to me' introduce an enfeebling tone of doubt or of the apologetically personal; there is now a swaying ('to me . . . to dying lips'). Tennyson had meant what he had written: sacramental, not sacred—the emphasis was on a solemn ceremony not only sacred in itself but having the power to make sacred. Tennyson would have done better to stand by his fiercely truthful hyperbole.

A similar thing happens with the pre-publication history of *In Memoriam*. In the first edition CXXIX ended,

> Strange friend, past, present, and to be;
>   Loved deeplier, darklier understood;
>   Behold, I dream a dream of good,
> And mingle all the world with thee.

The first two lines are superb; the suggestion of paradox in 'Strange friend' (the dead friend cannot but be a stranger) is beautifully taken up in 'Loved deeplier, darklier understood': when you love someone deeply, you do indeed understand them more and yet the understanding is not a simple illumination—love makes you more aware of the mysteriousness of another, makes you understand 'darklier' the person you understandingly love. It is not only the grave which darkens the relationship in such understanding (though that is Tennyson's starting point); to be loved deeplier even on earth would still be to be darklier understood. Yet the final two lines of the stanza are merely skilful, swathed in the Tennysonian. To FitzGerald, *In Memoriam* 'is full of finest things, but it is monotonous, and has that air of being evolved by a Poetical Machine of the highest order'. 'Behold', 'dream a dream', 'mingle': these here have something of the plangent tremulousness which comes when Tennyson is writing 'Parnassian'[3] verse. But, if Tennyson is remarkable at perfecting his own poetry, how is it that in the trial edition of *In Memoriam* this stanza is so much better? Because Tennyson became concerned, not to consummate his wording, but to retreat from a possibly offensive notion.

> Strange friend, past, present, and to be;
>   Loved deeplier, darklier understood;
>   Let me not lose my faith in good
> Lest I make less my love for thee.

Instead of Parnassian or Tennysonianisms, there is an austere confession that for Tennyson what counted supremely was not his faith in good but his love for Hallam. Because of the very mildness of tone, the effect is sharp to the point of paradox, and Tennyson must suddenly have realized that he had risked 'I could not love Honour so much, loved I not Hallam more.' Hence his retreat into the ripe fluency of Parnassian verse. His wording was always considered; sometimes it was too considerate.

3. Gerard Manley Hopkins's term for poetry that is skilful but mechanical [Editor].

There is much in *In Memoriam* that does not carry conviction. Its language falters or coarsens whenever Tennyson pretends that his life until the death of Hallam had been a happy one; whenever he swings into politics ('The blind hysterics of the Celt' is a line not without blindness and hysteria); whenever he refuses to admit that he cannot imagine heaven, let alone activity and energy in heaven; whenever he remembers his father; whenever he tries to feel that his love must daunt time, whereas it is time which does the daunting; whenever he makes any lordly claim about his attitude to death; whenever he has patent recourse to allegory (as in CIII); most of all, whenever he offers hopes which deep down he knows are hopeless.

'No, like a child in doubt and fear. . . . ' For it is the lack of conviction which carries the deepest conviction. 'It's too hopeful, this poem, more than I am myself.' At the last minute, he changed from the trial edition; he added the profound sincerity of VII, 'Dark house, by which once more I stand'; and LVI, with its bitter awareness of 'Nature, red in tooth and claw/With ravine'; and XCVI, in defence of 'honest doubt'. 'I should reproach Tennyson not for mildness, or tepidity, but rather for lack of serenity', said a poet whose deepest subject was his lack of serenity, T. S. Eliot: *In Memoriam* 'is not religious because of the quality of its faith, but because of the quality of its doubt. Its faith is a poor thing, but its doubt is a very intense experience.'

Where then should the stress fall? Pre-eminently on the poems of most intense feeling, and these tend to be the darkest. Tennyson was not simply 'a morbid and unhappy mystic' (in Harold Nicolson's words), since he was many things; but such is here the profoundest of his writing. II, 'Old Yew, which graspest at the stones'; VII, 'Dark house'; XV, 'Tonight the winds begin to rise'; L,

> Be near me when my light is low,
>   When the blood creeps, and the nerves prick
>   And tingle; and the heart is sick,
> And all the wheels of Being slow.

There are not many such sections, even when we add the supreme evocations of geological time, such as CXXIII, 'There rolls the deep where grew the tree'. Yet we should not underrate the very different evocations of 'tender gloom', the sections which have a Horatian elegiac serenity. Such sections—which constitute not the poem's faith, but its hope—do not evade the perplexity and questioning. They accommodate them within a world of imagined peace (that it is imagined is not disguised, so that the effect is at once calmative and tense), a world in which 'perplex' becomes a matter of the ship's gentle passage: 'All night no ruder air perplex/Thy sliding keel' (IX);

a world in which the answers to our direst questions, to our sense
that we are in a mist, might be as forthcoming, as heartening, as the
Christmas bells: 'The Christmas bells from hill to hill/Answer each
other in the mist' (XXVIII). One thinks of such sections as IX, 'Fair
ship, that from the Italian shore'; XI, 'Calm is the morn without a
sound'; XVII, 'Thou comest, much wept for'; XLIII, 'If Sleep and Death
be truly one'; LXXXIII, 'Dip down upon the northern shore'; LXXXVI,
'Sweet after showers, ambrosial air'; XCV, 'By night we lingered on
the lawn'; CXV, 'Now fades the last long streak of snow'; CXXI, 'Sad
Hesper o'er the buried sun'; and the magnificent moonlit landscape
in the epilogue. The modern sentimentality of darkness is discon-
certed by the truthful hope (a hope justified and sensitively circum-
scribed) such as is appropriate at the end of this epithalamium which
imagines the future offspring of a happy union as an augury of a
happier future.

Hopkins was perturbed in 1864 when he realized Tennyson's
imperfections. But he saw that there was already more danger of
being 'fooled' into underrating Tennyson than into overrating him:

> He is, one must see it, what we used to call Tennysonian. But
> the discovery of this must not make too much difference. When
> puzzled by one's doubts it is well to turn to a passage like this.
> Surely your maturest judgment will never be fooled out of saying
> that this is divine, terribly beautiful—the stanza of *In Memo-
> riam*, beginning with the quatrain

> > O [*read* Sad] Hesper o'er the buried sun
> >   And ready, thou, to die with him,
> >   Thou watchest all things ever dim
> > And dimmer, and a glory done.[4]

'And ready, thou, to die with him': muted and tender, distant but
immediate, it is one of Tennyson's finest evocations of what a mature
act of self-sacrifice should aspire to resemble. It does not speak of
Christ's sacrifice, but it hints at the mystery of the Trinity, for 'Sad
Hesper' and 'Bright Phosphor' are even better than one and the
same; they are also two and the same. The division within Tennyson,
especially the division between present and past, is here healed:

> Sweet Hesper-Phosphor, double name
>   For what is one, the first, the last,
>   Thou, like my present and my past,
> Thy place is changed; thou art the same.

In Memoriam, like so many of Tennyson's poems, stands obliquely
to its ending. As a sequence of poems, it is involved constantly in

---

4. Gerard Manley Hopkins, *Further Letters*, p. 219; 10 September 1864.

ending and then again beginning. Its untitled prologue, 'Strong Son of God, immortal Love', which precedes section I, has been described as 'a conclusion more truly than an opening to *In Memoriam*. Insofar as it is a prologue, it is one not so much to the poems it precedes as to the new way of life Tennyson was about to enter.'[5] Mrs Mattes notes too that the trial edition had this prologue before, and not after, the title *In Memoriam A.H.H. Obiit MDCCCXXXIII*, which made a considerable break and gave a different impression of the prologue's relationship to the succeeding poems.

In Memoriam both yearns for and fears an end. 'O last regret, regret can die!' (LXXVIII): can the immediate rebuke, 'No—', cancel such a fear?

> And saying; 'Comes he thus, my friend?
>   Is this the end of all my care?'
>   And circle moaning in the air:
> 'Is this the end? Is this the end?'
>
> (XII)

For the moaning fear is that the end (*finis*) may be something quite other than an end as a purpose or goal.[6] 'What end is here to my complaint?' He wishes not to be in pain, but it is his pain which is the living witness to his love.[7]

> Oh, if indeed that eye foresee
>   Or see (in Him is no before)
>   In more of life true life no more
> And Love the indifference to be
>
> (XXVI)

—then welcome death. What Tennyson most wants in all the world is to exorcise this fear about Hallam: that he is in his grave, and oh the indifference to be.[8]

On such a quest, to travel hopelessly is better than to arrive. Hence the felicity of Tennyson's choice of stanza for *In Memoriam: abba*, which can 'circle moaning in the air', returning to its setting out, and with fertile circularity staving off its deepest terror of arrival at

5. E. B. Mattes, *In Memoriam: The Way of a Soul* (1951), p. 98.
6. The manuscript of 'Ulysses' had included the haunting line 'As though to live were all the end of life'.
7. Sometimes Love vindicates itself, as in the beautifully paradoxical placing of 'fail' at the end of cxxv, where the rhythm and the buoyant persistence insist on a feeling of triumph not of life's failing:

> Abiding with me till I sail
>   To seek thee on the mystic deeps,
>   And this electric force, that keeps
> A thousand pulses dancing, fail.

8. Compare Wordsworth, "She dwelt among th'untrodden ways," lines 11–12: "But she is in the Grave, and Oh! / The difference to me" [Editor].

desolation and indifference. It is a stanza which rises to a momentary chime and then fades—but does not fade into despair or vacuity, only into dimness and regret, since after all (after all its lines) there comes the distant rhyme. It is the perfect embodiment of the true relationship of faith to faintness in the poem:

> I stretch lame hands of faith, and grope,
>   And gather dust and chaff, and call
>   To what I feel is Lord of all,
> And faintly trust the larger hope.
>
> (LV)

Faith, trust, and hope are there, but they are framed within something fainter, a fainter rhyme scheme. The very reasons which make the stanza so utterly unsuitable for sustained argument (and whose pressures help to make such sections of argument in *In Memoriam* so feeble and ill judged)—its continual receding from its affirmations, from what it momentarily clinches, so unlike the disputatious sequences of the heroic couplet: these make it the emblem as well as the instrument for poems in which moods ebb and flow ('There twice a day the Severn fills'), in which hopes are recurrent but always then dimmed—though never shattered. R. H. Hutton remarked that it was a feature of Tennyson's style, this 'air of moving through a resisting medium'; Henry James likewise saw the style as 'poised and stationary': 'the phrase always seems to me to pause and slowly pivot upon itself, or at most to move backward'. On the *In Memoriam* stanza itself, a most perceptive comment was made by Kingsley in 1850: 'their metre, so exquisitely chosen, that while the major rhyme in the second and third lines of each stanza gives the solidity and self-restraint required by such deep themes, the mournful minor rhyme of each first and fourth line always leads the ear to expect something beyond'. Tennyson senses what such a shape can do.

> Bring in great logs and let them lie,
>   To make a solid core of heat;
>   Be cheerful-minded, talk and treat
> Of all things even as he were by
>
> (CVII)

—where the birthday festivity for Hallam, the solid core of heat and of warm cheerfulness, is the solid core of the stanza itself.[9] Or the Christmas bells:

> Four voices of four hamlets round,
>   From far and near, on mead and moor,

9. Such festivity exists now only in the imagination, and pain is being staved off. Emily's journal, 6 August 1871: 'I think Alfred has a happy birthday though we do not mention it to him.'

> Swell out and fail, as if a door
> Were shut between me and the sound
> > (XXVIII)

—where the sense that the bells 'swell out and fail' is evoked through the stanza's own pattern of sounds.

The *In Memoriam* stanza is an instance of what Geoffrey Hartman has subtly explored as a relationship of ends to middles in the language of poetry. He quoted Milton's line 'Sonorous metal blowing martial sounds', suggesting that we look at it 'as generated from a redundant concept, "sonorous sounds", which we recover by collapsing the ends. The verse, from this perspective, is the separating out of "sonorous sounds"; a refusal, by inserting a verbal space between adjective and noun, to let them converge too soon.'[1] The *In Memoriam* stanza, though it permits convergence, does so on the strict condition that it be temporary—that it not be, in the strictest sense, final.

> And bless thee, for thy lips are bland,
> > And bright the friendship of thine eye;
> > And in my thoughts with scarce a sigh
> I take the pressure of thine hand.
> > (CXIX)

That last line has its tension and force—indeed, its pressure—from the way in which it declines to hurry or economize itself into 'I take thine hand'. So 'take' gains a gravity, a sense of endurance, and 'take the pressure' has something of taking a weight or a strain or a responsibility; the pressure is at once gently affectionate and pressing. At which point one notices that the last two lines themselves re-enact the form of the stanza, *abba*; set within the stanza with unobtrusive delicacy, the pattern refines itself to a conclusion: '*And* in my thoughts with scarce a *sigh/I* take the pressure of thine *hand*'.

And the poem's ending? It hated to contemplate the short-term eventuality, so to speak, but it could trust in the eventual, the 'event' of all time:

> That friend of mine who lives in God,
>
> That God, which ever lives and loves,
> > One God, one law, one element,
> > And one far-off divine event,
> To which the whole creation moves.

It is the distance which lends enchantment and might never ask for it back; one day the creation would arrive at the time 'when there

1. "The Voice of the Shuttle," *Beyond Formalism* (1970), p. 339.

should be time no longer' (Revelation 10:6–7). In the meantime, *E pur si muove*.[2] Again in the meantime, 'that friend of mine' receives his last tribute, for it was Hallam himself whose sonnet on the Three Fates had spoken of 'The Love/Toward which all being solemnly doth move'.

TIMOTHY PELTASON

[Reading *In Memoriam*]†

In Memoriam was so quickly and surely established as the representative poem of its age and of its author that it must always have been difficult to appreciate its extravagance and its idiosyncrasy. Taken most often as the comfortably conventional expression of conventionally comfortable feelings, especially by those who have not read it recently or carefully, the poem is, in fact, very oddly made: each of its 700-odd stanzas the product of daunting and obvious formal constraint; all of its stanzas collected together into a large and uncertain form the rules of which nobody can quite discern. And it looks oddly made with good reason. Even for Tennyson, whose methods of composition were never straightforward or regular, the making of *In Memoriam* was a protracted and peculiar and largely a hidden business. Moreover, the individual lyrics just do not sound like most of Tennyson's previous poetry, so in recognizing them as Tennysonian, we must widen the reference of that adjective. The shortness of the lines; the almost laconic sharpness and concision of many of them; the trying out of ideas that must have seemed to Tennyson's earnest fellow Apostles,[1] as well as to the harshly sensible critics of his first volumes, a bold striking out in new directions; the frankly autobiographical bearing of many of the lyrics: all of these signal Tennyson's possession of a new expressive idiom, an idiom that has arisen in response to new expressive needs and that reflects the exemplary strangeness of Tennyson's life and sensibility.

Begun in 1833 within a few weeks of Arthur Hallam's death, the sections of *In Memoriam* were written at many times and in many places over the next ten or fifteen years, but kept mostly out of sight while Tennyson revised the poems of his 1832 volume, wrote and rewrote the new poems that he would publish with his earlier work

---

2. "And yet it moves" (Italian); words attributed to Galileo, speaking of the earth's revolution around the sun [Editor].

† From *Reading* In Memoriam (Princeton: Princeton University Press, 1985), pp. 3–18. Copyright © Princeton University Press. Reprinted by permission of the publisher.

1. The society for intellectual debate to which Tennyson and Hallam belonged at Cambridge [Editor].

in 1842, wrote and then published *The Princess* in 1847, and lived the vagabond life that Robert Bernard Martin's recent biography has documented. Tennyson's father had died in 1831, and Hallam's death overturned the family once again, withdrawing suddenly the promise of some settlement in life, not just for Tennyson's sister Emily, who was engaged to marry Hallam, but for the whole family, whose connection to him must have seemed the connection to a world more securely and comfortingly ordinary than their own. In the seventeen years between Hallam's death and the publication of *In Memoriam* in 1850, Tennyson himself fell in and out of love with one woman, made and broke for ten years an engagement with another, worked on many different tasks, and lived and visited in many different inns and watering places and homes, none of them truly his own. And somewhere behind or between the narratable events of this period and the published poems, Tennyson was writing the different sections of *In Memoriam*, ranging widely in subject and mood, but keeping strictly to the four-line stanza and *abba* rhyme scheme that he had either chosen or fallen into as a way of binding together what he once considered calling his *Fragments of an Elegy*. Most of these fragments had probably been written by 1842, but they were not gathered together into the poem we now read until some time close to its official publication in May 1850, just a few weeks before Tennyson gathered together his private life as well, married Emily Sellwood, and settled at last into a home.

The finished poem records little of the external movement of this period of Tennyson's life, but registers finely and variously the psychic homelessness that accompanied it, the puzzled alternations of mood, the strange sense of starting over again with each new mood or moment, the persistent and frustrated search to put an end to this wandering among moods and to discover some stabilizing pattern in the history of recorded moments. For *In Memoriam* is exactly what Denis Donoghue has called all of Tennyson's poetry, "a Book of Moments,"[2] a book in which one moment, one lyric may continue from the last or may seem to replace it absolutely, leaving reader and poet together to confront the mysterious and unwilled changefulness of experience. The short sections of the poem, each divided into stanzas and each stanza closed in upon itself by rhyme, present to the reader discrete fragments of experience, momentary and present apprehensions. Even when individual lyrics look forward or back, as they regularly do, they are written from and for the present. The tentative organizations of experience achieved from within any moment can claim no final authority and must expose themselves to disruption or disproof in the moments that follow. And then these

2. In *The Ordinary Universe* (New York: Macmillan, 1968), p. 97.

moments, too, present themselves to be assimilated, organized, understood.

As a long poem made up of short poems, *In Memoriam* naturally interests itself in the way that short structures build into longer ones, the relations of part to part and part to whole. But this formalistic language hardly evokes our experience of the poem, and the parts and wholes of *In Memoriam* are not empty forms. The investigation that the poem conducts into the relationship of parts and wholes is an investigation also of the principles of psychic change and of the possibility of psychic integrity, conducted from within the history of a single troubled and speculative consciousness. And when this consciousness takes on itself the burden of the exemplary, it casts the questioning of its own integrity in time as a questioning of the larger possibility of historical connection, where history is both what happens between one moment and the next and between the beginning of time and the end.

Mediating between these two extremes is the appropriate task of a poem whose form is the attempt to register great change incrementally and whose speaker is, in Tennyson's own words, "not always the author speaking of himself, but the voice of the human race speaking through him."[3] Tennyson earned the poet laureateship by writing *In Memoriam*—it is hard to imagine a reward more fitting or more truly deserved—and the poem repeatedly offers itself as a representative unit of human history, a model, for better or worse, of the individual life and the life of the species. Yet there is resistance as well as encouragement to this identification of the poet with his kind. The relationship of the part to the whole is antagonistic as well as constructive, and many individual lyrics subvert or challenge the process by which they are assimilated into a large and exemplary narrative, declaring the sovereignty of the moment and the absolute privacy and idiosyncrasy of the poet's experience. At the same time, however, this process of assimilation necessarily goes forward as one lyric, one moment follows another and as the poet continues to put his experience before us. Neither the poem nor its readers can renounce the difficult task of gathering things together and seeing them whole, of giving a name to the uncertain shapes of history, of human experience, of *In Memoriam*.

What the whole of *In Memoriam* teaches, we must stand outside any one of its parts to determine. And yet it is inside the poem, in the lyric-by-lyric experience of reading it, that we are given such carefully leading advice about how such determinations might be made. The parts of *In Memoriam*, both in their evocations of the moment and in their readings of one another, teach that history is

3. [Hallam Tennyson], *Alfred Lord Tennyson: A Memoir* (London: Macmillan, 1897), I, 305.

Christian and redemptive, that it is evolutionary and progressive, that it is evolutionary and vicious, that it is meaningless and chaotic, that it is unreal, a travesty of the uniquely living moment. But whatever its models of human history, and even in its denials of history or of shared models for anything, the poem cannot help confronting the blank fact of change, a human mystery about which something must be said.

In section LXXVII, for instance, the poet thinks about the fate of his poem in history and the world.

> What hope is here for modern rhyme
> To him, who turns a musing eye
> On songs, and deeds, and lives, that lie
> Foreshorten'd in the tract of time?
>
> These mortal lullabies of pain
> May bind a book, may line a box,
> May serve to curl a maiden's locks;
> Or when a thousand moons shall wane
>
> A man upon a stall may find,
> And, passing, turn the page that tells
> A grief, then changed to something else,
> Sung by a long-forgotten mind.
>
> But what of that? My darken'd ways
> Shall ring with music all the same;
> To breathe my loss is more than fame,
> To utter love more sweet than praise.[4]

In the grimly reductive fantasy of the first two stanzas, history destroys the spirit, and the living, breathing language of the poet falls into the ludicrously material. The only resistance to this extreme materialism is in the extreme spiritualism of the last stanza, the defiant claim that value resides wholly in the self-sufficient act of the poet. He does not need history or an audience, but only the instantaneous fulfillment of his own expression. And lying between these two extremes is the poem's attractively modest and empirical description of itself; between the fantasy that it will have no worldly, historical career and the pretense that it needs none, the poem encounters its reader—the man browsing in the stall—and the inescapable fact that it is itself an action in time. Pages must be turned, grief changes.

"A grief, then changed to something else"; this perfectly captures

---

4. All citations from *In Memoriam* are from the edition of Susan Shatto and Marion Shaw (Oxford: Oxford University Press, 1982). Hereafter cited as Shatto and Shaw.

the oddity and suddenness of transition from one section to the next
of *In Memoriam*, or even from one line to the next within a section,
as well as the deep mystery of the poet's spiritual regeneration. Mood
succeeds mood according to some law or chance beyond the poet's
control. The pressing concern then is to account for these changes,
to ask how they come about and to ask if they constitute the coherent
history of an integrated self or only the "wild and wandering cries"
(Prologue) of a self in fragments. Or is there another form of coherence, another way to redeem these fragments besides their absorption into a genetic history? These questions are both evaluative and
analytic, questions about the success of Tennyson's effort to make a
long poem out of short poems, as well as about the content and
conduct of the poet's analysis of his own experience.

By "the poet" I do not mean the historical Tennyson, but the first
person of *In Memoriam*, a figure who inhabits the poem, but also
knows that he is creating it in words and meters: not Tennyson, but
not just a character or "the speaker."[5] The evaluative question is not
answered, but is at least asked more sympathetically and more
searchingly, when we recognize in this way that Tennyson has gone
before us and so arranged matters that the mourner's self-analysis is
also a poet's self-criticism. More and more often as the poem moves
forward, the poet is reading as he writes—"What words are these
have fall'n from me?" (XVI)—and asking himself what coherent and
speakable meaning can be extracted from the experiences that are
arranged before him. And this presses us to ask, as both a critical
and a philosophical question, what the very fact of arrangement
means for the discrete value of single lyrics and single moments. Is
the uniqueness and intensity of the moment betrayed or enhanced
by its assimilation into a larger whole? Is *In Memoriam* more or less
than the sum of its parts?

Much more, I think, and I have already started to say why in my
remarks on the enriching appropriateness of the poem's structure to
its subject matter. But I should address more explicitly the objections
of those critics for whom the structure of the poem is inadequate to
its large aims and irrelevant to an appreciation of its local excellences. And I should begin, as such critics generally do, with the
apparent depreciation of this structure by Tennyson himself.

"The sections [of *In Memoriam*] were written at many different
places," said Tennyson, "and as the phases of our intercourse came
to my memory and suggested them. I did not write them with any

5. Although I keep the poet and the author carefully distinct, I have not hesitated to call the
poet's friend "Hallam"—as he does not hesitate to call him "Arthur." Nothing is lost by
this identification, and it helps to keep down the elegant variations on "his friend," "his
lost friend," "his beloved friend," etc.

view of weaving them into a whole, or for publication, until I found that I had written so many."[6] Though often cited as evidence that *In Memoriam* is rather a collection of fragments than a single, long poem, this remark might as easily describe the value that Tennyson attached to the work of weaving as a distinct creative activity. This weaving is not the province of "the poet," whose moods, like ours, seem to come unbidden and whose will exerts itself against the massy personifications that figure forth his conscious experience—Love, Grief, the Hours, Sorrow, Nature: not the province of "the poet," but of the author, whose offstage manipulations give the poem its structure. For many modern admirers of *In Memoriam,* this separation of creative faculties requires little discussion, and the poem successfully imitates, in T. S. Eliot's phrase, "the concentrated diary of a man confessing himself,"[7] or, another of Tennyson's provisional titles, *The Way of a Soul.* But for many others the separation between the writer of the individual lyrics and their arranger, between the poet and the author, is insistently there to be described, or to be regretted.

Christopher Ricks, offering the most acute and explicit of recent challenges to the unity of the poem, will not settle for "the unity and continuity of a diary" perceived by Eliot. *"The Way of a Soul,"* says Ricks, "would indeed provide a graph, but a graph is not the same thing as an artistic unity."[8] Citing Charles Kingsley and Humphry House as allies, Ricks cannot find in *In Memoriam* the "conscious or organic method" or "single theme" that would unify the poem. The "links and cross-connections" among the sections do begin to weave the poem together, he acknowledges, but he does not think or make much of these and goes on to make an obscure, but apparently significant, distinction. "The Christmases, or the imagery of dark and light, of water and the human hand: these do much in the way of 'weaving them into a whole,' but it remains weaving, not growing or building." Ricks is distinguishing, I suppose, between an order imposed upon experience from without and an order that experience assumes, or convincingly seems to assume, in its own unforced unfolding. He wants *In Memoriam* to grow or to build as a piece of music builds, but not to be built—or woven—by an unseen hand. Alternatively, or perhaps in addition, Ricks and other critics of the poem's unity want a fuller and finer weaving of its parts, an arrangement that will show the relevance of each part to the whole and that

6. *Memoir*, I, 304.
7. *"In Memoriam,"* in *Selected Essays* (New York: Harcourt, Brace and Co., 1950), p. 291 [see above, p. 136].
8. *Tennyson* (New York: Macmillan, 1972), p. 214 [see above, p. 174]. Although I am here setting my own views in contrast to those of Mr. Ricks, I must gratefully acknowledge a large debt to his work on Tennyson, both to the critical book I have cited and to his superb edition of Tennyson's poems. He is the critic of Tennyson with whom I have most often been engaged in mental conversation in the writing of this book.

will complete the exposition of a single, great theme. Either the poet or the author must exert greater control over his material and claim greater responsibility for the organization of the whole. But if it is not clear that woven things are less adequately made than things that grow or build, neither is it clear that "unity" is what *In Memoriam* must be shown to have in order to justify a decision to read and value it as a whole, long poem and not just as a collection of lyric hits and near misses. Long poems may be separable into parts, uneven in quality, and wayward in exposition—*In Memoriam* is all of these—and still require our attentiveness to the arranged relations between their parts and to the implicit and explicit claims to significance made by these arrangements.

It is not, then, a question of voting "yes" or "no" on the unity of *In Memoriam*. Ricks does not define, and I cannot define, "unity" in a way that makes the question of its mere presence or absence an interesting one. The question is how and how much to talk about *In Memoriam* and especially about the "links and cross-connections" that Ricks acknowledges, but spends no time on in his survey of the poem. The emphasis on local excellences results, in fact, in a serious undervaluing of individual lyrics, a failure to appreciate the extent to which lyrics and groups of lyrics serve one another as context or as subject matter. I am coming back around, of course, to an emphasis on the relations of part to part and part to whole, relations to which *In Memoriam*, in the felicity of its design, cannot help calling attention. The sections of *In Memoriam* do not just echo and remember one another, as Ricks's designedly dull catalogue of "links and cross-connections" suggests, but place in sequence and opposition an array of different arguments for feeling one way or another, and an array of self-sufficient moods that deny the place of argument in feeling, but whose sequence nevertheless constitutes an argument. This anteriority of mood to argument—the sense that even our experiences of inwardness may be passively discovered as much as willed or created or rationally chosen—is essential to the distinctively Tennysonian feel of *In Memoriam* and militates against attempts to explain the poet's progress as the working-through of a necessary and rational plan. And yet the poet does progress. A single ecstatic or grief-stricken part of *In Memoriam* may deny the authority of the whole, while the whole determines and limits the significance of any part and claims a separate authority for its own large movement from grief to affirmation. This tension between the part and the whole is the poem's continuous criticism of itself, and subsequent criticism properly acknowledges and builds upon it.

To read the parts of *In Memoriam* against the background of the whole, it is necessary, first, of course, to read them, and Ricks's criticisms might reasonably be directed at those accounts of the poem that spend more time on the elaborated unity of the whole than on the complexity and resistance of individual lyrics. The large structure of the poem can be overvalued and overemphasized by readings of the poem that accept its progress uncritically and that identify meaning with narrative content or, even more reductively, with narrative outcome. Such readings pause only briefly over the language of individual lyrics in retelling one version or another of the poet's story, a story in which these lyrics have only the value of incidents or illustrations. This plot-oriented criticism originates in a respect that I share for Tennyson's powers of construction and can reveal new patterns and correspondences in the poem, as well as solve in one way the problem of talking about a long poem in a limited space. But the emphasis upon plot serves Tennyson ill, even so, because it is not the separable plot of *In Memoriam* that can compel assent or admiration from the unconverted reader.

A narrative account of the poet's progress offers no new or persuasive versions of religious truth or religious experience, nothing that enables the doubtful reader to join the poet in his passage to comfort, whether we see that passage as having been accomplished by crisis and redemption or by gradual evolution. Both the gradualist and the apocalyptic visions of human experience in *In Memoriam* are too familiar to shake the reader into any new understanding, and none of the possible models of human history that the poem proposes can settle the human experience it documents into a single meaningful shape. But this limitation need not diminish the poem, as it will appear to do in any reading that has no time for the careful examination of individual lyrics. This is because Tennyson does not have to be a great and original arranger of the history of the person or the race in order for *In Memoriam* to be a great and original poem.

In Memoriam is a poem about many things, but especially about the arranging impulse in human consciousness, about the conditions under which we find ourselves pressed into making new sense of experience. One of its discoveries is precisely that the great arrangements of human life are not original or idiosyncratic, but historically and tribally sanctioned. For the poet, the impulse to arrange his life into some meaningful order is simultaneously the impulse to identify his own life with all other lives and with the course of human history. And so he finds his loss of Hallam analogous to the fall of man and looks forward to reunion with Hallam as he does to the "far-off divine event" that is the goal of the race. Or he finds his history of trials and sufferings analogous to the geological history of the planet or the evolution of the species. Or he finds the model for his own expression of grief and renewal in the forms of pastoral and romantic elegy. In this variety of ways, the poet experiences and interprets and calls into question the gathering up of his life into some larger order, which is at once the gathering up of fragments into the whole of *In Memoriam* and the emergence of the suffering poet as "the voice of the human race." And this experiencing and interpreting and calling into question happen in the way that consciousness happens, as a sequence of virtually present moments, each one of which is both inside and outside the history that it at once examines and enters.

In Memoriam comes to us in a form that insists upon both the autonomy and the connectedness of the individual moment, the individual lyric, and, as form finds its appropriate content, upon both the autonomy and the connectedness of the person. The interest and value of the poem do not lie in its elaborate or persuasive rendering of any one arrangement of the human world, but in its power both to realize and to examine the experience of a single consciousness as it wakens to and resists its exemplary condition, an apprehension at once of community and of mortality. And this interest and value will hardly survive translation into the terms of a critical overview. The experience is real, the examination subtle and rigorous, and the resistance credible only in the language of individual lyrics.

I will turn in a few pages to the reading of these individual lyrics, to Tennyson's language as the justification for my own and as the only possible proving ground for my interpretation and my high evaluation of *In Memoriam*. But I have wanted to establish briefly the terms of my argument for the poem and especially for the artistic value of its special self-consciousness, for the ways in which it turns to account the oddity of its form and composition. The uncertain progress from one lyric to the next becomes an exemplary spiritual exercise, the work of weaving together discrete fragments becomes a poetic subject as well as a poetic problem, and this subject is dignified and enlarged by the experienced complexity of feeling that the poem offers. Self-reference is not an absolute good in poems, but when *In Memoriam* refers to itself it refers to significant human and poetic matters. The formalist critic who follows out these references does not abandon the great themes of the poem and of literary history, but examines them in the new ways that the poem itself makes possible.

Several of these great themes I have already touched upon in my suggestions that the productively troubled relationship of the part to the whole is at once the relationship of the moment to history, of consciousness to itself over time, and of the solitary self of the poet to all the different communities that he feels called upon to enter and to represent. The poem thus becomes an important event in, and an important commentary upon, Tennyson's own career—upon the notorious and intimately symbiotic relationship of "the two Tennysons"—and also upon literary history, particularly upon the history of Romanticism.

As a long poem made up of fragments, *In Memoriam* stands significantly between the long poems of the early nineteenth century and the self-conscious patchwork of such modern poems as *The Waste Land* and Pound's *Cantos*. The special interest of the poem as a link between the lyric practice of the early nineteenth and the early twentieth centuries is suggested by this passage from Robert Langbaum's *The Poetry of Experience*, one of the first of a distinguished and now various series of books to affirm the continuity of nineteenth- and twentieth-century poetry and the continuing dominance of Romanticism. Langbaum boldly names "the essential idea of Romanticism":

> That essential idea is . . . the doctrine of experience—the doctrine that the imaginative apprehension gained through immediate experience is primary and certain, whereas the analytic reflection that follows is secondary and problematical. The poetry of the nineteenth and twentieth centuries can thus be seen in connection as a poetry of experience—a poetry constructed upon the deliberate disequilibrium between experience and idea, a poetry which makes its statement not as an idea but as an experience from which one or more ideas can be extracted as problematical rationalizations.[9]

It is hard, as we read it, to take in and to test this assertion adequately, an assertion to whose explication Langbaum devotes the whole of an important and intelligent book. I would wish to demote "the" essential idea to an essential idea and to question the clear and sure hierarchy between primary and secondary, but I nevertheless think that Langbaum's formulation helps to bring into clearer relationship a great deal of obviously but obscurely connected material, from the first expressions of Romantic intuitionism and the quest for an "unmediated vision," to the prestige of "the objective correlative," to the latest assertion in poetry workshop or composition text of the superiority of "showing" to "telling." Langbaum's formulation helps to make clear another of the uses of *In Memoriam* and, especially, of the formal analysis of parts and wholes that follows the poem's reflections upon itself in the making. For it is precisely in the terms of Langbaum's formulation that Tennyson's works, especially *In Memoriam*, have often been depreciated as too much the mere statement of ideas. But *In Memoriam* is the book of intimately quo-

9. *The Poetry of Experience* (New York: Random House, 1957), pp. 35–36. Alan Sinfield also cites this passage in *The Language of Tennyson's "In Memoriam"* (Oxford: Basil Blackwell, 1971), p. 26.

tidian experience, too—"the concentrated diary of a man confessing himself"—and it may serve, if we will give full value to its experience and to its ideas and to their mutual criticism, as a profound meditation upon Langbaum's "essential idea" and as a central document in the history of Romanticism.

I should say something, too, about the great theme or themes that I will leave undiscussed, the themes of love and friendship. George Eliot said of *In Memoriam* that "the deepest significance of the poem is the sanctification of human love as a religion"[1] and Tennyson might well have agreed with her. But love and friendship are subjects of the poem only as they are idiosyncratically redefined by it. Although *In Memoriam* is obsessively concerned with a particular form of human relationship, this is not simply or precisely the relationship between loving friends. It is rather the relationship between a living friend and a dead one, between presence and absence, a relationship conducted over distance and through memory. Nor does memory do its work unaided in the poem. The poet does not commune with his absent friend in acts of pure introspection, but by reading the signs of his presence as they are secreted in landscapes, houses, and significant places, or as they are retained in his letters, or as they are absolutely created in imagination, with the poet writing stories of the history that never happened. Arthur Hallam himself is not a vivid presence, but a vivid absence, and the poet several times acknowledges his inability to commemorate his friend by depicting him or by reviving in narrative the experience of their friendship.

But this does not mean that Tennyson has followed his genius into solipsism or selfishness or that *In Memoriam* is a study of consciousness in isolation. It is, on the contrary, a poem about being in company, but particularly about the kind of company we are in when we read, about the company of the person who isn't there. Hallam is a "strange friend" (CXXIX) to the poet, a friend from the other side of a border or great divide. And the poet is a strange friend to his readers, of whose presence he becomes increasingly aware and whose companionship he solicits by offering his experience as representative.

A last great theme must be brought into view, if only to explain why I approach it so obliquely in the pages that follow. If *In Memoriam* is *a* great Romantic poem, it is surely *the* great agnostic poem, and God, as well as Hallam, is the absent friend whose uncertain signs the poet reads. But even the weirdly faithful agnosticism of the poem—the civil religion of the West for the last two centuries—looks more rigorous and can be looked at more rigorously through the analysis of poetic form, and this is the analysis that a close and

1. *Westminster Review*, October 1855. Quoted in Ricks, *Tennyson*, p. 221.

responsive reading of *In Memoriam* forces on us. Very late in the
poem, for instance, in section CXXVIII, the poet confronts the apparent chaos of human history and responds with an assertion of faith
characteristic both in its tentativeness and in its yoking of artistic
and cosmic order:

> No doubt vast eddies in the flood
>   Of onward time shall yet be made,
>   And throned races may degrade;
> Yet O ye mysteries of good,
>
> Wild Hours that fly with Hope and Fear,
>   If all your office had to do
>   With old results that looked like new;
> If this were all your mission here,
> . . . .
> Why then my scorn might well descend
>   On you and yours. I see in part
>   That all, as in some piece of art,
> Is toil coöperant to an end.

Although often quoted as evidence and illustration of Tennyson's
vision of order, the closing assertion of this lyric is, in fact, abrupt
and unsponsored and sends us back over the ground of the poet's
faith in this and previous lyrics. The "part" of human history from
which the poet has inferred his vision of order is apparently the
course of mourning and recovery recorded in the poem. But "seeing
in part" describes both a method of induction and its necessary limitation. The vision of order that has assisted in the poet's recovery is
now inferred from it and then arbitrarily linked to the meaningful
ordering of "some piece of art," a phrase that refers us inevitably to
In Memoriam and to a consideration of its larger order. And the
poet's relation to that order is neither innocent nor authoritative. On
the one hand, he imposes an order by writing a quotable (and often-
quoted) conclusion to his lyric that is itself an attempt at the justifying "end" that it describes. On the other hand, he can refer only
uncertainly to "some piece of art"—a slightly offhand phrase that
works against itself by suggesting the fragmentary where we expect
an image of exalted harmony. He makes this reference from inside
a work of art whose structure he is confronting as experience. The
providential hand of Tennyson the arranger he must take on faith,
just as we decide to believe or not in Tennyson's arrangement of
experience as truthfully or disinterestedly observed. Comparing an
order discovered to an order created, Tennyson makes an assertion
as arbitrary, as circular, as confessedly fallible, as temptingly and
aesthetically "right" as the act of faith.

So Tennyson's faith in a larger order is at least partly a faith in the
achieved wholeness of his own creation. And his celebrated failures
of faith are challenges to that wholeness, appearing in what may be
regarded as rebellions of the part from the whole. The unique self
and the unique moment rise up and refuse their membership in the
redemptive systems of community and of history, and they do so in
the space of memorable individual lyrics that refuse to cooperate
toward the end of the Epilogue, that refuse to be read as preparations
for "the one far-off divine event" to which the creation and the poem
both move. T. S. Eliot's preference for Tennyson's doubt over his
faith—"a poor thing" Eliot calls it—is well known and rightly influ-
ential, although it has surely influenced many people who hardly
share Eliot's special reasons for deprecating a faith so carefully cir-
cumscribed and uncertainly professed. But Eliot was responding to
what is there for every reader, to what James Kincaid has named as
"the darkness and irresolution that remain suspended"[2] in the poem
in spite of its closing affirmations. We can examine and enlarge upon
Eliot's response by recognizing that Tennyson's faith is not a religious
faith merely—not just a poor and vague version of the stricter faith
that Eliot had discovered—but a faith in psychic integrity, in historical coherence, in the possibility of community. Eliot, from his special and interested point of view, could deplore this contamination
of faith by historical and psychological and social experience, but
these are the versions of Tennyson's faith that we have hardly out-
grown and that we repose on far more unthinkingly than he does.
We can still learn from a poem that defines and tests its faith in so
many ways and that describes not just the mingled desire and reluc-
tance of doubt to yield to faith, but also of the part to yield to the
whole, of the unique self to become the voice of England, and of the
moment to surrender its significance to some far-off divine event.

ALAN SINFIELD†

The Strategy of *In Memoriam*

The 3,000 lines written over seventeen years which make up *In
Memoriam* witness to Tennyson's grief and anxiety at the death of
Arthur Hallam. As I observed in chapter 3, the poem turns upon an
experience, in section 95, very like Tennyson's trances, in which
'individuality itself seems to dissolve and fade away into boundless

---

2. James Kincaid, *Tennyson's Major Poems* (New Haven: Yale Univ. Press, 1975), p. 109.
† From *Alfred Tennyson* (Oxford: Basil Blackwell, 1986), pp. 113–22. Reprinted by permission of Blackwell Publishers.

being' (*Memoir*, p. 168). Tennyson manages, almost, to install his dead friend in the space reserved for the Nameless, as the transcendental signified which would finally guarantee the fulness of all our mundane signs. Also, Tennyson's persistence with his elegies witnesses to his intuition that this theme and manner answer very well to the difficulties and objectives of the mid-nineteenth-century poet, * * * those of negotiating a role for poetry in a developing bourgeois hegemony, addressed typically by constructing poetry as a superior mode of language. Hence Tennyson's success, for most of his readers, in centring himself as the natural laureate of that culture. Nevertheless, such an ideal resolution cannot be complete and, indeed, it is likely to raise new complications.

   We can see in the earliest written sections of *In Memoriam* how Tennyson struck immediately upon a vein which enabled him to write with a density of structure and resonance of personal and symbolic yearning. Section 30, written in 1833–4, has a structure almost as explicit as 'Now sleeps the crimson petal.'[1] The opening two stanzas relate feeling to landscape: the Christmas eve of the family fell sadly as 'A rainy cloud possessed the earth' and they made only 'vain pretence/Of gladness'. The shape of the next four stanzas is set by 'We paused' and 'We ceased' at the start of the first and third; revising the poem between 1842 and 1845, Tennyson enhanced this effect by writing 'And silence followed' at the end of the third, corresponding to the silence at the end of the first (instead of 'We kissed each other').

> We paused: the winds were in the beech:
>   We heard them sweep the winter land;
>   And in a circle hand-in-hand
> Sat silent, looking each at each.
>
> Then echo-like our voices rang;
>   We sung, though every eye was dim,
>   A merry song we sang with him
> Last year: impetuously we sang:
>
> We ceased: a gentler feeling crept
>   Upon us: surely rest is meet:
>   'They rest', we said, 'their sleep is sweet',
> And silence followed, and we wept.
>
> Our voices took a higher range;
>   Once more we sang: 'They do not die
>   Nor lose their mortal sympathy,
> Nor change to us, although they change'.

1. One of the lyrics in Tennyson's long poem, *The Princess* (1847) [Editor].

Initially, in the first stanza quoted, the outside scene figures the family's discouragement and they hold hands in a circle against it, seeking containment and reciprocity within the human; the syntactic structure moves against the rhyme scheme, coherence is precarious. The song they sing in the second stanza is backward-looking, last year's, and again the stanza form is disturbed, suggesting their hesitancy and precipitate commitment. The silence of the third stanza is different from that of the first (repetition with difference is the primary strategy in the incremental structure of *In Memoriam*). The outside scene no longer impinges and the family feeling is no longer an echo or forced; the silence frees explicit grief and, in the fourth stanza, singing in 'a higher range', reaching beyond the mortal. The diction so far is relatively (perhaps surprisingly) conversational, but the syntax corresponds increasingly with the stanza shape and there is increasing use of incantatory repetition. These effects intensify as the last two stanzas give the rest of their song, and a concluding hymn of the poet which is both more personal and more general:

> 'Rapt from the fickle and the frail
>   With gathered power, yet the same,
>   Pierces the keen seraphic flame
> From orb to orb, from veil to veil'.
>
> Rise, happy morn, rise, holy morn,
>   Draw forth the cheerful day from night:
>   O Father, touch the east, and light
> The light that shone when Hope was born.

As Tennyson envisages a realm beyond the human, the writing becomes incantatory—poetic music seems to fill up the sign and remedy the defect of language—guaranteeing, as it seems, the metaphysical reality toward which it points. Thus it is the family's singing which gives them confidence in something which transcends mortality: in the silences they experience emotions beyond language, but the singing both represents and goes beyond those emotions.[2]

  Arthur's soul is said to advance 'With gathered power, yet the same'. Here in an early poem we see already the characteristic incremental strategy of *In Memoriam*: the stanza form is repeated and within it phrases, images and syntactical structures are taken up and developed, and through it all there is an onward and upward movement which manages, still, to keep in touch with its starting point. This effect may be seen as giving to the whole sequence the harmony and unity which, from Tennyson's time to the present, has been

---

2. On language in the poem, see Peter Allan Dale, " 'Gracious Lies': The Meaning of Metaphor in *In Memoriam*," *Victorian Poetry*, 18 (1980), 147–67.

taken as the hallmark of art's transcendence. The original reviewers mostly discovered such a unity:

> The *Morning Post* said, 'Not only is the unity of design and of subject apparent throughout, but the thoughts follow each other in a natural sequence, the continuity of which renders it necessary to contemplate the work as a whole in order fully to appreciate its beauties'. The *Eclectic* declared, 'An organic unity informs the whole; unity of feeling and of interest'. And Lushington in *Tait's* asserted that the poem was 'perfect and unique as a whole, to a degree and in a style very rarely reached'.[3]

Section 30—and this is the measure of Tennyson's immediate intuition of how these poems could work for him—anticipates not only the characteristic structural movement of *In Memoriam* but even its thematic development. The section moves from grief, concrete localities and personal circumstances to hope, an explicitly transcendent notion of reality and a more public discourse—the last stanza, especially, is like a hymn.[4] Reviewers appreciated this generalizing movement. The *Examiner* said it 'is a pathetic tale of real human sorrow . . . with varied and profound reflections on individual man, on society, and on their mutual relations'; and the *Eclectic* saw an 'outlet of personal feeling and sympathies' whose 'expression is enlarged into relevance with universal humanity'.[5]

The significance of *In Memoriam* was that it seemed to validate and even extend the current construction of poetry. I showed in chapter 2 that the main alternatives for poetry in the wake of the Shelleyan conjunction of political and imaginative freedom were the exploration of states of mind and direct incorporation into the hegemonic ideology. In *In Memoriam* Tennyson attempts to refuse the marginalization implicit in the cultivation of intense states of mind: he explores a personal grief, but asserts nevertheless that it is of universal significance. Thus he lays claim to a poetic 'I' that can stand without the indirection of dramatic monologue.

Now that we are familiar with the poem, it takes a little thought to recover the boldness of its strategy—even Tennyson did not at first see quite how much he could include. In 1842 he was planning a poem whose pretensions were not much larger than his personal elegy for Arthur Hallam.[6] The sections acknowledging the limited

3. Edgar Finley Shannon Jr., *Tennyson and the Reviewers* (Cambridge, MA: Harvard University Press, 1952), p. 147.
4. See Marion Shaw, '*In Memoriam* and Popular Religious Poetry', *Victorian Poetry*, 15 (1977), 1–8.
5. Shannon, *Tennyson and the Reviewers*, pp. 142, 152.
6. Tennyson, *In Memoriam*, ed. Susan Shatto and Marion Shaw (Oxford: Clarendon, 1982), pp. 11–5, 312–5, 317–20.

scope of his writing were in it (now 48, 49, 75, 76, 77) and there was little to contradict them

> If these brief lays, of Sorrow born,
>   Were taken to be such as closed
>   Grave doubts and answers here proposed,
> Then these were such as men might scorn.
>   (section 48)

But the poem as published in 1850 has much larger pretensions, and its readers by and large accepted them. It takes up troublesome issues like science, religion and political change and declares that 'all is well', claiming that its speculations are validated by the intensity of the poet's imaginative experience, by love:

> And if the song were full of care,
>   He breathed the spirit of the song;
>   And if the words were sweet and strong
> He set his royal signet there.
>   (section 125)

In effect, as Terry Eagleton argues, Arthur 'is nothing less than the empty space congregated by a whole set of ideological anxieties concerned with science, religion, the class-struggle, in short with the "revolutionary" decentring of "man" from his "imaginary" relation of unity with his world.'[7] (To avoid suppressing the intimacy of the poem, which some perhaps find embarrassing, I am writing 'Arthur' where commentators normally put 'Hallam'. In the text, after all, he is 'Arthur' and we wouldn't think of calling Beatrice or Laura by their formal second names.)[8]

In the terms I used earlier, the margins bid for centrality. Tennyson repudiates the choice between individual states of mind and the major concerns of his society, and challenges directly the positivism of the ideology of machinery:

> I trust I have not wasted breath:
>   I think we are not wholly brain,
>   Magnetic mockeries;
>   (section 120)

He denies that poetry is 'wasted breath', it has its own, superior validity, founded in the spiritual nature of humanity. Of course, all these assertions are insecure, shot through with 'doubt'. But that is

---

7. Terry Eagleton, 'Tennyson: politics and sexuality in *The Princess* and *In Memoriam*', in *1848: The Sociology of Literature*, ed. Francis Barker et al. (University of Essex, 1978), p. 104.
8. Beatrice and Laura are the women addressed in the poems of Dante and Petrarch, respectively [Editor].

not the point. The faith/doubt 'question' proclaims in its very construction the priority of 'spiritual' matters which poetry, in that culture, seemed specially equipped to handle, and the fact that 'faith'
is always just beyond grasp suits excellently the strategies and themes
of loss and yearning which Tennyson was perfecting.

Yet the transfigured Arthur affords only an apparent resolution. It
is more interesting and necessary, now, to read *In Memoriam* for the
discontinuities which convey a more complex sense of the human
subject and its insertion in history and ideology. I pointed in chapter
3 towards Tennyson's awareness of the limitations of the self/Name-
less opposition: by projecting his love onto eternity he forgoes the
human contact which was its motive force. Tennyson remarked to
James Knowles about section 47: 'Love protests against the loss of
identity in the theory of absorption'.[9] Yet absorption is pretty much
what has happened to Arthur by the end. In section 82 the poet
complains, 'We cannot hear each other speak' and in 130 he
declares, 'Thy voice is on the rolling air.' But they are two different
things, the connection is little more than metaphorical. Tennyson's
discomfort with this shuffle is manifested quintessentially in section
95, where he wrote 'His living soul was flashed on mine,/And mine
in his was wound', but changed it in 1872 to 'The living soul' and
'mine in this'. Tennyson commented: 'The Deity, maybe. The first
reading . . . troubled me, as perhaps giving a wrong impression.' Neither 'impression' is adequate because, to close the argument of *In
Memoriam*, Tennyson needs it to be *both* Arthur *and* the deity. The
awkwardness of the attempt at closure has been argued recently by
James R. Kincaid, Kerry McSweeney and Peter Hinchcliffe. Kincaid,
somewhat hampered by the allegedly archetypal system of Northrop
Frye, finds that *In Memoriam* does not move securely from the
'ironic' to the 'comic' pattern: from section 100 'the assurances lose
power and images of profound irony intrude' and 'instead of a genuine conclusion, we are given a series of skilful but inadequate sub-
stitutes.'[1] McSweeney is keen to distinguish 'Romantic naturalism',
which sees 'man as most creatively alive and most rooted when in
vital reciprocal contact with the world around him', from super-
naturalist religion, and he stresses the extent to which Tennyson tries
to force the one to become the other.[2] Hinchcliffe doubts that Hallam can 'really be type and friend at the same time' and argues that
although the concluding epithalamium may take 'the subsidiary anxieties of the sequence and close them off, one by one', it cannot
'finally divert us from the emptiness of heart with which *In Memo-*

9. Quoted in *In Memoriam*, ed. Shatto and Shaw, p. 211.
1. James R. Kincaid, *Tennyson's Major Poems* (Yale University Press, 1975), pp. 105, 109
   and chapter 5 generally.
2. Kerry McSweeney, *Tennyson and Swinburne as Romantic Naturalists* (Toronto University
   Press, 1981), p. xiii and chapter 3.

riam ends. For Arthur Hallam has not been recovered and retained.'[3]

The split between the earthly and heavenly Arthurs appears precisely in Tennyson's ideas about how to preserve what I called, in chapter 2, bourgeois freedom. We are told that Arthur had

> A love of freedom rarely felt,
>   Of freedom in her regal seat
>   Of England; not the schoolboy heat,
> The blind hysterics of the Celt.
>   (section 109)

His would have been

> A life in civic action warm,
>   A soul on highest mission sent,
>   A potent voice of Parliament,
> A pillar steadfast in the storm,
>
> Should licensed boldness gather force.
>   (section 113)

The last line quoted and the ensuing seven were taken by Tennyson from 'Hail Briton!', the longest and most elaborate of the poems of 1831–3 about bourgeois freedom. From this we can see the specific role designed for Arthur: it is the role taken in the seventeenth-century English Revolution by John Hampden. In 'Hail Briton!' Hampden is invoked as 'A single voice before the strife . . . In whom the spirit of law prevailed/To war with edicts' (lines 59, 61–2); in 'England and America in 1782' bourgeois freedom is traced to 'that deep chord which Hampden smote'. Hampden's main role was as a parliamentarian, one who, as Tennyson imagines of Arthur, 'tracts of calm from tempest made' (112)—Macaulay admires him for his judicious pacification of the House of Commons: " 'We had sheathed our swords in each other's bowels', says an eye-witness, 'had not the sagacity and great calmness of Mr Hampden, by a short speech, prevented it'."[4]

Within the terms of nineteenth-century parliamentary politics, the role required of Arthur and the implicit programme for society are clear enough. But suppose they prove inadequate? The agrarian and Reform Bill disturbances of 1830–2 had been followed in England by Chartism, which had presented petitions for universal male suffrage to parliament in 1839, 1842 and 1848; in France, Germany, Italy, Hungary and Ireland there had been revolutionary uprisings in 1848. This is what Tennyson meant by 'licensed boldness gather[ing] force', 'the red fool-fury of the Seine' and 'The blind hysterics of the

3. Peter Hinchcliffe, 'Elegy and Epithalamium in *In Memoriam*', *University of Toronto Quarterly*, 52 (1983), 241–62, pp. 257–9.
4. Thomas Babington Macaulay, *Essays, Historical and Literary* (London: Ward, Lock, n.d.), p. 243.

Celt' (113, 127, 109). His imagery in *In Memoriam* is that of earth-
quake and volcano—

> They tremble, the sustaining crags;
> The spires of ice are toppled down,
>
> And molten up, and roar in flood;
> The fortress crashes from on high,
> The brute earth lightens to the sky,
> And the great Æon sinks in blood.
> (section 127)

The imagery was not uncommon. Joseph Stephens told a Poor Law
repeal meeting in 1838: 'England stands on a mine—a volcano is
beneath her; you may dance on it—you may pluck the flowers from its
surface, but it only sleeps.'[5] It represented a recognition, perhaps
obscure, that a discontented proletariat is not an occasional malfunc-
tion in the bourgeois state but a necessary contradiction at its deepest
foundation.[6] Can Arthur's 'reverence and charity' cope with such a
profound source of disturbance?—this was the class fear of 1848.

When Hampden had failed to control the situation through parliament, he took up arms and died fighting against the king's army
(as Tennyson notes in 'Hail Briton!', 63–4). But Arthur is not envisaged as doing this. Of course, Hampden was fighting *for* the revolution, for bourgeois freedom against oppressive monarchy; Arthur
is to defend the status quo against a new claim for freedom. Perhaps
this is why, in the face of this ultimate threat, and with his uneasy
negotiation of bourgeois freedom out of imaginative and political
freedom, Tennyson has no political programme. Having failed to
achieve bourgeois ends through parliament Arthur is withdrawn
neatly to his fall-back position in eternity:

> thou, dear spirit, happy star,
> O'er lookst the tumult from afar,
> And smilest, knowing all is well.
> (section 127)

The earthly Arthur is a model for a parliamentary statesman, but
when the situation becomes more extreme the spiritual closure is
called for—'A deeper voice across the storm' rather than 'A potent
voice of Parliament' (127, 113). The function of the heavenly
Arthur—to handle that which cannot be coped with by human
means—is apparent.

* * *

5. Patricia Hollis, ed., *Class and Conflict in Nineteenth-Century England* (London: Routledge, 1973), p. 208.
6. Cf. Karl Marx and Friedrich Engels, 'Manifesto of the Communist Party,' in Marx, *The
Revolutions of 1848*, ed. David Fernbach (Harmondsworth, UK: Penguin, 1973), p. 79.

JEFF NUNOKAWA

In Memoriam and the Extinction of the Homosexual†

"So what do I know about being mature. The only thing mature means to me is *Victor* Mature . . ."
—Mart Crowley, *The Boys in the Band*

"Descend, and touch, and enter; hear/The wish too strong for words to name" (*In Memoriam*, 93.13–14).[1] It is difficult for a contemporary audience to read these lines, in which Tennyson prays for Hallam's embrace, without thinking that the wish too strong for words to name is the love that dare not speak its name. Tennyson's critics have often resisted such interpretations by reminding us that expressions of devotion must be situated historically. Gordon Haight, for example, argues that "the Victorians' conception of love between those of the same sex cannot be understood fairly by an age steeped in Freud. Where they saw only pure friendship, the modern reader assumes perversion . . . Even *In Memoriam*, for some, now has a troubling overtone."[2] As Haight's comment suggests, there is often more homophobia than history in the traditional appeal to the differences between Victorian and contemporary discourses of desire. Christopher Ricks, no sympathizer with Hellenistic readings of *In Memoriam*, dismisses the claim that such readings are necessarily anachronistic: "As so often, the position of the historical purist is itself unhistorical. . . . Some Victorians, who found Shakespeare's *Sonnets* troubling, found *In Memoriam* troubling."[3] *The Times*, for example, condemned *In Memoriam* for its "tone of amatory tenderness."[4] Tennyson's own trouble with this tone may be registered in his famous protest that while Hallam lived, he never called him "dearest."[5]

---

† From *English Literary History* 58:2 (1991) 427–38. Copyright © 1991 by The Johns Hopkins University Press. Reprinted by permission of the publisher.
1. *The Poems of Tennyson*, ed. Christopher Ricks (London: Longman, 1969). All subsequent citations of *In Memoriam* refer to Ricks's edition.
2. Gordon Haight, *George Eliot: A Biography* (New York: Oxford Univ. Press, 1968), 496.
3. Christopher Ricks, *Tennyson* (New York: Macmillan, 1972), 219.
4. Quoted by Ricks, *Tennyson* (note 3), 219.
5. Quoted by Valerie Pitt, *Tennyson Laureate* (London: Barrie and Rockliff, 1962), 117. The point that I am rehearsing here, that the homoeroticism of *In Memoriam* has troubled even its first readers, is made most decisively by Christopher Craft, in his investigation of the poem's homosexual rhetoric, " 'Descend, and Touch, and Enter': Tennyson's Strange Manner of Address," in *Genders* 1 (1988): 85–86. See also Craft's analysis of the sometimes complex strategies deployed by generations of Tennyson's readers to evade or contain the homosexual elements of the elegy (86–87). Craft's reading of *In Memoriam*'s "same gender eroticism" (87) touches my own. See note 8.

But the historical particularity of Tennyson's passion in the troubling passages of *In Memoriam* can be taken up to define, rather than deny, its homosexual character: what construction of the homosexual is registered and reproduced in the parts of *In Memoriam* which Victorians themselves could designate as such?[6] I want to begin with the suppressed phrase which has elicited so much attention from critics interested in denying or affirming the homosexual character of Tennyson's poem. The invitation to matrimony that Tennyson excised from the manuscript version of section 93 ("Stoop soul and touch me: wed me") has been taken by various readers, including, perhaps, Tennyson himself, as a figure of homosexual desire. But it is the revision rather than the original, or better, the revision's relation to the original which we may more accurately designate as homoerotic: the site of homoerotic desire is constituted as the negation of the heterosexual figure of marriage. To apprehend the homoerotic in *In Memoriam* as that which is defined *against* heterosexuality is to gain a sense of it as part of the nineteenth-century formation of sexual abnormality that Michel Foucault points to, a formation which is constituted by, and in turn constitutes its opposite: sexual normality.[7]

And if, according to a logic that Foucault has made familiar to us, the homosexual in *In Memoriam* is formed by its relation to the heterosexual, the heterosexual is formed by its relation to the homosexual. More specifically, *In Memoriam* proposes a developmental model of male sexuality which establishes the homoerotic as an early phase that enables and defines the heterosexual. "The wish too strong for words to name" is not a desire for matrimony, but rather a primary stage in the formation of the husband and the father:

> How many a father have I seen,
> A sober man, among his boys,
> Whose youth was full of foolish noise,
> Who wears his manhood hale and green:
>
> And dare we to this fancy give,
> That had the wild oat not been sown,
> That soil, left barren, scarce had grown
> The grain by which a man may live?
>
> (53.1–8)

---

6. See, of course, Michel Foucault, *The History of Sexuality: Volume 1. An Introduction*, trans. Robert Hurley (New York: Pantheon, 1978) for an account of sexual categories as the product of historically specific discursive practices, rather than timeless essences.
7. See especially part 2 of *The History of Sexuality*, "The Repressive Hypothesis."

The "wild oats" and "foolish noise" which make up the patriarch's prehistory may be aligned with the boyhood love that Tennyson sets against the marital contract in section 59 of *In Memoriam*. This boyhood love is another version of early passion which makes way for, and a way for, heterosexuality:

> O Sorrow, wilt thou live with me
> No casual mistress, but a wife
> . . . .
>
> My centered passion cannot move,
> Nor will it lessen from to-day
> But I'll have leave at times to play
> As with the creature of my love.
>   (59.1–2, 9–12)

Tennyson's post-Marlovian proposal of marriage is preceded and occasioned by the loss of his earlier pastoral play: his bride is a metonym for the loss of Hallam, and his heterosexual situation is thus defined as the ghost of prior passion; marriage is an elegy for earlier desire.[8]

I will seek shortly to demonstrate more specifically how *In Memoriam* identifies these early regions of passion as homoerotic, but before I do this, I want to recall the historical situation of Tennyson's

8. Here is the most significant point of convergence between my reading of *In Memoriam* and Christopher Craft's. Like Craft, I locate the homosexual in Tennyson's poem as a primal moment in a developmental narrative that terminates with a form of heterosexual desire that appears removed from the earlier stage that precedes and enables it. But my sense both of the character of this developmental narrative and of its calibrations—the categories homosexual and heterosexual—differ from Craft's. While Craft emphasizes the status of this narrative as "a disciplinary trajectory" (95), more or less continuous with the project of sublimation that Havelock Ellis prescribed for same-gender desire, my reading takes up an evolutionary narrative in the poem, which casts the homosexual not as the target of proscription or aversion, but rather as something that a person, or population, naturally, necessarily, outgrows. Craft's reading, like my own, is inflected by a Foucauldian recognition of the dialectical dependence which marks the relation between the heterosexual and homosexual. Craft reads this dependence as the condition of what he sees as the ambivalent persistence of the homosexual within the very structure of the heterosexual: "The erotics of such a substitutive structure are irreducibly ambivalent: since the homo is lost or banished only to be rediscovered in and as the hetero (which is itself thus constituted as a memorial of a former undifferentiated sameness) all longing remains longing for the homo even as it submits to the mediation of the hetero. Difference itself thus bespeaks a desire for sameness—speaks, like the poet, *in memoriam*." (97–98) My reading, on the other hand, seeks to describe a version of heterosexuality characterized by the radical abandonment of a prior homoeroticism which also supplies the condition of its existence. Craft's conviction that the "homo" persists in the very structure that displaces it depends on his identification of the homosexual with the general category of sameness, and, correlatively, of the heterosexual with the general category of difference. (This identification is compactly performed in Craft's abbreviation of heterosexual and homosexual in the passage I have just quoted.) My reading of the heterosexual and homosexual in Tennyson's poem seeks to consider a different construction of these terms.

ordering of male desire. The conception of the homoerotic as an early term in the tutelary itinerary of the bourgeois British male, an itinerary which ultimately installs him in the position of husband and father, is a staple of Victorian and post-Victorian ideology. Certainly the definitive site of this erotic apprenticeship is the English public school[9] where, in the words of one Etonian, "It's all right for fellows to mess one another a bit. . . . But when we grow up we put aside childish things, don't we?"[1]

In *Between Men: English Literature and Male Homosocial Desire*, Eve Kosofsky Sedgwick examines the ideological efficacy for the Victorian bourgeoisie of this evolutionary model of male desire. Sedgwick suggests that the social distinctions within the class of Victorian gentlemen were figured as different developmental stages within an individual psychic career in order to promote "the illusion of equality . . . within that class."[2] We may begin to sense that importance of such a softening of social distinctions for Tennyson in his relation to Arthur Hallam when we recall the difference between Tennyson's rather vexed and confused class and financial circumstances, and Hallam's far more secure possession of wealth and aristocratic position. The difference in their social circumstances, while perhaps not dramatic to our eyes, was sufficiently significant that, in the words of Robert Bernard Martin, "it is surprising that the most celebrated friendship of the century should ever have begun at all."[3]

Sedgwick argues that the Victorian narrative of individual psychosexual development served as the form in which economic and social

9. Boarding school, equivalent of American "prep school" [Editor].
1. Michael Nelson, *Nobs and Snobs* (London: Gordon & Cremonski, 1976), 147, as cited by Eve Kosofsky Sedgwick, *Between Men: English Literature and Male Homosocial Desire* (New York: Columbia Univ. Press, 1985). In *The Worm in the Bud: The World of Victorian Sexuality* (1969; reprint, Harmondsworth, Middlesex: Penguin Books, 1983), Ronald Pearsall discusses the remarkable extent and intensity of homoerotic activity in the English public schools in the nineteenth century, and the comparatively tolerant or indifferent attitude of school authorities towards even overtly sexual relations amongst students (551–60). (See also Louis Crompton, *Byron and Greek Love: Homophobia in Nineteenth-Century England* [Berkeley: Univ. of California Press, 1985]). While the figuration of male homoerotic activity as schoolboy love, a term in the growth of the patriarch, casts this version of such activity as a part of, rather than apart from heterosexual hegemony, this is, of course, not to suggest that all instances of sexual intercourse between males in Victorian England were tolerated by or instrumental to heterosexual authority. Pearsall quotes William Stead's observation during the Wilde trial about the discrepancy between the prevailing attitude toward fleshy versions of schoolboy love and the fierce prosecution of homosexual behavior when it took place beyond the bounds of early development: "Should everyone found guilty of Oscar Wilde's crime be imprisoned, there would be a very surprising emigration from Eton, Harrow, Rugby and Winchester to the jails of Pentonville and Holloway. . . . boys are free to pick up tendencies and habits in public schools for which they may be sentenced to hard labour later on" (Pearsall, 555).
2. Sedgwick (note 1), 178. Sedgwick's book first alerted me to the activity during the Victorian period of the notion that homosexuality is "just a phase."
3. Robert Bernard Martin, *Tennyson: The Unquiet Heart* (New York: Oxford Univ. Press, 1980), 69.

distinctions within the bourgeoisie were made to appear. In Tennyson's poem, the figure of evolutionary scale not only promotes a conception of potential equality between terms situated at different stages
of development, but also replaces a model of social organization
where there is no such potential equality between vertically distinct
terms. In other words, in *In Memoriam*, we can witness the decision
to rewrite what the poem first designates as unchanging social differences as different moments in a narrative of development, a narrative
which includes, as one of its passages, the exodus of the male subject
out of the blighted pastoral regions of the homoerotic.

Throughout *In Memoriam*, Tennyson pictures the difference
between himself and his dead friend as an insuperable vertical distance:

> Deep folly! yet that this could be—
> That I could wing my will with might
> To leap the grades of life and light,
> And flash at once, my friend, to thee.
> (41.9–12)

In section 60, Tennyson describes this difference in height as a difference of class; the terms that he employs here to measure the
distance between himself and Hallam describe his sense of loss as a
sense of socioeconomic inferiority:

> He past; a soul of nobler tone:
> My spirit loved and loves him yet,
> Like some poor girl whose heart is set
> On one whose rank exceeds her own.
>
> He mixing with his proper sphere,
> She finds the baseness of her lot,
> Half jealous of she knows not what,
> And envying all that meet him there.
>
> The little village looks forlorn;
> She sighs amid her narrow days,
> Moving about the household ways,
> In that dark house where she was born.
>
> The foolish neighbors come and go,
> And tease her till the day draws by:
> At night she weeps, 'How vain am I!
> How should he love a thing so low?'
> (60.1–16)

In the four sections of *In Memoriam* that follow, Tennyson enlists
various models of organic progression which recast and qualify the

class difference figured here. The distinction between Tennyson and Hallam becomes, in section 61, the difference between a "dwarf'd . . . growth" (7) and the "perfect flower of human time" (4). For Tennyson to define himself as a dwarfed growth is, implicitly, to attribute to himself the unrealized potential for *full* growth. While the "soul of nobler tone" is simply inaccessible to what is below and behind him, the "perfect flower of human time" figures a completion of development which the stunted plant could have attained. In section 63, Tennyson collates the distinction between himself and Hallam with differences between lower and higher species of animals, and if this seems to substantiate rather than diminish their separation, we need to remember Tennyson's endorsement of both phylogenic and ontogenetic versions of evolution. In section 118, for example, the forlorn desire to "leap the grades of life" is rewritten as a prescription for a personal practice of evolutionary process: "Move upward, working out the beast,/And let the ape and tiger die" (27–8). And if the figure of lesser development can rise to a higher stage, according to the evolutionary models that Tennyson sets forth in sections 61 through 65, the higher rises by means of the lower. The inferior term of the developmental hierarchy is cast as the seed that moves the superior term to "noble ends" (65.12).

Tennyson thus relieves class differences by replacing the simple social barrier between the "poor girl" and the "soul of nobler tone" with a permeable boundary: the "dwarf'd growth" and the "perfect flower of human time" are related as figures situated at different stages of the same evolutionary narrative. I want to suggest that the scenario of social ascent that Tennyson sets forth in section 64, in which Hallam is pictured not as a noble, but instead as a case study of upward mobility, registers the ideological force of these developmental models. The description of Hallam as "some divinely gifted man,/Whose life in low estate began . . . who breaks his birth's invidious bar" (1–2, 5) is enacted by means of an implicit analogy to the scenarios of natural evolution that surround it.

Identified with these evolutionary models, the scale from homosexual to heterosexual is defined as another version of the developmental range that displaces the class differences of section 60. Here is Tennyson addressing Hallam in section 61:

> If thou cast thine eyes below,
> How dimly character'd and slight,
> How dwarf'd a growth of cold and night,
> How blanch'd with darkness must I grow!
>
> Yet turn thee to the doubtful shore,
> Where thy first form was made a man;

> I loved thee, Spirit, and love, nor can
> The soul of Shakespeare love thee more.
>   (61.5–12)

When the stunted, shadowed growth locates his devotion to Hallam with Shakespearean love, he identifies his desire with a standard Victorian figure for the male homoerotic. It was the homoerotic reputation of the Sonnets which made some of Tennyson's contemporaries uneasy about his fondness for them. Benjamin Jowett, for example, was relieved by what he regarded as Tennyson's retreat from his devotion to the Sonnets. To do otherwise, Jowett, opined, "would not have been manly or natural. . . . The love of the sonnets which he [Tennyson] so strikingly expressed was a sort of sympathy with Hellenism."[4] Certainly it was the taint of Hellenism attached to the Sonnets which prompted Henry Hallam to "wish that Shakespeare had never written them."[5]

Tennyson begins section 62 by again affiliating his lower species of love for Hallam with Shakespearean devotion:

> Tho, if an eye that's downward cast
> Could make thee somewhat blench or fail,
> Then be my love an idle tale,
> And fading legend of the past.
>   (62.1–4)

These lines allude to the conclusion of Sonnet 116: "If this be error and upon me proved,/I never writ, nor no man ever loved" (13–14).[6] We need now to notice what Tennyson does with Sonnet 116, and why he does it. If *In Memoriam* takes up the Victorian conception of the Sonnets as an exemplary figuration of male homoerotic passion, it revises the terms of Shakespearean desire to fit with the modern formation of the homosexual which gained hegemony in the nineteenth century. While Shakespeare's devotion is "the marriage of true minds" in Sonnet 116, it is defined as that which is *not* marriage in *In Memoriam*. In keeping with the construction of the homoerotic as an early point on the developmental agenda of male desire, a stage which *precedes* and is terminated by matrimony, Tennyson's poem draws marriage away from the form of devotion that Victorians attributed to the Sonnets and situates it at a height where that form

---

4. Hallam Lord Tennyson, *Materials for a Life of Alfred Tennyson* (privately printed, no date). Quoted by Ricks (note 3), 215. For a detailed discussion of the complicated career of "Hellenism" as a signifier of male homosexuality, see Crompton (note 1), especially chapter 2.
5. Henry Hallam, *Introduction to the Literature of Europe* (1839), 3:501–4. Quoted by Ricks, *Tennyson*, 215.
6. *The Sonnets, Songs and Poems of Shakespeare*, ed. Oscar James Campbell (New York: Schocken Books, 1964). All subsequent citations of Sonnet 116 refer to this edition.

has been transcended. Tennyson goes on in section 62 to compare his Shakespearean passion for Hallam with Hallam's own ascent to the higher species of heterosexuality:

> And thou, as one that once declined,
> When he was little more than boy,
> On some unworthy heart with joy,
> But lives to wed an equal mind.
>
> (62.5–8)

Shakespeare measures the permanence of his love in 116:

> Love's not Times fool, though rosy lips and cheeks
> Within his bending sickle's compass come;
> Love alters not with his brief hours and weeks,
> But bears it out even to the edge of doom.
>
> (9–12)

But Tennyson, again subjecting the sonnet to the Victorian conception of the homoerotic as an early stage of male erotic development, declares the impermanence of the devotion that it expresses, casting it as a kind of schoolboy passion which "wholly dies" (10), or becomes "matter for a flying smile" (12) when boys put away childish things to become husbands and fathers.

Thus, Tennyson's claim that his passion for Hallam rivals Shakespeare's, works less to aggrandize his own passion than to diminish Shakespeare's. The constitution of the homoerotic in *In Memoriam* is most fully registered in its revision of Sonnet 116, a revision which converts Shakespeare's claim for the deathlessness of his desire into an announcement of its mortality.

I want now to examine a subtler announcement of the failure of Shakespearean devotion in *In Memoriam*. Tennyson alludes in section 62 to Shakespeare's designation of the permanence of his passion as the grounds upon which his writing rests: "If this be error and upon me proved,/I never writ nor no man ever loved." While Tennyson's echo of these lines slightly alters Shakespeare's contract, ("if an eye that's downward cast/Could make thee somewhat blench or fail,/Then be my love an idle tale,/And fading legend of the past"), I nevertheless want to suggest that the connection that Shakespeare sets forth between the existence of his text and the permanence of his passion remains in place in Tennyson's poem, only now in a negative form. When he recasts the passion of the sonnet as temporary rather than permanent, Tennyson cancels the condition upon which Shakespeare's text depends. And the proof of Shakespeare's error is registered by the figure of Shakespearean devotion in section 61 that I referred to earlier, the figure who is "dimly character'd and

slight." This fading legend of Shakespearean love is the negative real-
ization of Shakespeare's covenant in Sonnet 116: here, the text disappears since the love that it represents is ephemeral, rather than
eternal. The Shakespearean text is dimmed and slighted according
to the terms of its own contract and according to the Victorian conception of its content.

The negative version of the Shakespearean contract which inhabits Tennyson's text suggests that "the wish too strong for words to
name," another instance of desire contradistinguished from marriage, might as well be called the wish too *weak* for words to name.
In "the wish too strong for words to name," the consequence of
Tennyson's cancellation of Shakespeare's claim for the durability of
his love is fully realized. The marriage of true minds is described now
as the ephemeral predecessor of marriage, a transitional, transitory,
and thus wordless "wish." Shakespeare's contract enables us to identify the place in *In Memoriam* where the homoerotic is extinguished,
the place where Tennyson's love for Hallam is matured and his
Shakespearean devotion expunged. Tennyson's fear that Hallam's
death left him a dwarfed growth, permanently arrested at the stage
of schoolboy love, is allayed in section 81 of the poem, where Death
declares that through its intervention, Tennyson's devotion to Hallam was fully ripened:

> Could I have said while he was here,
> 'My love shall now no further range;
> There cannot come a mellower change,
> For now is love mature in ear.'
>
> Love then had hope of richer store:
> What end is here to my complaint?
> This haunting whisper makes me faint,
> 'More years had made me love thee more.'
>
> But Death returns an answer sweet:
> 'My sudden frost was sudden gain,
> And gave all ripeness to the grain,
> It might have drawn from after-heat.'
>   (81.1–12)

We may locate the repository of the ripened grain of Tennyson's
matured love when we gather together an allusion that is dispersed
in sections 81 and 82, an allusion to Keats's "When I Have Fears":

> When I have fears that I may cease to be
> Before my pen has gleaned my teeming brain,

> Before high-piled books, in charactery,
> Hold like rich garners the full ripened grain.
>   (1–4)[7]

Tennyson takes up not only the occasion of Keats's poem (the prospect of premature death), but also two of its figures—the grain in section 81, ("My sudden frost was sudden gain/And gave all ripeness to the grain") and, in 82, the garner that Keats pictures as the container for that grain:

> For this alone on Death I wreak
> That wrath that garners in my heart;
> He puts our lives so far apart
> We cannot hear each other speak.
>   (82.13–16)

By reconstituting the reference to Keats's text in these sections of *In Memoriam*, we can discern the harvest of Tennyson's matured love in the rancor of his heart, a rancor whose source is the impotence of speech.

The dispelling of the homoerotic in these lines becomes visible when the resentment that Tennyson garners in his heart is placed next to the *words* that Keats garners, the "high-piled books, in charactery," which "hold like rich garners the full ripened grain." Tennyson's wrath, which, I have suggested, may be identified with his ripened love, represents two linguistic failures; not only his inability to hear or be heard by Hallam, but also the absence of the words, the "charactery," that Keats pictures as the ripened harvest that fills the garners. And according to the Shakespearean formula active in Tennyson's poem, a formula which equates the termination of what the Victorians constructed as homoerotic desire with verbal disappearance, this absence tells us that the maturation of Tennyson's love is the conclusion of its homoerotic phase. The ripening of love is built upon the disappearance of prior characters, the proof of Shakespeare's error. This verbal absence appears at the conclusion of a section of *In Memoriam* which includes a survey of the stages of evolutionary progress:

> Eternal process moving on,
> From state to state the spirit walks;
> And these are but the shatter'd stalks,
> Or ruined chrysalis of one.
>   (82.5–8)

The "wild oat" of section 53, an early version of male desire whose passing is defined by verbal effacement, may be construed amongst

---

7. *The Poems of John Keats*, ed. Miriam Allott (London: Longman, 1972).

the "shatter'd stalks" and "ruined chrysalis" as something else aban-
doned by that which is ripe. The absence of any reminder of this
early desire may be the poem's most eloquent elegy for the homosexual; unlike the grain and the butterfly, matured male love leaves
behind no mark, no souvenir of a kind of devotion whose failure can
have no trace.[8]

But if the homoerotic disappears within the course of male desire
as it is charted by Tennyson, this inexorable early loss is incessantly
rewritten in subsequent constructions of the homosexual, rewritten
and transliterated. If the homosexual is a stage, fated for extinction
in the nineteenth-century conception of the homosexual that *In
Memoriam* helps to construct, the doom attached to it is visited upon
a population as the category of the homosexual passes from stage to
subject in the years that follow Tennyson's elegy.[9] The funeral that
Tennyson hosts for his own puerile homoerotic desire in *In Memoriam* has its afterlife in the glamorous rumor of preordained doom
that bathes the image of live-fast-die-young gay boys such as Dorian
Gray, Montgomery Clift, James Dean, Joe Orton, and, most recently,
a French-Canadian airline steward who came to be known as Patient
Zero, the spoiled child in whom the dominant media apprehended
the embodiment of the lethal effects of a new virus. The youthful
fatality of homosexual desire, the youthful fatality which *is* homosexual desire in Tennyson's poem, prepares the way for the story of
the bathhouse boy's frolicsome progress to an inevitable early grave.
"Blanch'd with darkness" still, the figure "dimly character'd and
slight" helps explain why the dominant media inaccurately identifies
AIDS with, even *as*, the early death of gay men. The "dwarf'd"
"growth of cold and night" haunts such representations of the current crisis, the "dwarf'd" "growth of cold and night" that defines the
homosexual as that which dies young.

8. The psychosexual itinerary that I have sought to identify in *In Memoriam* is, of course, an
   exclusively masculine model of improvement. It is in section 60 of the poem, where the
   vertical distance between Hallam and Tennyson is figured as an impermeable boundary,
   that the difference between lower and higher is the difference between a woman and a
   man. The replacement of "some poor girl" in section 60 with the figure of Shakespearean
   desire in the sections that follow reflects a crucial dimension of the strategy that Tennyson
   enacts in *In Memoriam*; to convert a masculine itinerary of desire into a social program
   for upward mobility is to confirm the position of women as a permanent underclass,
   excluded categorically from the potential for ascent. The embarrassed maiden of section
   60 serves to remind us of who must be left behind by Tennyson's stairway scenario.
9. On the construction of homosexuality as a subject position, see Foucault (note 6), and
   Jeffrey Weeks, *Coming Out: Homosexual Politics in Britain, from the Nineteenth Century
   to the Present* (London: Quarter Books, 1977). Eve Kosofsky Sedgwick considers how the
   discourse of evolution that I have sought to isolate in Tennyson's construction of the
   homosexual informs contemporary homophobic accounts of AIDS. See "*Billy Budd*: After
   the Homosexual," in *Epistemology of the Closet* (Berkeley: Univ of California Press, 1990),
   185–190.

W. DAVID SHAW

The Paradox of Genre: Impact and Tremor in Tennyson's Elegies†

"When the commonplace 'We must all die' transforms itself suddenly into the acute consciousness 'I must die—and soon,' then death grapples us," George Eliot's narrator says in *Middlemarch*, "and his fingers are cruel" (bk. 4, chap. 42). In *The Thread of Life* Richard Wollheim makes a similar distinction between an "impact" and a "tremor." The terrible news of a friend's sudden death makes an "impact." News that I have terminal cancer, provided it is accepted and believed, induces a "tremor." As Wollheim says, "the tremor is a part of our natural sensibility, and we may think of it as a sensible index of self-concern."[1] An event that makes an impact, even when it throws an elegist offbalance, as if he had received a blow, is usually artfully staged, like the ritual of leave-taking in Tennyson's "Ulysses" or "The Passing of Arthur." By contrast, in his postscript to "Tiresias," news of Edward Fitzgerald's death catches Tennyson offguard. He continues to reel from the shock. And in *In Memoriam* Hallam's death has the same tremulous effect on Tennyson that the new astronomy has on Donne or Pascal.

Elegies generate their tremors in two main ways: by creating the tremulous ripple effect of a verbal ambiguity or two-way meaning, and by transgressing a code, as Tzetvan Todorov suggests in his essay "The Origin of Genres."[2] Let me consider the verbal and rhythmic nuances first. To generate a tremor an elegist may use late-breaking caesuras that signal closure or the skipping of a heartbeat, as in Ben Jonson's poem on the death of his son: "Farewell, thou child of my right hand, and joy;/My sinne was too much hope of thee, lov'd boy" ("On My First Sonne," ll. 1–2). Tennyson often creates similar tremors of feeling by using two-way syntax or phrases that hover ambiguously between contrasting emphases. Is "a glory done" in *In Memoriam* (121.4) a *glory* done or a glory *done*? Even a simple echo-like repetition can send tremors of feeling down a lyric. The death-ward declensions in Frost's "Nothing Gold Can Stay," for example, are so lightly insistent that they quaver with subdued feeling like the first leaves of spring. Occasionally, as in Browning's lyric, "A Toccata of Galuppi's," a controlled stage death alternates with a death that

† From *Elegy and Paradox* (Baltimore: The Johns Hopkins University Press, 1994), pp. 210–11; 214–17; 221–24; 233–35. Copyright © 1994. Reprinted by permission of the Johns Hopkins University Press.
1. Richard Wollheim, *The Thread of Life* (Cambridge, MA, 1984), p. 237.
2. Tzetvan Todorov, "The Origin of Genres," *New Literary History* 8 (1976): 159–70.

is uncontrolled and real. Browning movingly portrays the contrast between the nostalgic impact of music that commemorates the "Dear dead women" with the golden hair (l. 44) and the tremor of a "cold music" that, in foretelling the speaker's own death, "creep[s]" silently "through every nerve" (l. 33).

More generally, a tremor is induced whenever an elegy, in trying to establish itself by transgressing some norm, juxtaposes a convention and a tolerant, humane testing of that convention. One paradox of genre consists in this, that the norms of a literary kind become fully visible only when transgressed. As Todorov explains, "the fact that a work 'disobeys' its genre does not make the latter nonexistent; it is tempting to say that quite the contrary is true. And for a twofold reason. First, because transgression, in order to exist as such, requires a law that will, of course, be transgressed. One could go further: the norm becomes visible—lives—only by its transgressions. . . . But there is more. Not only does the work, for all its being an exception, necessarily presuppose a rule; but this work also, as soon as it is recognized by its exceptional status, becomes in its turn . . . a rule" (160).

Failure to deviate at all from an elegiac formula is found at its most extreme in an obituary notice. To read the words, "Hallam, Arthur, on Friday, 13 September, suddenly in Vienna, son of the historian Henry Hallam," might produce an impact. But they create none of the tremors of feeling we experience when reading *In Memoriam*. One way Tennyson's elegy produces its effect is by transgressing the convention that the traditional language and ancient symbols of a pastoral elegy like "Lycidas" should exorcise the terror of dying. Unlike Milton, Tennyson fears that the God who consigns Hallam to an early grave in *In Memoriam* is a "wild Poet," working "Without a conscience or an aim" (34.7–8). In a world "red in tooth and claw," a savage world that is still strangely evanescent, turning hills into shadows and "solid lands" into melting mist (123.7), the death of Tennyson's friend may be of the same order as the melting of an icicle. This is why the melancholy of many nineteenth-century and modern elegists seems deeper, more tremulous, than the melancholy of Milton or Donne. By exploring six more specific ways in which Tennyson's elegies transgress earlier conventions, I hope to illuminate Todorov's paradox that the norms of a genre would be hard to recognize apart from the slight tremors of subversive questioning that are continually testing these norms and loosening their hold.

* * *

Forgetting and Remembering

Elegy is always "in memoriam"—an art of re-viewing and recollecting the past, as opposed to merely remembering it. Yet Tennyson also transgresses this convention by reminding us, often with a slight shock of recognition, that elegy is equally an art of forgetting. Indeed, until the mere impact of a sensory impression of the dead is effaced, until the dead are forgotten, they cannot be genuinely recalled either. Recollection is an art; and, as Kierkegaard observes, "what is recollected is not indifferent to recollection as what is remembered is indifferent to memory."[3] The mere impact of a photograph or of a setting remembered in photographic detail may distract the elegist from the act of recollection that turns the Somersby rectory or the "Dark house" in Wimpole Street into a geography of his mind. Like the composition of place in an Ignatian meditation, the scenes over which the elegist continues to brood tremulously are recollections, not mere memories. Without recollection there could be no meditation, and without meditation no discovery and growth.

Tennyson transgresses an elegiac code whenever he tries to forget rather than remember. But how is this possible? To write an elegy at all is implicitly to commemorate and recollect. One way to forget is to disguise an elegy as something else, as Tennyson does in his verse epistle to Dufferin.[4] His son's death, as we shall see later, is precisely what Tennyson tries to elide or repress. The elegist wants to forget his son until he can assimilate the loss and better commemorate it. An alternative solution is to evoke a lost place or person as an absent presence. In section 101 of *In Memoriam* Tennyson anticipates a scene of neglect and oblivion after his family leaves Somersby and the garden boughs and flowers fall into ruin. Yet the power of the negatives, "Unwatched," "Unloved," "Uncared for" (ll. 1, 5, 9, 13), depends, in one critic's words, "on the unsaying of the very detail" they seem "to present."[5] "Unloved," the repeated adjectives at the head of lines insist on saying. But also "loved," and deeply so, by the elegist who discovers, with a slight tremor of elation, that no mirroring of place, however bleak, can be unhinged from the memorial of a self-conscious mind. In James Richardson's words, "there is a palimpsest, a dimness" in such lines. "No," they say, "but yes." Because "Tennyson's simplest and most profound delight in language is with its ability to say yes and no at the same time" (32), he finds he can best remember Somersby or Hallam when he seems to forget.

Merely to remember a death is not to commemorate it. An elegy

---

3. Søren Kierkegaard, *Stages on Life's Way*, tr. David F. Svenson and Walter Lowrie (Princeton, 1940), p. 30.
4. "To the Marquis of Dufferin and Ava" (1889), Tennyson's elegy for his son Lionel [Editor].
5. James Richardson, *Vanishing Lives* (Charlottesville, 1988), p. 32.

recollects and re-presents an event; unlike a death or an obituary, it
does more than just transcribe it. Mere memory is to authentic recollection what descriptive language is to performative language. An
elegist who merely remembers what is close at hand will develop no
skill in recollection. Though people can mourn together in a funeral
ode, they recollect in private. Death may have changed Wellington
into "Something far advanced in State" ("Ode on the Death of the
Duke of Wellington," l. 275). Yet when the pun on "State" invites
the elegist to imagine the change, he can think of nothing more
inspiring than an apotheosis of machine-like simplicity and practical
capacity: "There must be other nobler work to do/Than when he
fought at Waterloo,/And Victor he must ever be" (ll. 256–58). The
funeral ode is versified obituary that does nothing to alter Wellington
in its act of remembering him. By contrast, a private recollection
often sets free both the mourner and the person who is mourned.

Once again *In Memoriam* provides the best example of how an
elegy replaces the random unfolding of a mere memory, which is an
indifferent act, with the ordered sequence of a recollection, which
involves imaginative effort and discovery. One critic complains that
when Tennyson speaks of Hallam's "noble breast" early in the poem
(11. 19), "the adjective is sentimental, not because it is sentimental
to call a friend 'noble,' but because of a failure of expression. Tennyson has given no particular occasion and no analogy."[6] Later, however, the mourner uses intimate particulars ("Sweet human hand and
lips and eye," 129.6) and a number of precise oxymorons ("known
and unknown; human, divine," 129.5) to evoke Hallam as a "Strange
friend, past, present, and to be" (129.9). By the end of the elegy the
vagueness of a mere memory has been replaced by the defining
details of an authentic recollection.

A mourner may suppress a painful memory. Until it is recollected,
like repressed material coming into focus under psychoanalysis, neither the memory itself nor the pain associated with it can be forgotten or assuaged. At first, only grim antipuns, by fending off the dark
meanings built into them, can help Tennyson place the traumatic
events far enough away to re-present and evaluate them: "I seem to
fail from out my blood/And grow incorporate into thee" (2.15–16).
"Fail" unlocks "ail," another form of "sick" ("Sick for they stubborn
hardihood," l. 14). Even the preposition "for" may mean "because
of." To cure the sickness caused by his unhealthy longing dark
secrets have to be confessed. Just as Rousseau says he writes his
Confessions to rid himself of the guilt of falsely accusing an innocent
servant girl of stealing a worthless ribbon, so Tennyson seems to
write his elegy to expiate an inexplicable guilt he feels: "Behold me,

6. Reuben Brower, *The Fields of Light* (New York, 1962), p. 35.

for I cannot sleep,/And like a guilty thing I creep/At earliest morning to the door" (7.6–8). But what possible offense can Tennyson have committed against Hallam?

I think the very act of survival leads to guilt. Like many survivors of the holocaust, the mourner has the awesome feeling that he is not worthy of survival; he has not survived enough. It is therefore important that in the elegist's imagination the ghost who may feel pitched into a grave, like Shakespeare's Banquo, whose death is somehow undeserved, a source of guilt to the living, or even painfully unfair, should be made to sleep well. Paradoxically, the best way to forget the dead by giving them a quiet grave is first to remember them. Only a past that has been genuinely recollected can also be forgotten.

Gerhard Joseph offers a different explanation. He ingeniously suggests that "the prime source" of the mourner's elegiac "dis-ease" is the guilt he feels over "cannibalizing [Hallam] for purposes of aesthetic self-aggrandizement."[7] There may also be a third source of anxiety: in mourning the death of someone who has taken up residence in himself, Tennyson keeps running the risk of incest. Unable to marry his sister, the woman Hallam was engaged to, Tennyson ends by marrying someone with the same name.[8] Meanwhile, he continues to identify with Hallam's bride in fantasy, assuming her part and speaking of her "widowed . . . heart" as if it were his own (85.113). Even in elegies by Hardy and Housman, the marriage of the dead man's beloved to the survivor may be a disguised act of homage or love. Leading his life backward in memory, Tennyson is also able to lead it forward again, slowly easing the conscience of the "guilty thing" who creeps outside the dark house in Wimpole Street, a victim of unlocalized malaise, like one of Nietzsche's "pale criminals," whose wavering sense of being both traitor and betrayed at once precedes and motivates his evil dreams about God and nature being at strife.

Forgetting becomes unhealthy whenever we repress what we know. Momentarily forgetting the object-specific nature of his loss— not just the death of Hallam but also the eclipse of any lodestar for faith in the burned-out universe predicted by the Second Law of Thermodynamics—the mourner in *In Memoriam* allows his free-floating melancholia to create a more generalized impact by diffusing at large over life. Tennyson may forget because he is afraid to remember a loss more personal and poignant than mere generalized grief. More wholesome than his free-floating melancholia is his hard-edged, because object-specific, mourning, which may bring slow detachment from Hallam in its wake. Forgetting must not come too soon, otherwise Hallam may seem betrayed. But release should come

7. Gerhard Joseph, *Tennyson and the Text* (Cambridge, 1992), p. 18.
8. Tennyson's sister and his wife were both named Emily [Editor].

before the elegy is over, since life is for the living and no grief should last forever, not even in an elegy that "can go to extraordinary figural lengths to keep itself alive" (Joseph, 17).

As Antony H. Harrison reminds us in his essay on Wordsworth and Swinburne, there is also a "politics of mortality," a politics of remembering and forgetting, which bears upon the topic.[9] In his elegies Tennyson is writing as both the Burkean conservative of "Love thou thy land" and as the transgressor of norms, as the subversive poetic equivalent of the political radical in "Locksley Hall Sixty Years After." Committed to remembering the past and conserving the impact of tradition, the elegist owes allegiance to Burke's continuum of the dead, the living, and the unborn. But as a radical he also wants to forget. T. S. Eliot is surely right about Tennyson: he was "the most instinctive rebel against the society in which he was the most perfect conformist."[1] The impulse toward coherence and stability in literature and politics, toward remembering a past they want to conserve, is deeply rooted in the consciousness of Tennyson's mourners. But faced with the unknown, they also waver between hope and fear. Having destroyed something, can death, like radicalism in politics, put something better in its place? Whatever one's politics, death the leveler is always a highly visible radical. A constant reminder of human equality, it is also the great transgressor of norms.

*   *   *

Brokenness and Continuity

Most elegies invite us to read across events, to discover continuities between the first and second anniversaries of Hallam's death, for example, the first and second Christmas, the earlier and later uses of the infant crying in the dark, and so on. Even when later occurrences of the burial ship or yew tree are not meant to supersede what came before, as an antitype is thought to supersede its type in a figural reading of Scripture, we are asked to register the continuities over an interval of time. As Eric Griffiths says, the continuities between Hopkins and the sailor who is pitched to his death in *The Wreck of the Deutschland* "are the constituents of a span of timed thought, and it is the span we are asked to realize."[2]

If one norm of elegy is the search for some stabilizing continuity in the midst of discrete fragments of change, then it must be conceded, I think, that Tennyson, like many elegists, transgresses this

9. Antony H. Harrison, *Victorian Poets and Romantic Poems: Intertextuality and Ideology* (Charlottesville, 1990), pp. 177–204.
1. See the penultimate paragraph of Eliot's essay, p. 139 herein [Editor].
2. Eric Griffiths, *The Printed Voice of Victorian Poetry* (Oxford, 1989), p. 349.

norm as often as he observes it. The glorious ascent of Lycidas makes an impact on the reader. But because nothing in *In Memoriam* can claim comparable authority, the provisional organizations of meaning achieved within any moment of a poem Tennyson once considered calling his *Fragments of an Elegy* must expose themselves to the tremor of "disruption or disproof in the moments that follow."[3] Often Tennyson uses the momentary indecision created by a line break to suspend us between two kinds of brokenness, between a breakdown and a breakthrough.

> He is not here; but far away
>   The noise of life begins again.
>   (*In Memoriam* 7.9–10)

The first line is hard to scan, because as Eric Griffiths says, "the words seem to require four even stresses or four even absences of stresses." If we pause at the line ending, and speak the line as a regular iambic tetrameter, we hear an echo of the angel's words to Mary Magdalene in the first three Gospels: "He is not *here*, but *far away*." Yet the run-on drops the line "into the blank space of the page," as Griffiths notes, "to re-emerge from it as something quite alien to hope: 'But far away/The noise of life begins again.' What revives is not the friend he misses but the beat of regular iambics and 'the noise of life,' the daily round, they represent" (127). As tremulous as the light that flickers through the drizzling rain is the mourner's evocation of "the long unlovely street" (7.2). Broken apart by strong caesural pauses, the phrase wavers between a spatial, adjectival use of "long" and a temporal, adverbial use. The street's long prospect is devoid of charm. But it is also "unlovely" in a deeper sense, since emptied now of Hallam's love. The breaking of day at the end of the lyric is equally ambivalent. Does the light sift through a sickly filter of drizzling rain only to break apart on the bald street? Or does the recollection of the tomb from which Christ is resurrected allow the day to break out of blankness? Do we experience the impact of something breaking down or the tremor of something breaking through?

There are comparable tremors of brokenness and indecision in the oracular ninety-fifth section of *In Memoriam*. When the sunken "day-star," having repaired "his drooping head" in "Lycidas," "Flames in the forehead of the morning sky" (ll. 168–69, 171), the spectacle of death and resurrection affirms a marvelous continuity. By contrast, in the corresponding sequence in *In Memoriam*, line breaks, ellipses, and two-way grammar allow oddly broken sounds to be heard like echoes, then pondered and remembered in silence.

---

3. Timothy Peltason, *Reading* In Memoriam (Princeton, 1985), p. 5 [See above, p. 189].

> And strangely on the silence broke
>   The silent-speaking words, and strange
>   Was love's dumb cry defying change
> To test his worth; and strangely spoke . . .
>   (*In Memoriam*, 95.25–28)

When an oxymoron ("silent-speaking") finds itself repeated in a second oxymoron ("love's dumb cry") everything we hear starts to be heard tremulously, two or three times, like echoes. Because echoes give the impression of having traveled great distances, they are the auditory equivalent of section 123's time-lapse photograph of the earth extending over billions of years. As Gerhard Joseph says, "sound like sight is most evocative—and melancholy—when it is experienced at a far, far remove from its original source" (97). As the reversing pattern *abba* locks the two forms of silence into a chiasmic vise ("strangely," "silence," "silent-speaking," "strange"), these echoes prove astonishingly stubborn, not at all faint or attenuated. The second use of "strange" is picked up by an adverbial version of itself at the end of the quatrain, where it rides expansively across the break between stanzas: "And strangely spoke [stanzaic break] The faith, the vigour, bold to dwell/On doubts" (*In Memoriam*, 95.28–30). Further protracted by a timeless infinitive phrase, "bold to dwell," the "faith" and "vigour" are left poised for a moment over the empty space at the end of line 29. We expect the infinitive to be completed by a prepositional phrase beginning with "in": to dwell "in hope," perhaps, or even "in God." But because the mourner is dwelling on his doubts, hovering or brooding over them, he is using a different sense of "dwell" to evoke that very experience of wavering or trembling shared by readers who are trying to decide how Tennyson will cross the slight break between lines and complete his run-on.

Even the meaning of the noun "change" is unexpectedly allowed to change. When Tennyson speaks of "love's dumb cry defying change/To test his worth" (95.27–28), is love defying change in order to test its own worth, as we originally assume? Or is love challenging change to do the testing? Is change the adversary that love must defy, or is change the secret ally, the agent that conducts the testing and so proves love's worth? The momentary uncertainty about the grammar, which is made more uncertain by the brief hovering over the line break, imparts an elegiac tremor to the lines. So does Tennyson's revival of the verb "fluctuate" 's odd transitive meaning of "making tremulous by throwing into wavelike motion": "And fluctuate all the still perfume" (95.56). The mourner uses as well as mentions the idea of a tremor by allowing "fluctuate" to fluctuate for an instant between its normal intransitive and its much stranger transitive meaning.

The New Criticism, or old formalism, in which many students of the 1950s and 1960s were trained, looked for order and coherence in Tennyson. Post-structuralism sees discontinuities, disorders, breaks. Many critics would now agree that the sheer length and repetitiveness of *In Memoriam* refuse to fulfill the generic promise of a pastoral elegy, which isolates and contains the mourner's grieving. Even after Hallam's culminating communication with Tennyson in the garden, the action of the elegy is still in urgent progress. A drama continues even after the story should formally conclude. In controlling grief, the elegist also transgresses norms by trying *not* to make the reader feel that art is totally coherent and controlled. The comfortable framework of art confines the reader to a knowable universe. But death is an unmanageable, mind-expanding event. A wholly controlled elegy makes at most an impact on a mourner and a reader. But an elegiac tremor is induced whenever Tennyson chooses to break down boundaries and create a sense that his elegy, like his life, is simultaneously continuous and broken. Hallam's poetry of mere reflection is to his poetry of sensation in his 1831 review of Tennyson's poems what the *impact* of bad news that we continue to remove from us and contemplate at some distance is to the *tremor* of a more immediate concern, a brokenness we experience like the taste of self-knowledge, and which is often accompanied by profound inner change.

*   *   *

The Power of Genre: A Pragmatic Criticism

Any study of elegy is a study of genre; and generic criticism is a traditional enemy of the literary text. To correct the tendency of a generic critic to search for axioms and norms, a rhetorical critic shows how elegies are as distinctive as a tremor of grief, or as a shock wave of pain, and are never wholly explicable in general terms alone. To talk about the tremor induced by Tennyson's verse epistle to Dufferin is to talk about the way it transgresses an elegiac norm. Its grief is most acute when most hidden, and its power to heal most apparent when consolation is renounced altogether and the elegiac germ of the poem is disguised as something else: as a letter of thanks to a friend. A close reader of elegy will make us aware of the difference between a theory of the genre and Tennyson's idiosyncratic conduct of a given poem. Alert to the tremors of feeling created by line breaks and caesural pauses, a rhetorical critic will seek the most suggestive misfit between prescribed rules and what Helen Vendler has called "the imp of the perverse, the Muse of the unpredictable next line."[4]

A second advantage of rhetorical criticism is that it is pragmatic: it helps readers make better or more convincing arguments. As pragmatists we seek in a theory of genre the least willful distortion of what we experience as we read. It is the explicit incompleteness of any explanatory theory of elegy that "creates the seeming completion or fullness" of a poem like *In Memoriam* that we are trying to explain. The theory's incompletion "makes the literary text seem to elude us, to contain more than we can know."[5] For this reason it may even be useful at a certain stage of criticism to treat each elegy sui generis, since drawing attention to family resemblances may blunt the strangeness of an elegy. And strangeness is like death: it keeps us in touch with elusiveness and mystery. No one has any specialized knowledge of death; in this area there are only the ideologies that inhibit freedom and limit hope.

Like the distinction between strong and weak mourners, which crosses historical boundaries and is justified not just historically or theoretically but also pragmatically, the distinction made in this chapter between an impact and a tremor is to be used as a tool of critical explanation. It engenders power, not by what it enables a magician or seer, a Christ-Orpheus, to do inside a pastoral elegy like "Lycidas," but by what it enables an enterprising reader to do. The alternative to such flexible pragmatic criticism is to assume, like Dr. Johnson, that a poem's uniqueness lies only in its typicality: "Lycidas" is merely an example of its genre, "a pastoral, easy, vulgar, and therefore disgusting"—a pronouncement that inhibits critical inquiry and that displays what one commentator has called a peculiarly "classical form of stupidity."[6]

The impacts and tremors I have been tracing in Tennyson's elegies also describe the process of a genre's breakdown and renewal. When an elegiac convention, instead of making its anticipated impact, generates a tremor of unbelief or critical questioning, it may lead a poet to write more idiosyncratically and honestly. Instead of trying to emulate Milton or Shelley, Tennyson may discover that "*In Memoriam* is also a poem about making do, about submitting to the flow of moments, to the uncertainties that succeed every certainty" (Peltason, 46). If the first shock of unbelief is followed by an aftershock of recognition, by a discovery that "There lives more faith in honest doubt" (*In Memoriam*, 96.11) than in a merely pro forma affirmation of belief, the poet may discover a new way of writing elegy. With

4. Helen Vendler, *The Music of What Happens: Poems, Poets, Critics* (Cambridge, MA, 1988), p. 25.
5. Adena Rosmarin, *The Power of Genre* (Minneapolis, 1985), p. 44.
6. Francis Sparshott, "Notes on the Articulation of Time," *New Literary History* 1 (1970): 311–34, p. 332.

time, any initial shock effect will probably wear off, and the subversive questioning of a new kind of mourner, of someone like the wife in Frost's "Home Burial," may be needed to generate new tremors of dissatisfaction and grievance. Such serial shocks and aftershocks even describe the genesis of chapters in this book. Dissatisfied with traditional accounts of elegy, which too often assume that all mourners aspire to the condition of the pastoral elegist, I wanted to show how norms live and become visible by transgressing other norms. Judged by the criteria of pastoral elegy, there is too much Tennyson in *In Memoriam* and too little Hallam. But because no one would ever make the same criticism of Augustine's *Confessions* or Newman's *Apologia*, I began to suspect that we may be requiring such an elegy to meet the wrong norms. When I found that lyric anxiety and even a touch of confessional egotism cannot be assimilated without residue into the tragic catharsis prescribed by pastoral elegy, I also discovered that this same stubborn residue can be made into the nucleus or germ of a second genre: confessional elegy. And when I found again that a core of silence and a brokenness at the heart of eloquence cannot be reconciled with confessional elegy's huge trajectories of grief, thrown like an arch across long spans of time, I discovered that two of the defining norms of Romantic and modern elegy, respectively, were at last coming into clearer focus for me.

SARAH GATES

Poetics, Metaphysics, Genre: The Stanza Form of *In Memoriam*†

The vacillation between opposite aspects of a theme or between opposing states of mind (such as hope and despair) that turn out not to oppose but to define each other is a crucial *modus operandi* in *In Memoriam*. In the past, critics tended to align themselves "in defense" of one side or the other. T. S. Eliot, for example, asserted of the faith/doubt theme that "its faith is a poor thing, but its doubt is a very intense experience,"[1] while Carlisle Moore argued, on the other hand, that this "doubt" really only serves the "faith" by proving its strength.[2] J.C.C. Mays synthesizes these positions by treating such apparent conflicts as interrelated and mutually constitutive

† From *Victorian Poetry* 37 (1999) 507–19. Reprinted by permission of *Victorian Poetry*.

1. T. S. Eliot, "In Memoriam," in *Tennyson: In Memoriam: A Casebook*, ed. John Dixon Hunt (London: Macmillan, 1970), p. 135. [See above, p. 138.]
2. Carlisle Moore, "Faith, Doubt, and Mystical Experience in 'In Memoriam,' " in Hunt, pp. 241–259.

dichotomous oppositions that animate the progress of the poem, arguing that each half only comes to know itself through the other half, so that the "whole progression of the poem is through opposition playing against itself" with the resolution occurring only in time.[3] In a similar tangle of apparently contradictory positions, studies of the poem that treat its structural form have tended to enlist it into the ranks of essentially narrative genres—"confession" or "autobiography," for example[4]—while others cast it as essentially lyric —as "fragment," "elegy," "sonnet sequence," "collection of aphorisms"—thus addressing each side of an apparent formal contradiction between the poem's lyric concentration and its narrative drift.[5] Although these formalist considerations seem less susceptible to the kind of synthesizing achieved in the thematic studies, David Shaw has made a detailed and illuminating examination into the generic affiliations of this narrative in lyrics and the ways in which Tennyson "tests" or expands the conventions of the genres he uses.[6] He suggests in *Tennyson's Style* that "even if there is no final generic reconciliation in *In Memoriam* (and I know of no study that convincingly demonstrates that there is), the poem as a whole does manage to achieve [a] kind of continuity in change" (pp. 146–147). In this essay, I would like to propose a way to understand this "continuity in change," by adapting some of Jean Starobinski's ideas about autobiography to a lyric format along the way, and especially by making a detailed exploration of poetics, of the peculiar appropriateness of Tennyson's *abba* stanza form as a vehicle for embodying and signifying his intellectual and spiritual conflicts (the thematic material), and his own journey through them (the autobiographical structure).[7] It seems clear to me that if we want to

3. J. C. C. Mays, "*In Memoriam*: An Aspect of Form," *UTQ* 35 (1965):28.
4. W. David Shaw discusses *In Memoriam* as a "confession" in "*In Memoriam* and the Rhetoric of Confession," *ELH* 38 (1971): 80–103 and later as "spiritual autobiography" in *Tennyson's Style* (Ithaca: Cornell Univ. Press, 1976), p. 132. Hereafter referred to as *Style*.
5. Donald Hair claims that "the fragment . . . is the essential form of the work" in *Tennyson's Language* (Toronto: Univ. of Toronto Press, 1991), a claim he supports in his analysis of the "theories of language" that "underwrite" the poem (p. 89). Peter Hinchcliffe analyzes *In Memoriam* as an "elegy" resolved at the end by an "epithalamium" in "Elegy and Epithalamium in *In Memoriam*," *UTQ* 52 (1983):142–162. He includes the list of "competing" "generic signals" the poem seems to provide which have been treated as "formal models" for understanding the poem in the past. Peter M. Sacks regards it as an "elegy" in his psychoanalytic study of the genre in *The English Elegy: Studies in the Genre from Spenser to Yeats* (Baltimore: Johns Hopkins Univ. Press, 1985). Shaw reads the poem as an elegy in *Elegy and Paradox: Testing the Conventions* (Baltimore: Johns Hopkins Univ. Press, 1994), in which he explores the ways *In Memoriam* "tests" the conventions of that genre, especially in its Darwinian context, which was undermining the spiritual kinds of consolation that had historically granted their resolutions.
6. See W. David Shaw, *Tennyson's Style*; *Elegy and Paradox*; and *Alfred Lord Tennyson: The Poet in an Age of Theory* (New York: Basil Blackwell, 1996); hereafter referred to as *ALT*.
7. My model for this study is John Freccero's "The Significance of *Terza Rima*," in John Freccero, *Dante: The Poetics of Conversion*, ed. Rachel Jacoff (Cambridge: Harvard Univ. Press, 1986), pp. 258–271, which explores the interaction of thematics and poetics in a specific verse form.

understand the "coherence" (the term Peter Hinchcliffe prefers, quite reasonably, to "unity" [p. 242]) of this extraordinarily self-contradictory, fluidly granulated work, we might start with a look at the only constant—and an obsessive constant it is—to be found in it.

Critics have often commented in passing upon the effect of the *abba* stanza form which, Christopher Ricks, for example, says "can 'circle moaning in the air', returning to its setting out, and with fertile circularity staving off its deepest terror and arrival at desolation and indifference." In his analysis, the *abba* form enacts in the outer rhymes the mourner's desire to "travel" rather than to "arrive," to continue missing Hallam rather than to cease loving him. The fourth line circles back to the first line via the rhyme; the stanza returns to its beginning; and thus, like the thoughts of the mourner,

> reced[es] from its affirmations, from what it momentarily clinches, so unlike the disputatious sequences of the heroic couplet: these very reasons make it the emblem as well as the instrument for poems in which moods ebb and flow, . . . in which hopes are recurrent but always then dimmed—though never shattered.[8]

This wonderful description itself enacts exactly the feel of the *In Memoriam* stanza. More recently, David Shaw has pointed out that the middle lines of the stanzas "contract the meaning, while the first and fourth lines tend to diffuse it," and "that the whole energy of the last line is directed forward, while the energy of the first line is directed back," a dynamic which produces "frequent stalemates . . . between forces of closure and delay" (*ALT*, p. 33), and Peter Sacks has mentioned that the self-enclosed quality of the stanzas enacts a kind of frozenness in the present that is symptomatic of melancholia (p. 169). These descriptions are helpful and put us on the right path, but more can be said about the *abba* form.

The fourth line does gesture back to the first, but it does not enact a complete return, for it can only do so after the reader has passed through the two middle lines whose couplet form gives so much strength to their rhyme. Thus, the outer rhyme of a--a is distanced; the second "a" recollects only dimly the first "a," which by then has become a faint echo and seems, in spite of the rhyme, to have been something different than the "a" we are now reading. The effect of this pattern was aptly described by Charles Kingsley in 1850: "The mournful minor rhyme of each first and fourth line always leads the ear to expect something beyond."[9] The second "a" "returns," but it

---

8. Christopher Ricks, *Tennyson* (New York: Macmillan, 1972), p. 228. [See above, pp. 185–6.]
9. Quoted in Christopher Ricks, *Tennyson*, p. 228.

also leads "beyond" because it is different from the middle couplets and only faintly recollects its partner. The movement, then, is one of vacillation (a to bb, and back to a), of gesturing backward (a ← a), and of leading beyond (bb → a). Rather than characterize this movement as a circle, I would call it a spiral, a figure that includes the backward forward gesturing of vacillation, the repetition risking stasis (the central concentration), but also the outer diffusion, the movement beyond. The ends do not quite meet: the first "a" raises the anticipation of the second, but the intervening couplet interrupts the closure, or deflects the rhyme, so that the second "a" recollects, but differs from, the first. The outer lines, therefore, gesture toward enfolding the inner lines, but at the same time, the inner lines break through, or refuse this enfolding gesture.

These enfoldings and interruptions can act upon each other in turns, especially if we expand our focus from individual stanza to the level of whole lyric: once the intervening middle deflects the closure of the enfolding ends, it becomes dominant. But then its very dominance becomes in turn vulnerable to deflection by the material it has interrupted. (Every "clinching" is in this poem ephemeral, as Ricks has already pointed out.) We can see this process quite clearly in section 127: the peace of the phrase "All is well" begins and ends the lyric, but is disrupted by the vivid and violent descriptions of revolution that fill the middle:

> And all is well, though faith and form
> > Be sundered in the night of fear;
> > Well roars the storm to those that hear
> A deeper voice across the storm,
>
> Proclaiming social truth shall spread,
> > And justice, even though thrice again
> > The red fool-fury of the Seine
> Should pile her barricades with dead.
>
> But ill for him that wears a crown,
> > And him, the lazar, in his rags:
> > They tremble, the sustaining crags;
> The spires of ice are toppled down,
>
> And molten up, and roar in flood;
> > The fortress crashes from on high,
> > The brute earth lightens to the sky,
> And the great Aeon sinks in blood,
>
> And compassed by the fires of Hell;
> > While thou, dear spirit, happy star,

> O'erlook'st the tumult from afar,
> And smilest, knowing all is well.[1]

The peace at the end prevails, in large part, because of the shifting placement of its imagery within the construction of the stanzas. It moves from the position of fragile enclosure in the outer lines of stanza 1 (the "And all is well, though" and "A deeper voice" in the first and fourth lines which surround, but fail to enclose, the "sundering" and "roaring" of lines 2 and 3) to the position of solid core in the middle couplet of stanza five ("While thou, dear spirit, happy star,/O'erlook'st the tumult from afar"). The violence which disrupts stanza 1 with the "sundering" and "roaring" possesses the middle of the lyric—stanzas 3 and 4—but enters only the first of the outer rhyming lines of the last stanza. Thus, what is at first an interrupting core of violence becomes an encompassing force, which is in turn interrupted and calmed (or settled) by a new core of peace which is ushered in by the "dear spirit, happy star" in the middle couplet of the last stanza. In the end, the last line, which fulfills the anticipatory "All is well, though" of line 1, is both a return and a movement beyond. The first "And all is well" is qualified by the subsequent "though" which introduces all the violence, while the last "all is well" follows strongly upon the "smiling" of this "happy star" and the over-looking "from afar" which immediately precede it. This chiastic structure is a larger version of the stanzaic *abba* in which the final rhyme gestures toward, yet recalls only faintly, its antecedent. The final "all is well," because it has conquered the middle disruption and because it comes from a heavenly plane that lies above both the disruptions and the peace that characterize the vicissitudes of earthly existence, recalls only faintly the first unsure "And all is well, though." Its context is much wider; its "well-being" has been earned. The spiral has swung next to, but past, its origin.

Moving from the level of individual lyric to broader theme, I would like to turn to sections 5 and 19, a pair of meditations on expression, silence, and grief which addresses the theme of "expressing the inexpressible." Together, they yield the insight that the inexpressible nature of the mourner's grief comes from the inner intensity of feeling and the inadequacy of words. Characteristically, however, they make this claim in the sort of spiraling vacillation through opposite positions in an idea or state of mind, which the *abba* form so clearly enacts. At first, in section 5, "words" do not provide a channel for the release of inner feeling, but instead "half conceal" it:

> I sometimes hold it half a sin
> To put in words the grief I feel;

---

1. Citations are from *The Poems of Tennyson*, ed. Christopher Ricks (Berkeley: Univ. of California Press, 1987). Lyric and line numbers will appear parenthetically within the text.

> For words, like Nature, half reveal
> And half conceal the Soul within.
>
> But, for the unquiet heart and brain,
>   A use in measured language lies;
>   The sad mechanic exercise,
> Like dull narcotics, numbing pain.
>   (1–8)

The outer garment of words, which in section 19 will allow the expression of grief, here prevents it. It enfolds, "half reveals and half conceals" the feeling, at best providing "dull narcotics" to "numb pain." As we might expect, these silencing (because inadequate) "words" and "language" appear interruptingly in the middle couplets, and hamper the expression of the "Soul's" feeling—the "sin," the "despair," the "pain," the "unquiet heart and brain" which extend uncertainly across the outer lines. But in the final stanza, "words" move into those outer lines:

> In words, like weeds, I'll wrap me o'er,
>   Like coarsest clothes against the cold:
>   But that large grief which these enfold
> Is given in outline and no more.
>   (9–12)

We begin a movement toward the other side of the spiral's loop, where "grief" will appear in the middle position and "words" in the outer. In the above stanza, "words" have begun a transformation into the early phase of expression—the "outline"; when we get to section 19, we will find a full exploration of this answering "opposite" (and at its close, the return "beyond"):

> There twice a day the Severn fills;
>   The salt sea-water passes by,
>   And hushes half the babbling Wye,
> And makes a silence in the hills.
>
> The Wye is hushed nor moved along,
>   And hushed my deepest grief of all,
>   When filled with tears that cannot fall,
> I brim with sorrow drowning song.
>   (19:5–12)

Now it is not the language (as container or garment), but the filling (the content) that silences. The fullness of grief imaged in the filling of the Severn and the Wye with "the salt sea-water" silences the surrounding hills just as the overwhelming ocean of unshed and unsheddable tears drowns the mourner's "song." Whereas in section 5 the inadequacy of words in the middles—words as concealment—

had silenced, here at the far side of the loop, the density and concentration of grief in the middles—the tidal act of the "filling"—"hushes." But in the last stanza we swing around once again, just beyond the point in section 5 where "words" became the "outline":

> The tide flows down, the wave again
>   Is vocal in its wooded walls;
>   My deeper anguish also falls,
> And I can speak a little then.
>
> (13–17)

The draining allows "vocality," the "falling" anguish allows speech. Here, though, the "tide flows down" in the first outer line, almost as though the full stillness in the middle couplets has begun to drain into, or even through, those outer lines, as the mourner begins to "speak a little." He equates the tide's flow, the water's drainage, with his own speaking by setting "The tide flows down" and "I can speak" into the rhymed pair of outer lines—thus "draining" and relieving a too full container of its contents. Importantly, this means that the "flowing," "vocality," "anguish," and "speaking" occur in every line of the stanza, making this "expression" fuller. The anticipated "expression" given in "outline" in 5 is completed—but beyond—in this repetition with a difference. "Speaking a little" recollects "To put in words," but it is more "expressive"; it allows more grief to flow. In this thematic spiral of silencing-expression-silencing-expression, the anticipatory "outline" is "filled" and then "drained" in a more relieving expression, "speaking" that "rhymes" with the first "outline" of expression but moves beyond it as well.

No doubt we could trace more loops in this theme, in which more grief, more reticence, or less adequacy would disrupt this newly won expression, for this process, like the spiral as a form, is potentially endless. However, I would rather trace such a longer set of revolving vacillations below, in the movements of Tennyson's general metaphysical discussion in *In Memoriam*. For now, I want to turn briefly to the recurrence of images and events in *In Memoriam*—the yew tree and the dark house, the Christmases, and the anniversaries of Hallam's death with which the mourner marks his emotional progress. In each case, the fulfillment "returns" to the motif established in anticipation, but also transcends the original scope. This pattern is perhaps clearest in the "Christmas" lyrics. Both sections 28 and 104 begin with the same lines: "The time draws near the birth of Christ:/The moon is hid; the night is still" (28:1–2, 104:1–2), and continue with the same image of bells in the mist: "The Christmas bells from hill to hill/Answer each other in the mist" (28:3–4) and "A single church below the hill/Is pealing, folded in the mist" (104:

3–4). But the cluster of images in section 104 has been replaced, in that the family has moved from the home of section 28, and re-felt, for the mourner has moved beyond the despair of sections 28–30 ("This year I slept and woke with pain,/I almost wished no more to wake,/And that my hold on life would break" [28:13–15]) and the quieter grief expressed in section 78 ("But over all things brooding slept /The quiet sense of something lost" [7–8]), to a larger sense of poetic vocation. The bells whose "merry, merry" "voices" bring "sorrow touched with joy" in section 28 can boldly "ring out the old, ring in the new" by section 106, signaling the mourner's readiness for higher poetic achievement: "Ring out, ring out my mournful rhymes,/But ring the fuller minstrel in" (19–20). Thus the vacillation and spiraling revolutions of the *abba* rhyme scheme, which characterize the individual stanzas, also characterize the broader movements among recurring images and events in the poem as a whole.

So, too, will it prove characteristic of the poem's metaphysical discussions. The vacillations between faith and doubt supply one of those "animating" forces that run through the poem—one that fails to settle even in the very frame that is supposed to resolve and close it. Before taking up this frame in detail, however, I would like to pick up the faith/doubt spiral in the famous central "trance" lyrics (sections 95 and 96), where we will see the spiraling vacillation characterized by the same enclosing/deflecting process I have been tracing. At first, doubt enfolds or encloses the possibility of faith while the mourner despairs. Then faith emerges from the center of this doubt, only to be struck through the center again by doubt, and so on. Beginning in section 95, the mourner's soul is swept up into Hallam's spirit, right out of the center of his heart's "hunger" (and at the center of the lyric-stanzas 7 and 8):

> A hunger seized my heart; I read
>   Of that glad year which once had been,
>   In those fallen leaves which kept their green,
> The noble letters of the dead:
>
> And strangely on the silence broke
>   The silent-speaking words, and strange
>   Was love's dumb cry defying change
> To test his worth; and strangely spoke
>
> The faith, the vigour, bold to dwell
>   On doubts that drive the coward back,
>   And keen through wordy snares to track
> Suggestion to her inmost cell.

So word by word, and line by line,
    The dead man touched me from the past,
    And all at once it seemed at last
The living soul was flashed on mine,

And mine in this was wound, and whirled
    About empyreal heights of thought,
    And came on that which is, and caught
The deep pulsations of the world,

Aeonian music measuring out
    The steps of Time—the shocks of Chance—
    The blows of Death. At length my trance
Was cancelled, stricken through with doubt.
                                    (95:21–44)

It is a most powerful doubt, having struck through and "cancelled"
such a rapturous, "empyreal" faith as is this one with which the spirit
has "whirled" up the mourner. Moreover, true to the spiral pattern
of enclosing and deflecting middles and ends, it is from the middle
of this new rapturous faith—and the line—that the mourner is
"stricken through," and returned to the earthly world, where the
"doubtful dusk" shows the "knolls" and "the white kine" (50–51). It
is a doubt, we could say, that "rhymes" with, yet moves "beyond" the
earlier doubt—the "hunger" that begins the lyric. But out of this new
doubt arises a new faith in section 96: "There lives more faith in
honest doubt,/Believe me, than in half the creeds" (11–12). This
recovered faith has a stronger quality because it, in turn, is wrung
out of the powerful doubt just expressed in section 95, as the lyric
goes on to recount (here, the mourner is speaking of Hallam, but is
clearly using him as the model for his own process of regaining faith
as well):

He fought his doubts and gathered strength,
    He would not make his judgment blind,
    He faced the spectres of the mind
And laid them: thus he came at length

To find a stronger faith his own. (96:13–17)

Like the final "all is well" of section 127, the faith of section 96 has
been regained on a different plane; it has lived through and encom-
passed the earlier doubt and now comes from the surer grounding
in "judgment" which overcomes such "spectres of the mind" as, for
example, the "spectral" experience recounted in section 95. Thus,

this opening chime, the "spectral" faith of 95, has become only an echo to this new, surer faith that has come with the fulfillment of that early anticipation. But this new faith is, of course, susceptible to new doubts—the spiral does not stop—as we find in studying, for example, section 122. Here, the mourner runs up against that "judgment," which made the faith of section 96 so strong, in the doubts of "reason," expressed as anxiety about the reality of the experience reported in section 95: "Oh, wast thou with me, dearest, then?" (122:1) and "*If* thou wert with me" (122:9, emphasis added). However, by section 124 he spirals around again to another faith—one felt in the "heart," one which "melts" away the outer "freezing reason" from within, from a warmer center of feeling in the "breast":

> A warmth within the breast would melt
> The freezing reason's colder part,
> And like a man in wrath the heart
> Stood up and answered "I have felt."
>   (124:13–16)

The strength of the heart's "stand" rhymes with the earlier "judged" faith of section 96, but also moves beyond it: it has spiraled through and overcome the doubts produced by reason (and fed the "hunger" of the "heart" in section 95 as well).

These movements between faith and doubt and from Christmas to Christmas which trace the development from "mournful rhymes" to "fuller minstrel" bring me to another aspect of the poem, the mourner's evolution or "way of a soul." Alan Sinfield treats this idea thematically, as one of those dichotomies that animate the poem— this one between "Tennyson the private man" and "Tennyson the public poet," Tennyson the Romantic who expresses personal grief because he cannot help it ("piping but as the linnets sing") and Tennyson the Enlightenment classicist who makes a work of art by shaping his language carefully ("All as in some piece of art,/Is toil coöperant to an end"). These two natures struggle: the private man must turn his grief into art, thus allowing the public poet to appear; in turn, the "artifact" created by the public poet gives expression to the personal grief of the private man. One continually gives way to the other in a constant vacillation that, I would argue, is reflected in the *abba* stanza form.[2] However, I would like to cast my discussion of this issue in terms of genre rather than theme. For it seems to me that this development manifests itself in large part as a kind of *abba* spiraling vacillation between the fugal linearity and the centrifugal force of autobiographical "narrative" and the gravitational concen-

---

2. See the chapter, "*In Memoriam:* The Linnet and the Artifact" in Alan Sinfield, *The Language of Tennyson's* In Memoriam (New York: Barnes and Noble, 1971), pp. 17–40.

tration and the centripetal force of lyric "moment." Studies of *In Memoriam* have wrestled with just this structural conflict between the basic narrative thrust of the whole and the (also basic) lyric stasis of the parts. Ralph Rader describes the first as "a sense throughout of the poem as a serially staged existential projection into time, in which the later stages were not for poet, any more than for speaker/ actor, foreseen at the earlier stages,"[3] while Timothy Peltason evocatively describes the experience of reading each lyric moment:

> Reading a single section of *In Memoriam*, we fall into its lyric space only to pass through it and emerge blinking on the other side. Our experience as readers thus matches that of the poet, for whom consciousness is a constant series of repetitions, enchantments, and reawakenings.[4]

David Shaw addresses generic structure more formalistically, claiming variously that "individual sections have the concision of gravestone inscriptions but the poem as a whole is digressive. It has the amplitude of spiritual autobiography" (*Style*, p. 132), and that "Tennyson tries to accommodate elegy's high style and decorum to a diary's informalities and to the intimacies of a verse epistle" (*ALT*, p. 1). To my mind, it is exactly these opposing energies that propel what I would like to call its generic spiral, which is reflected in the *abba* stanza form. To clarify what I mean, however, I need to call upon some structural theory of autobiography—specifically, a passage from Jean Starobinski's "The Style of Autobiography," which articulates his notion of the "double deviation" of the autobiographical "I":

> The narrator describes not only what happened to him at a different time in his life but above all how he became—out of what he was—what he presently is. . . . The chain of experiences traces a path (though a sinuous one) that ends in the present state of recapitulatory knowledge.
>
> The deviation, which establishes the autobiographical reflection, is thus double: it is at once a deviation of time and of identity.[5]

I wish to secure two points from this passage: first, that the narrator is a present "I" who recollects the links in the "chain of experience" between him- or herself and the protagonist, the past "I"; second, that the "deviation" between narrator and protagonist is one of both

---

3. Ralph Rader, "Notes on Some Structural Varieties and Variations in Dramatic 'I' Poems and their Theoretical Implications," *VP* 22 (1984): 117.
4. Timothy Peltason, *Reading* In Memoriam (Princeton: Princeton Univ. Press, 1985), p. 84.
5. Jean Starobinski, "The Style of Autobiography," trans. Seymour Chatman, in *Autobiography: Essays Theoretical and Critical*, ed. James Olney (Princeton: Princeton Univ. Press, 1980), pp. 78–79.

time and identity. These points can help translate what have been the kind of experiential articulations of the poem's effect (such as those quoted above) into structural terms. Both deviations are at work in *In Memoriam*, although the lyric format of this "auto-biography" requires some adaptation of terminology. The speaker is not a present narrator, who, by recollecting a past self as protagonist gives his experience shape and coherence (or, as Starobinski says, the "contour of a life" [p. 73]), but is instead a present protagonist, who "speaks" these experiences and selves as they occur, in a series of lyric comments which slowly add up to something like a "contour of life." In other words, because of the lyric format of *In Memoriam*, the autobiographical deviations are dynamically reversed. Tempo-rally, we see the protagonist encounter his vicissitudes through his own eyes as they occur, and not through those of a resultant presid-ing consciousness recollecting them from a later time. The protag-onist raises his anticipations and voices his desires for his future self; his temporal deviation comes between the present "I" and the hoped for future "I": "Men may rise on stepping stones/Of their dead selves to higher things" (1:3–4). The deviation of identity is similarly reversed. The mourner does not cast back and examine the man he used to be and how he became the man he is, but instead longs for Hallam, the lost and future ideal self he would like to rejoin in either this world or the next. The "life" of *In Memoriam* or the mourner's "autobiography" is the story of "I" in a state of becoming, or, as Chris-topher Ricks says, of traveling rather than arriving.

Thus we can see, once again, the suitability of the *abba* stanza form. The mourner at the beginning, like the stanza in its first line, must live through the difficult experience of middle time in order to arrive at his final state, as the stanza arrives at its closing rhyme. Just as the first line raises the anticipation of its partner in the fourth line but then fades into a faint echo as that partner spins past closure, the mourner's hopes for himself and Hallam anticipate their reunion, although when it comes, the "reunion" differs from the original anticipation. The double deviation created by the mourner at the beginning is never closed because the nature of the mourner himself changes through the experiences described—or more accurately, lived—in each lyric, just as the intervening bb couplets transform by interruption the a- -a rhyme. The mourner at the end "rhymes" with, but yet has evolved beyond, the earlier mourner. The spiritual reun-ion with Hallam in section 103, for example, fulfills its anticipation, but not as that anticipation had originally imagined. Hallam does not come back to earth, nor does the mourner die; rather, their "spirits" meet in the dreamed higher sphere that makes of the original desire a faint echo, or a dim recollection, of a past self, a "dead self"—the "stepping stone" to this higher place. The mourner at the end of *In*

Memoriam desires neither an earthly reunion with Hallam nor a heavenly one (through death), any more than he desires to return to his early despair.

It is difficult to imagine a form better suited to accommodate both the evolutionary movement toward the "fuller minstrel" or the "higher race" and the self-enclosed, concentrated, individual lyric moments of fear, despair, or rage. However, its principle of spiraling revolution can also help to explain what Shaw (among others) has found to be "weak" closural gestures, for it is a form that seems particularly unsuited to the sealing and transcending requirements of "resolution." First, there is no interlacing between stanzas in the rhyme scheme (as there is in *terza rima*, for example)—a form that gives the stanzas what Peter Sacks calls a "self-encysted quality, an effect of being withheld from time" (pp. 168–169) and therefore, also, from time's discursive equivalents, narrative and the closures that mark its shapes. As in the flux of life (and the feel of *In Memoriam* seems to me closer to that flux than the most "realistic" of narratives), a sense of wholeness and overarching shape is difficult to perceive or to produce; the vacillations in thought, identity, or state of mind can continue forever, just as the stanzas can replicate themselves in self-enclosed, "lapidary" granules ad infinitum (*Style*, p. 132). Moreover, the spiral itself is an infinite, an endless, "closure-less," linear sort of "shape" that can only be brought to a stop arbitrarily (unlike other geometrical shapes that close themselves). This "stop" (the exact term is difficult to choose, for one cannot say "resolution," "closure," "conclusion," or even "finish" since none of these sealing actions takes place here) is just what the framing Prologue and Epilogue attempt to impose: an arbitrary stoppage to the spiraling doubts, faiths, expressions, silences, progressions, and regressions. (As David Shaw remarks: "The long elegy seems endlessly to end, and so never ends at all, except by a kind of optional stop rule that says, 'now we shall have an epithalamium that writes "finis" to our story' " [*ALT*, p. 32]). The frame itself gets swept up in the power, I believe, of the stanza form it shares with the rest of the poem and in its most intractable thematic incarnation, the vacillation between faith and doubt. So in the Prologue, we have a prayer to the "Strong Son of God, immortal Love" for faith, for a closing or bridging of the abyss between human and divine wisdom: "And in thy wisdom make me wise" (44). In the Epilogue, this faith is forged, this abyss is bridged, from the earthly side by the child to be conceived on the wedding night, the "closer link/Betwixt us and the crowning race/Of those that, eye to eye, shall look/On knowledge" (127–130), and from the heavenly side by Hallam's spirit, the "noble type/Appearing ere the times were ripe/That friend of mine who lives in God" (138–140).

This new bridge, the fulfillment of the prayer in the Prologue, has been earned in the interposing lyrics of *In Memoriam* which perform all the vacillating labor of doubting and finding faith, losing and regaining Hallam, so that, as fulfillment, it represents, like all the others, a movement beyond its anticipation. However, in the final stanza of the Epilogue, just as "That God" seems at last "one" with the creation (with no bridges needed), a new, wider abyss opens out:

> That God, which ever lives and loves,
>   One God, one law, one element,
>   And one far-off divine event,
> To which the whole creation moves.
>   (141–144)

Just at the end of the solid rhyming "oneness" invoked in the middle couplet, we find the fourth line once again pulling away, opening a gap. The "divine event" is suddenly "far off," and the "whole creation" just as suddenly lagging behind, having to "move," to cross another, vaster abyss which is signified in the assonance of the outer lines: God "loves" and it "moves." They reach, they yearn toward one another but cannot close, and we find ourselves swinging around another side of another loop, one whose "movement beyond" remains, this time, unrecorded—perhaps the only possible "stop" to this singular lyric narrative-narrative lyric.

Tennyson: A Chronology

1809   Born (August 6) at Somersby, Lincolnshire.
1811   Arthur Henry Hallam born (February 1).
       Emily Tennyson born.
1827   Together with two of his brothers publishes a small volume of poetry.
       Enters Trinity College, Cambridge.
1828   Hallam arrives at Trinity.
1829   Meets Hallam some time in the spring; invites him to Somersby (December), where Hallam meets Emily.
1830   Publishes *Poems, Chiefly Lyrical*.
       Travels with Hallam in southern France (summer).
1831   Death of his father, George Tennyson (March); returns to his family in Lincolnshire without finishing his degree at Cambridge.
       Hallam publishes a favorable review of *Poems, Chiefly Lyrical*.
1832   Hallam's engagement to Emily finally recognized by Hallam's parents.
       Publishes *Poems* with Hallam's encouragement.
1833   Hallam dies in Vienna of a cerebral hemorrhage (September 15). Tennyson receives the news in early October; begins writing sections of *In Memoriam* later that month.
       Ship bearing Hallam's body arrives in England in late December; the funeral, which Tennyson does not attend, takes place in early January 1834.
1837   Arranges for his family to move from Somersby to High Beech, Epping.
       Engaged to Emily Sellwood.
1840   Engagement broken off.
1842   Publishes *Poems* in two volumes, his first book of verse since Hallam's death.
       Marriage of Cecilia Tennyson (b. 1817), described in the "Epilogue" to *In Memoriam*.

1850   Publishes *In Memoriam* to great critical acclaim (May).
        Marries Emily Sellwood (June).
        Named poet laureate by Queen Victoria (November).
1892   Dies (October 6) and is buried in Westminster Abbey.

Selected Bibliography

• indicates items included or excerpted in this Norton Critical Edition.

I. EDITIONS

The major editions of the poem are as follows:

The Works of Alfred, Lord Tennyson. Ed. Hallam, Lord Tennyson. London: Macmillan, 1907–08 (the "Eversley Edition").
> Volume 2 contains not only the final version of *In Memoriam* overseen by Tennyson, but also a number of notes, both by Tennyson and by his son Hallam, prepared specially for this edition.

The Poems of Tennyson. Ed. Christopher Ricks. 2nd ed. Berkeley: University of California Press, 1987.
> This landmark in Tennyson scholarship, first published in 1969, is the standard edition for all of Tennyson's poetry; it contains a full textual apparatus and a concise and informative introduction to the poem. There is also a one-volume *Selected Poems* drawn from the Ricks edition (published by Longman), which contains all of *In Memoriam*.

In Memoriam. Ed. Susan Shatto and Marion Shaw. Oxford: Clarendon Press, 1982.
> This is the most complete edition of the poem available. It includes extensive notes on each section, a detailed description of all the manuscripts and printed texts, and appendices containing additional poems that were once part of *In Memoriam* but were not included in the final version. The introduction describes the growth of the poem and very usefully discusses classical analogues.

II. BIOGRAPHIES AND BACKGROUND

The most useful sources are the following (in order of publication):

• Hallam, Lord Tennyson. *Tennyson: A Memoir.* London: Macmillan, 1897.
> Hallam Tennyson's memoir of his father has been an indispensable resource for subsequent Tennyson studies. The chapter on *In Memoriam* contains extensive comments by the poet concerning his intentions.

T. H. Vail Motter, ed. *The Writings of Arthur Hallam.* New York: Modern Language Association, 1943.
> Motter's edition reproduces Hallam's poems, criticism, and theological writings, many of which directly influenced the writing of Tennyson's poem.

Sir Charles Tennyson. *Alfred Tennyson.* London and New York: Macmillan, 1949.
> This biography by the poet's grandson fills in gaps left by the *Memoir*, including details of the poet's troubled boyhood with his brooding father.

Robert Bernard Martin. *Tennyson: The Unquiet Heart.* New York: Oxford University Press, 1980.
> The best of several good modern biographies, by a writer who was also a respected critic of Victorian literature.

James A. Hoge, ed. *Lady Tennyson's Journal.* Charlottesville: University Press of Virginia, 1981.
> Emily Sellwood married the poet shortly after the publication of *In Memoriam*. Her journal offers a fascinating insight into their lives in the years 1850–74.

III. CRITICISM

Critical literature on the poem is extraordinarily extensive, including at least four full-length monographs (by Bradley, Mattes, Sinfield, and Peltason, all of them represented in this volume). Joseph Sendry's bibliographic article provides an extremely readable and wide-ranging analysis of criticism up to 1980. The following list therefore concentrates on articles and book chapters that have appeared since the publication of Sendry's article.

Adams, James Eli. "Woman Red in Tooth and Claw: Nature and the Feminine in Tennyson and Darwin." *Victorian Studies* 33 (1989): 7–27.
    Adams astutely analyzes the gendering of the poem's evolutionary models, particularly the personification of Nature as a betraying "demonic woman."
Albright, Daniel. "The Muses' Tug-of-War in *In Memoriam*." *Tennyson: The Muses' Tug-of-War* (pp. 176–213). Charlottesville: University Press of Virginia, 1986.
    In a fresh take on an old theme, Albright explores the polarities of Tennyson's poem, particularly the binaries of heavenly and earthly, expressive and inexpressive.
Armstrong, Isobel. "Tennyson in the 1850s." *Victorian Poetry: Poetry, Poetics and Politics* (pp. 252–83). London and New York: Routledge, 1993.
    As her book's title indicates, Armstrong explores the intersection of poetry and history, and particularly of poetic form and political ideology. The dense, complex chapter on *In Memoriam* considers the influence of Victorian science and language theory on Tennyson's notion of "type."
Baum, Paull F. "In Memoriam." *Tennyson Sixty Years After* (pp. 105–33). Chapel Hill: North Carolina University Press, 1948.
    Baum's book, part of a protracted critical reaction against Tennyson in the first half of the twentieth century, sharply disapproves of *In Memoriam* for its lack of unity and for its mingling of vague theological speculation with trivial personal detail.
• Bradley, A. C. *A Commentary on Tennyson's In Memoriam*. London and New York: Macmillan, 1901.
    Bradley's was the first important book-length study of Tennyson's poem; in addition to a section-by-section commentary, it contains an excellent introduction. The section of the introduction concerning structure usefully divides the poem into four parts, hinging on the Christmas poems, and further identifies thematic subgroups.
Craft, Christopher. " 'Descend, and Touch, and Enter': Tennyson's Strange Manner of Address." *Genders* 1 (1988): 83–101.
    An excellent reading of the link between death and homoerotic desire in *In Memoriam*. Craft lucidly summarizes earlier critical anxiety about the sexuality of the poem, and his reading has strongly influenced later gender-based readings.
• Eliot, T. S. "In Memoriam." *Essays Ancient and Modern* (pp. 175–90). London: Faber and Faber, 1936.
    Eliot's brief but enormously influential essay discusses the nature of Tennysonian doubt and memorably analyzes the poem's confessional structure.
• Gates, Sarah. "Poetics, Metaphysics, Genre: The Stanza Form of *In Memoriam*." *Victorian Poetry* 37 (1999): 507–19.
    Gates relates the poem's most distinctive formal feature, its *abba* stanza, to larger structural units—individual sections, groups of sections, and finally the whole evolutionary narrative.
Gigante, Denise. "Forming Desire: On the Eponymous *In Memoriam* Stanza." *Nineteenth-Century Literature* 53 (1999): 480–504.
    Beginning with Tennyson's Renaissance precursors, Gigante argues persuasively that the *In Memoriam* stanza encapsulates a form of desire that is simultaneously thwarted, endless, and anonymous.
Gold, Barri J. "The Consolation of Physics: Tennyson's Thermodynamic Solution." *PMLA* 117 (2002): 449–64.
    Gold explores the similarities between *In Memoriam* and the developing science of thermodynamics in the mid-nineteenth century, focusing on the balance between the laws of conservation of energy and entropy.
Hair, Donald S. "Tennyson's Domestic Elegy." *Domestic and Heroic in Tennyson's Poetry* (pp. 7–46). Toronto: University of Toronto Press, 1981.
    The poem's domestic imagery, Hair suggests, functions as pastoral conventions do in earlier elegies, as a means of rendering the speaker's private grief familiar and universal.
Hayward, Helen. "Tennyson's Endings: *In Memoriam* and the Art of Commemoration." *English* 47 (1998): 1–15.
    Following the lead of earlier critics, notably Ricks (as she acknowledges), Hayward surveys the whole poem to show how Tennyson's elegy resists closure.

Joseph, Gerhard. "Producing the 'Far-Off Interest of Tears': Tennyson, Freud, and the Economics of Mourning." *Victorian Poetry* 36 (1998): 123–33.
    Joseph offers a succinct analysis of the poem's conscious quest to derive gain from loss.
• Mattes, Eleanor Bustin. *In Memoriam: The Way of a Soul*. New York: Exposition Press, 1951.
    Mattes considers various influences on Tennyson's poem, including Hallam's own writings. The most important chapters are those that analyze how Tennyson's study of science affected his faith and gave rise to the poem's idiosyncratic treatment of the concept of evolution.
• Nunokawa, Jeff. "*In Memoriam* and the Extinction of the Homosexual." *English Literary History* 58 (1991): 427–38.
    Along with that of Christopher Craft, this article provides one of most persuasive queer readings of the poem. Nunokawa suggests that sexuality, like everything else in *In Memoriam*, follows an evolutionary model, in which schoolboy homoeroticism eventually gives rise to normative heterosexual marriage.
• Peltason, Timothy. *Reading* In Memoriam. Princeton, NJ: Princeton University Press, 1985.
    Peltason's reader-response approach sets itself against generations of critics who have sought unity in the poem (or objected to the lack of it) by celebrating the moment-by-moment vacillations that the reader necessarily shares with the poet.
• Ricks, Christopher. *Tennyson*. 2nd ed. New York: Macmillan, 1989.
    Ricks's lively, penetrating study, first published in 1972, remains the standard critical biography of Tennyson. The chapter on *In Memoriam* provides the account of the poem from which most subsequent readings, especially formalist and queer criticism, begin.
Sacks, Peter M. "Tennyson: *In Memoriam*." *The English Elegy: Studies in the Genre from Spenser to Yeats* (pp. 166–203). Baltimore and London: The Johns Hopkins University Press, 1985.
    Sacks moves through the poem from Prologue to Epilogue, illuminating the poet's work of mourning at each stage in the context of the elegiac tradition.
Sendry, Joseph. "*In Memoriam*: Twentieth-Century Criticism." *Victorian Poetry* 18 (1980): 105–18.
    Sendry's article surveys the poem's critical history through the first eight decades of the twentieth century, offering analyses of all of the major contributions. The same issue of *Victorian Poetry* that contains this article also contains five further essays on *In Memoriam*, all of them valuable, concentrating on such issues as the poem's descriptions of writing, its metaphors, and its prosody.
• Shannon, Edgar Finley, Jr. *Tennyson and the Reviewers*. Cambridge: Harvard University Press, 1952.
    The chapter on *In Memoriam* forms the culminating point of this study of Tennyson's reputation and of the influence that reviews of his early poetry had upon his revisions and his subsequent writings.
Shaw, W. David. "The Autobiography of a Mourner: *In Memoriam*." *Tennyson's Style* (pp. 132–67). Ithaca and London: Cornell University Press, 1976.
    Shaw enumerates the forms of catharsis Tennyson achieves, concentrating on the paradox that although *In Memoriam* uses the conventions of personal confession, it nevertheless relies upon indirect or "veiled" language.
• ———. "The Paradox of Genre: Impact and Tremor in Tennyson's Elegies." *Elegy and Paradox: Testing the Conventions* (pp. 212–35). Baltimore and London: Johns Hopkins University Press, 1994.
    Shaw's sophisticated analysis puts Tennyson's poem in its generic context by examining traditional elegiac binaries that *In Memoriam* embodies without ever resolving.
• Sinfield, Alan. *The Language of Tennyson's* In Memoriam. Oxford: Basil Blackwell, 1971.
    Sinfield provides often brilliant close analyses of syntax, imagery, sound, and rhythm, all contributing towards a sustained reading of the poem's double voice: immediate, yet carefully controlled. The chapter on diction argues against earlier critics who considered the poem either vague or needlessly ornate, by showing how Tennyson coaxes meaning out of simple verbal collocations.
• ———. *Alfred Tennyson*. Oxford: Basil Blackwell, 1986.
    An important Marxist reading. The chapter on *In Memoriam* contains a concise account of the poem's social and political self-positioning; it describes how *In Memoriam*, though in so many ways a private elegy, nevertheless became a work of central importance to "the bourgeois state."
Tucker, Herbert F. "*In Memoriam A.H.H.*: Transient Form." *Tennyson and the Doom of Romanticism* (pp. 376–406). Cambridge: Harvard University Press, 1988.
    Tucker's rich and witty book offers extraordinary close readings of major poems from the first half of Tennyson's career. The chapter on *In Memoriam* describes "the reciprocal, historically conditioned impingement of self and society."

Wheeler, Michael. "Tennyson: *In Memoriam*." *Death and the Future Life in Victorian Literature and Theology* (pp. 221–64). Cambridge: Cambridge University Press, 1990.

    Wheeler considers Tennyson's heartfelt universalist hope—that every individual will live on after death—in the context of Victorian theology.

• Willey, Basil. *More Nineteenth-Century Studies: A Group of Honest Doubters* (pp. 79–105). London: Chatto and Windus, 1956.

    This account is one of the sharpest and most readable of the many critical discussions of the poetic debate between faith and scientific knowledge.

Index of First Lines